Russian Tanks and Armored Vehicles 1917-1945

Wolfgang Fleischer

Russian Tanks and Armored Vehicles

1917-1945

An Illustrated Reference

Wolfgang Fleischer

Schiffer Military History
Atglen, PA

Acknowledgement

The author thanks all those who made information and photographs available and contributed to the success of this work. Special thanks in this respect to Messrs. Eiermann (Sinsheim), Faustka (Vienna), Hildebrandt (Bad Doberan) and Hulansky (Würzburg).

Photo Credits

Federal Archives (3), Caye (4), Eiermann (10), Faustka (6), Fleischer (426), Grössner (2), Hildebrandt (10), Hulansky (30), Jurga (1), Keczycki (1), Klotzsche (4), Matzat (3), MHM (4), MTM (9), Regeniter (2).

Book Design by Ian Robertson.

Library of Congress Catalog Number: 99-62850

Printed in China.
ISBN: 0-7643-0913-7

We are interested in hearing from authors with book ideas on related topics.

Published by Schiffer Publishing Ltd.
4880 Lower Valley Road
Atglen, PA 19310
Phone: (610) 593-1777
FAX: (610) 593-2002
E-mail: Schifferbk@aol.com.
Visit our web site at: www.schifferbooks.com
Please write for a free catalog.
This book may be purchased from the publisher.
Please include $3.95 postage.
Try your bookstore first.

In Europe, Schiffer books are distributed by:
Bushwood Books
6 Marksbury Road
Kew Gardens
Surrey TW9 4JF
England
Phone: 44 (0)181 392-8585
FAX: 44 (0)181 392-9876
E-mail: Bushwd@aol.com.

Try your bookstore first.

Contents

Foreword

On February 10, 1943, a remarkable article appeared in a German daily newspaper under the title "Where do the many Soviet tanks come from?" The question that introduced this article indicates a certain astonishment at the unshaken strength and vigor with which the Soviet tanks attacked the German positions on the eatsern front. How could the Soviet Union's armament industry, after the course of the war to date and the very large numbers of tanks lost at the front, manage to replace these losses? It must be realized that the most important coal and iron depots, as well as important tank factories, were in German hands at that time, or as in the case of the tractor factory in Stalingrad, had been destroyed during the war. Under these conditions the constantly growing numbers of modern Russian tanks appearing at the front had to cause amazement. Such mass production, as the Germans knew from their own experience, called for decades of preparation. It was the result of an armament program carried on by the Russian government with all its energy, and without regard for the cost, beginning long before the National Socialists had come to power in Germany. In fact, the history of the Red Army's armored troops ranks as one of the astonishing phenomena of twentieth-century military history. Tanks had proved their military usefulness in the course of World War I. Like no other weapon of war, they united mobility and firepower under a protecting armored shell. Success in the capturing of large areas was no longer imaginable in the age of technology without motorized, mechanized or armored armies. No less a person than the theoretician and leader of the Bolshevik Revolution in Russia, V. I. Lenin, had analyzed the conditions under which wars were waged in the Machine Age and come to the conclusion that, without using the results of technological progress for military aims, victory on the battlefield could not be achieved. "The advantage belongs to the one . . . who has the best technology, organization and machines. . . ."[1] If the Soviet leadership wanted to promote their long-range goal of supporting world revolutions from the territory of the Soviet Union, they had to prepare their most important instrument of force, the Red Army, to meet the demands of modern military technology. The People's Commissar for Defense, K. J. Voroshilov, spoke on this theme at the celebratory meeting on the 15th anniversary of the founding of the Red Army on February 23, 1933, mentioning the "planned technical reconstruction of the Red Army with consideration for all the demands of modern warfare and modern combat. . . ." Strong armored troops certainly had the best consideration of the Soviet leadership's plans and were given a certain priority in the process of rearming.

The first job was to turn the Soviet Union, a scarcely industrialized country that had been weakened by World War I and the subsequent revolution, into a modern industrial power. Appropriate plans had been made in May 1929. The Fifth Soviet Congress approved the plans for the first Five-year Plan (1928-1933). Thus the material prerequisites were created to, as it says again and again in official documents, "strengthen the defensive power of the Red Army . . .". Within the parameters of the economic program that was effectively turned to reality, the motor vehicle and tractor industry made an unparalleled advance, necessary for mass motorizing and mechanization, between 1928 and 1933. As a result, the yearly production of tanks could be tripled between 1931 and 1938. At about the same time as the realization of the first Five-year Plan, the Soviet military dealt with the theoretical basis of tank use.

Wolfgang Fleischer
Freital, Germany
November 1998

1. V. I. Lenin, Works, Vol. 27, (East) Berlin 1960, p. 183.

Introduction

The cooperation with Germany that was thus practiced at first was broken off in the early thirties. Each nation strove for its own purposes. The German and Soviet military theorists very quickly concentrated on all questions of the offensive use of tanks. This is shown by numerous reports published in the specialist press at that time. As early as 1929-1930, the first motorized units had been established for testing purposes. In the course of tests, the utility of theoretical knowledge was put to the test. Experiences in other countries, particularly in Britain, and partially controversial discussions about the use of the tank weapon were followed alertly in the Soviet Union. Tank models imported from Britain and the USA also influenced the technical development of Soviet tanks gradually until the end of the thirties. The very number of 20,000 tanks produced by the end of the thirties emphasizes the importance of armored troops to the Soviet Army. The USSR thus owned more tanks than the armies of all other nations on earth put together. By 1936 the formation of larger armored units, of divisions and corps, had begun.

The development of antitank defense by the mid-thirties and the experiences of tank use gained during the Spanish Civil War of 1936-1939 made it necessary to modify basic combat qualities of the tanks. They needed armor that would provide protection from the armor-piercing shells of antitank guns. To be able to combat enemy tanks and antitank artillery effectively, the increasing of firepower through the use of high-powered tank guns was called for. In further development of this technical-tactical concept, Soviet engineers created completely new tanks like the T-34 and KV, whose combat qualities could no longer be brought into agreement with either the organizational basis or the tactical and operational principles of the Red Army. These had to be developed further. Typical of this new generation of tanks was the combination of armor protection, firepower and mobility, the last in keeping with the geographical conditions of the land, which succeeded ideally in the T-34. Their appearance at the beginning of the warfare between Germany and the Soviet Union in 1941 was an unpleasant surprise for the German troops.

The Soviet leadership had originally planned to reequip the armored troops by 1943. But as a result of the German attack, almost all of the old-type tanks had been lost by the summer of 1942. Thanks to the capable armament industry located on the far side of the Ural Mountains, the losses could be made up very quickly, and in fact the numerical superiority of the Russian armored troops could be established. This was what inspired the author of the article quoted at the beginning to raise the question of the origin of the many Soviet tanks. During the course of the war, and unaffected by high losses, they took over the decisive role on the battlefield. In January 1945 a high-ranking German officer had to recognize resignedly that only the tanks had made the difference on the battlefield, and he meant above all others the tanks of the Soviet Union. A flood of them poured toward Central Europe in 1945, essentially changing military thinking after World War II. Soviet tanks became an important export article, capable of putting down any opposition to the spread of the Communist reign of power.

1

The Beginning of the Tank Weapon in Tsarist Russia - A Retrospect

In Soviet military historical writings, the attempt was made over and over after the end of World War II to portray Tsarist Russia and the Soviet Union as the cradle of the tank weapon. Thus wrote the scholar of technical science, Engineer Colonel V. D. Mostovenkov, in the book "Tanki," published in Moscow in the fifties: "The first creator of a military vehicle project which later came to be called a tank or armored vehicle was the designer V. D. Mendeleyev (1886-1922), the youngest son of the famous Russian scientist D. I. Mendeleyev. V. D. Mendeleyev worked in the shipbuilding department of the Cronstadt Institute of Naval Engineering from 1903 to 1906, and as a designer in various shipyards in St. Petersburg until 1916. Between 1911 and 1915 he worked without a contract on various combat vehicle projects. In this he put to use his experiences in the field of Russian naval shipbuilding. One variant of Mendeleyev's combat vehicles is said to have weighed 170 tons, had an eight-man crew and reached a top speed of 24 kph. The planned thickness of the armor plate was considerable: 150 mm in front and 100 mm on the sides and rear. A 120 mm tank gun was to be mounted in the front part of the vehicle as its primary weapon. In addition, a machine gun in a turning turret was planned. V. D. Mendeleyev developed interesting technical solutions. They included pneumatic shock absorbers, the possibility of moving the vehicle on rails, and a turning mechanism with pneumatic servo drive and friction clutch. Similar to the means of ammunition feed on warships, loading the 120 mm tank gun was to be mechanized. The project was far ahead of its time and thus was regarded as the technical fantasizing of an imaginative designer.

A further tank project was the off-road vehicle (Vesdechod: everywhere-driver) that was presented to the chief executive of the "Special Committee of the Air Fleet for the Support of Aerial Combat Forces through Voluntary Contributions" in August 1914, just after the beginning of World War I, by its inventor, A. A. Porokovstchikov. He foresaw two design possibilities:

1. A vehicle with a broad, endless chain track. Taking curves and turning would be done by means of two wheels, attached to the sides at the front end, which would be steered with a steering wheel like those of a car. The track was located under the body of the vehicle. It did not touch the ground when driving on paved roads, but on softer ground, when the side wheels pressed deeper into the ground, it provided a good weight distribution. Thus a low specific ground pressure resulted. By turning the front wheels, the turning moment needed for changes in direction was created.

2. A second variant of the vehicle was to be propelled by two chain tracks.

In terms of design and production, the first variant was simpler, and it was recommended for testing. At first, though, the project seemed to be doomed when the Russian Army's main office for military technology was not willing to provide the means to build a prototype. Only when the Chief of Technical Provision of the Northwest Front learned of the proposal to build such a vehicle and put it to military use were the needed 9,660 rubles authorized.

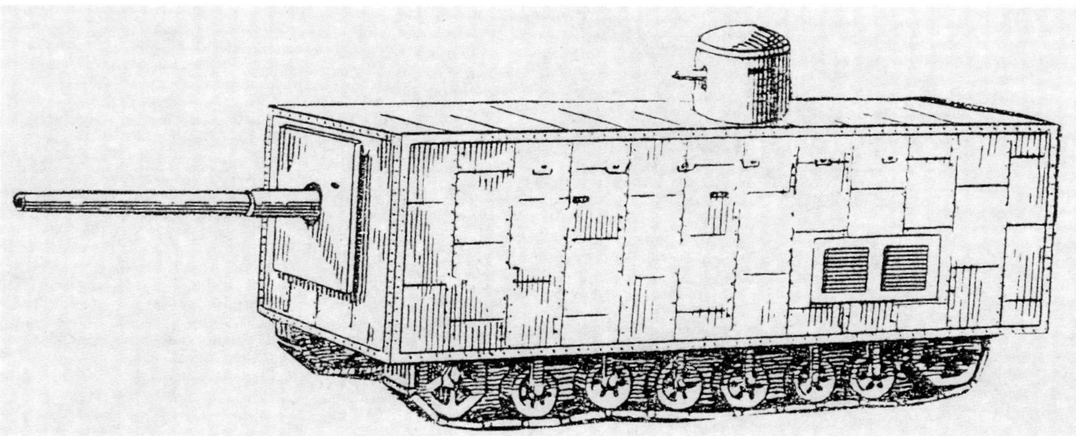

The heavy tank project by V. D. Mendeleyev, from 1916. The armament, powerplant, and eight-man crew of the 170-ton heavy tank were to be protected by armor with a maximum thickness of 150 mm.

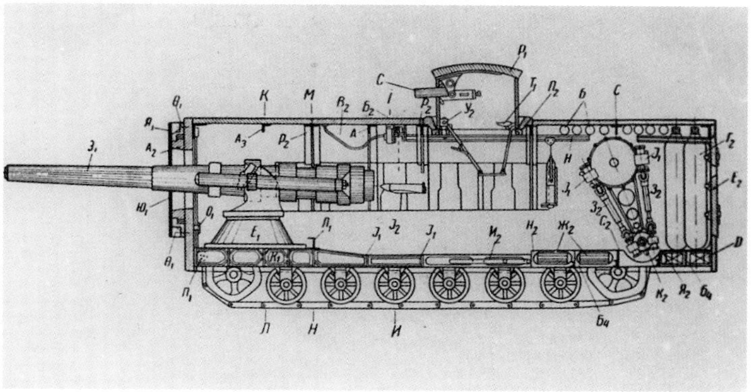

A cutaway drawing of Mendeleyev's tank project. It was planned to mount the engine in the rear of the vehicle. Mendeleyev had projected a 120 mm ship's cannon as the primary weapon, to be joined in a turning turret by a machine gun.

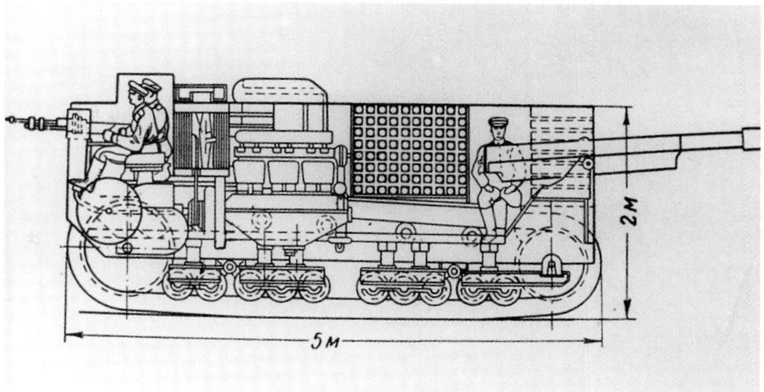

Another Russian tank project was a 20-ton tank of 1915. Note the similarity to the French St. Chamond tank, which was first built in 1916. The Russian tank was to have a four-man crew, be armed with a 107 mm gun and a machine gun, and be able to move at seven kilometers per hour. The thickness of the armor plate was projected at 10 to 12 millimeters.

On February 1, 1915, work began in an especially established workshop in Riga, and on May 18, 1915, the prototype could already be tested. In the records of the testing commission, dated July 20, 1915, it can be read: "It was shown that the aforementioned off-road vehicle moved easily over sand of any depth, whereby it reached a speed of 25 Werst (26.75 kph); in addition, the off-road vehicle drove over a trench some 4 Arshin (2.84 meters) wide and 1 Arshin (0.71 m) deep at medium speed. All large holes and uneven spots in the troop training camp at which the test took place were overcome by the off-road vehicle without trouble at top speed. The mobility is completely satisfactory, the off-road vehicle covered ground and terrain that is impassable for normal motor vehicles."

The vehicle's powerplant had been taken from motor vehicle production. The motor produced 20 horsepower. The flexible track was located under the bottom of the "Vesdechod" and was raised at the front so it could overcome obstacles better. The great surface area of the track resulted in a low specific ground pressure and thus good off-road capability. The chassis was protected from damage by a covering.

For its use as a combat vehicle, the vehicle was to be fitted with armor to afford protection from infantry fire. As its armament, a machine gun was planned for. The fighting weight then amounted to 3.5 to 4 tons. It was a light and relatively fast vehicle. As a result of the project, it could also be made amphibian. But the work on it was not finished. The chief administration for military technology even made sure that the work of finishing the test model had to be stopped despite the positive testing results. The chief of this agency even posed the question: "What do we need this machine for?" Only after the first reports of the use of British tanks in Western Europe appeared in the Russian press in September 1916, and questions were raised in the Duma, was the developmental work resumed again. There appeared an improved off-road vehicle, Number 2, of which only one example was built. The running gear included elements of both wheeled and tracked motor vehicles, meant to guarantee the movement of the vehicle on either roads or off-

The "Vesdechod" (attack driver) project was first introduced in 1914. Building a prototype was begun at the start of 1915. The small tank's two-man crew was protected by light armor. It was to be armed with a machine gun in series production.

The inventor of the "Vesdechod" (attack driver), A. A. Porochovstshikov (left), with his tank. Despite good test results, the project was not followed up.

To contemporaries it was like a vision of a destructive machine from a distant world: the 40-ton tank designed by N/ N/ Lebedenko in 1917. During its very first test drive, the tank got stuck. Work was halted, and the tank was scrapped in 1923.

The light tank from the "Krasnoye Sormovo" (Red Sormovo) factory weighed seven tons and much resembled its French model, the Renault mle. 1917light tank. Only the armament, a 37 mm gun and a 7.62 mm machine gun, was new.

Fourteen light tanks were built at Sormovo by 1922. Except for their stronger armament, they could scarcely be told externally from captured and repaired French Renault mle. 1917 tanks.

The MS-1 (T-18) of 1929 was a comparatively small tank (4380 mm long, 1760 mm wide, 2120 mm high). It could climb slopes with a gradient of 35 degrees, cross trenches with a width of 1300 mm, climb obstacles 600 mm high, and wade in water 700 mm deep.

A captured British Mark V "Ricardo" heavy tank used by the Red Army in the early twenties. Lack of a tank design forced the Red Army leadership to depend on foreign tanks.

The MS-1 light tank of 1927. Besides the 37 mm gun, a twin 7.62 mm machine gun was planned as its armament at first. Because of the cramped conditions in the turret, it was decided to install just one machine gun.

This MS-1 (T-18) built in 1929 had a 37 mm tank gun and a 7.62 mm machine gun. It carried 250 shells for the tank gun and 3,000 bullets for the machine gun. The fuel capacity for the four-cylinder in-line engine was stated at 90 liters.

Left, Below: The MS-1 light tank (T-18) seen during a parade on Red Square in Moscow. This type of tank was regarded as well-designed and proved to be superior to the Renault tank.

This MS-1 (T-18) built in 1930 has been equipped with a 40 HP engine. Despite the higher weight (to 6.3 tons), mobility could be improved. Speeds to 22 kph could be attained/ The range is stated as 110 km.

road terrain. Armor with a thickness of 8 millimeters was planned. The armament consisted of three or four machine guns, two or three of them mounted in a turret. No records of the completion of work on this armored vehicle exist.

Numerous Russian inventors worked independently of each other on the creation of armored combat vehicles between 1914 and 1917. From the many designs, that of N. N. Lebedenko, which led to the construction of a prototype in 1915-17, stands out. Typical of this vehicle, which weighed about forty tons, were two big front wheels, with a diameter of some nine meters. With their help, the required off-road mobility was to be attained. A third wheel of smaller diameter, attached to the rear, was to provide steering. To build Lebedenko's combat vehicle, the impressive sum of 210,000 rubles was approved. In testing, though, the hind wheel got stuck and the vehicle could not move farther. The work was halted, possibly also from the realization that such a big tank would very quickly be put out of action by enemy artillery fire. Until 1923 it remained near the railroad station in Orudievo, not far from the city of Dmitrov, and was then scrapped.

In the thirties, MS tanks were turned over to civilian organizations for pre-military youth training in Soviet Russia. By 1931, 960 tanks of this type had been delivered.

The riveted armor of the MS-1 (T-18) was 8 to 16 mm thick and offered protection from handgun fire and shell fragments. The driver and commander sat one behind the other in the vehicle. The latter was also the gunner and loader of the tank gun and the machine gun.

During the battles on the East Chinese Railway in the summer of 1929, one company with MS-1 light tanks saw action. Despite their small numbers (ten tanks), they made a lasting impression on the Chinese soldiers and added much to the offensive success of the 36th Rifle Division.

Light tanks of the MS-1 type appeared in small numbers during combat against the German Wehrmacht in the summer of 1941. This tank veteran was photographed by a German soldier in the streets of a large Russian city the next spring.

The T-17 was created in 1929 as a small one-man tank weighing only 2.4 tons. The vehicle was armed with a twin or single 7.62 mm machine gun. The armor was 10 to 14 mm thick. The 18-HP engine allowed a top speed of 16 kph.

A variant of the MS-1 (T-18) was the T-23 light tank of 1931. It weighed 3.5 tons, had a two-man crew, and was armed with a 7.62 mm machine gun. The armor was 6 to 10 mm thick and offered protection from handgun fire.

That comparable ideas and projects, and a few prototypes of armored vehicles, existed in other lands at that time is long since known. Thus they do not need to be mentioned here. The notable point is the parallelism. This shows that war machines were gaining ground in the military realm, as a result of increasing industrialization in human society, independent of national boundaries. This being so, the contention of Mostovenko and other Soviet authors that Russia or the Soviet Union had a pioneering role in the development of tanks is not tenable. It simply lacks any evidence. The first useful battle tanks came from Britain. Their combat usefulness was first recognized there and, against much opposition in their own country, they first saw action on the front against German troops. In any case, the first functioning tanks that were put into action by the Red Army during the 1917-1922 Revolution came from Britain and France. They were captured. In March 1919, after the battles in the vicinity of Odessa, several French Renault light tanks made in 1917-18 fell into Red Army hands. One of the captured Renault tanks was sent to Lenin in Moscow as a gift from the 2nd Ukrainian Red Army. A short time later, several British Mark V "Ricardo" tanks were captured in the Ukraine. In the autumn of that year, a further twenty heavy tanks were captured by the Red Army in combat with the White Russian troops of General Denikin. The availability of several dozen captured or repaired tanks in usable condition was the prerequisite for the establishment of motor vehicle units in the Red Army in January 1920. Their specified strength was given as three tanks, two or three cars, three or four trucks, and a few motorcycles.

In September 1920 the "Instructions for the use of Tanks in the Red Army of Workers and Farmers" appeared. The use of tanks was foreseen for the following purposes: Penetrating fortified enemy positions, eliminating barbed wire and other obstacles, fire support for their own troops, and destroying communication and

The further development of the MS-1 (T-18), the T-19 light tank, was displayed in 1931. The performance of the engine was raised to 60 HP, and various elements of the powerplant were improved.

By using components of the MS-1 (T-18) light tank and an engine imported from Germany, the T-24 medium tank was developed at the end of the twenties, and 25 of them were delivered to the Red Army in 1931. Its riveted armor was 8 to 20 mm thick. Note its heavy armament, with a 45 mm gun and four 7.62 mm machine guns, built at three levels.

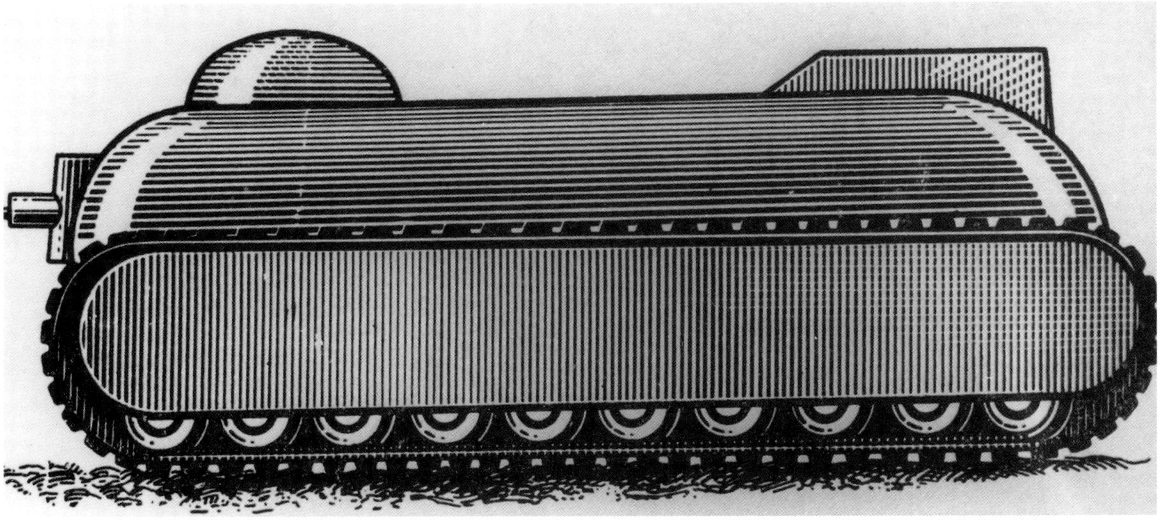

A reconstruction of a light tank design by engineer Maximov. The tank, carrying only one man, was to be protected by 10 mm armor. It was to be armed with a light machine gun. The project did not become reality.

transport in the enemy's hinterlands. Fortified points should be engaged and held until the troops arrived. The artillery was to be used to support tank attacks. Tanks should also come into action in defense and in counterattacks. Their main task was seen as the direct support of the infantry. To this extent there were no differences from the British Army's uses. The incompleteness of the tanks of those times, in particular their slow speeds and meager ranges, made their use in expending breakthroughs impossible.

Along with tanks, the Red Army had more than 100 armored trains in service in 1920, plus more than 150 armored vehicles of various types. They were often used in connection with the motorized armored units. The armored trains, which were limited to use on the rail network, often were given the task of supporting other troops with their artillery fire.

In 1919 the engineer Maximov completed the design for a light tank, which was called "Shield-bearer." It weighed 2.25 tons, had a 40-HP engine and armor 10 mm thick, and was armed with a 7.62 mm caliber heavy machine gun. Maximov had tried to create a small, simple, and inexpensive combat machine. The commander of the tanks had to take up a lying position in combat, a highly unpleasant position from which to steer the tank and operate the machine gun. His chances of getting a good view of the battlefield were only meager. These mistakes were still made in years to come by the designers of several one-man tanks.

The basis of Soviet tank construction was only created at the end of 1919. In that year the "Krasnoye Sormovo" works began, as instructed by the Soviet government, to manufacture the first Soviet tanks. They were actually copies of the light French Renault tank of 1917, a goodly number of which had been captured by that time. For the powerplant of the Soviet version, the AMO works (later the "Lichatchov" automobile works) was responsible. The armor plates, 8 and 16 mm thick, were delivered by the Ishor works. Between October and December 1919 all the designing and drawing work had been finished. Seven months later the first Soviet tank left the factory. It was given the name "Fighter for Freedom, Comrade Lenin." Great difficulties had to be overcome in its production. The appropriate production experience and necessary machines were lacking. The assembly of individual components was done by hand. By 1922, fourteen more tanks had been built in this manner, and each had its own name:

"Paris Commune"	"Victory"
"Proletariat"	"Red Warrior"
"Storm"	"Ilya Muromez"

and others. In addition, captured light Renault tanks were given a general overhaul and newly equipped.

The most important modification of the Soviet version was in its armament. In the French original, enough room had been provided to allow the turret gunner, who was also the tank commander, to operate the gun, by installing either a 37 mm tank gun or a machine gun. On the battlefield, the differently armed tanks were supposed to support each other mutually. In the Red Army, though, ergonomic problems made it favorable for tanks to have greater firepower and less armor. After the building of the first tank at Sormovo, the tanks were armed with a 37 mm tank gun and a 7.62 mm machine gun. The other data were:

Fighting weight: 7 tons
Crew: 2 men
Engine power: 33.5 HP
Top speed: 8.5 kph
Range: 60 km

Like the French original, this tank had a taillike lengthening of the rear body to increase its trench-spanning ability.

In 1920 a first competition was authorized. Designers were to submit designs for tanks. The first prize was won by a design for an amphibian tank, designated Motor Vehicle Type AM. Following this design, work commenced at the Ishor factory to build two amphibian tanks. There is no documentation of the results of this work.

A second competition was authorized in 1922. Seven designs were submitted and evaluated. Nothing is known of whether they were used, and the work of manufacturing copies of the French Renault tanks indicates that there were no factories capable of building armored vehicles. This is presumably also the reason why the leadership in tank construction was taken over in 1923 by the administration of the armament industry. It established the following focal points:

1. Evaluation of available experience in tank building in the soviet Union,
2. Training of personnel for the armored troops,
3. Study of tank construction,
4. Development and manufacture of new tank models for testing purposes.

Cooperation with industry had been improved, as well as with the training facilities and tank units of the Red Army. In addition, the administration of the armament industry had founded a technical bureau. There the design of a new tank was worked on until 1925; it showed obvious similarities with the British tank designs of World War I.

In 1927 the MS-1 light tank was developed; after improvements to its running gear, it was designated T-18. Its concept was still based on the light French tanks, but it had undergone important design improvements. The air-cooled engine was united with the transmission to form one block. The power train to the tracks utilized inside-geared wheels. The return rollers with rubber coverings were also new. A considerably more compact design could also be attained by installing the motor transversely to the main axis. A simple differential drive provided for turning. Such design innovations helped to make the fighting compartment larger, so that the crew had more room to operate the retained 37 mm tank gun and a machine gun. The weight could even be reduced to 5.5 tons while the same thickness of armor (8-16 mm) was retained. The first version of the tank reached 17 kph, and with improved running gear it even attained 22 kph.

After the necessary manufacturing requirements had been created by the chief administration of the armament industry, series production of the MS-1 light tank could be commenced at the Leningrad Weapon Factory in 1928. By 1931, 960 tanks of this type had been produced. Production of the BA-27 armored vehicle (some 100 were made) ran parallel to it. Light tanks of the MS-1 type saw action in 1929 during the combat for the East China Railroad.

In the course of MS-1 production, in which the last-produced modernized versions were designated MS-2 and MS-3, other types of light tanks were created. These were the T-19 and T-20 tanks. The T-20, unlike the MS-1 (T-18), had a more powerful engine that produced 60 horsepower. Side friction couplings and steering brakes provided for steering. In addition, the running gear had been modified. One version of the MS-1 (T-18) was the T-23 tank. Following a general trend in tank design at that time, it had a turretless or casemate design. The vehicle was thus lighter, weighed only 3.5 tons, and reached a top speed of 35 kph. The T-17 was also conceived as a light tank. It had an air-cooled two-cylinder engine that produced 18 horsepower. Here a principle developed in France had been taken over.

The MS-1 (T-18) light tank formed the basis for a further tank model, designated T-1-12. This type was not very successful. It formed the transition to the T-24 medium tank, 25 of which were built in 1929-1930. This tank reached a weight of 18.5 tons and a speed of 22 kph. Elements of the running gear came from MS-1 (T-18). The powerplant consisted of the German BMW M-6 engine with a planetary gearbox. This engine produced 300 HP. The armor plate offered protection from infantry weapons up to large-caliber machine guns. With the three-gun arrangement of the weapons, the Red Army was folllowing the lead of the USA's T-1 medium tank developed in 1925. For the first time in a Soviet tank, a 45 mm gun was installed in the main turret along with two machine guns. On it was a separate turning turret with a machine gun, and a fourth machine gun was mounted in the hull. On account of design errors and mechanical unreliability, the Red Army did not have this tank put into production. A whole series of special features characterized the TG heavy tank, which caught the eye because of its streamlined external form. It went back to a 1929-30 design for a medium tank. The TG had a 76.2 mm gun and four machine guns. The weight was stated as 25 tons, the crew as five men. The 300 HP engine gave it a speed of 32 to 40 kph. Of technical interest is the servo steering system, which was activated via a mechanical gearbox.

The TG heavy tank was built as a test model. It had an eye-catching modern silhouette, was heavily armed with a 76.2 mm and a 37 mm gun plus four machine guns. The armor was also comparatively heavy (10-50 mm).

The Christie fast tank was tested by the U.S. Army under the designation of T-3, but this type of tank was not introduced. Thus [p. 4] it could be obtained for testing as a wheel/track tank by a special commission of the Institute for Mechanization and Motorization in the Central Command of Armored Troops in the Red Army. The BT wheel/track tank was based on it.

This, though, turned out to be its weak point; the steering was very delicate, and only test models were built.

What typified the Soviet tank development until the beginning of the thirties? In view of their tactical-technical requirements and design-technical layout, the Red Army, in cooperation with the chief administration for the armament industry, followed whatever developmental trends they recognized outside Russia. The emphasis was at first on tanks to support the infantry. The influence of the leading tank-producing countries, particularly France and Britain, but also the USA, was clearly obvious. In a technical sense, though, military cooperation with Germany scarcely brought any results worth mentioning. Since 1926 Germany had maintained a "test station" in Kazan, where various tank models developed within the secret German rearmament program were tested. At the same time, future tank officers were being trained, and Red Army officers took part in the training.

In the Soviet Union, the responsible agencies made every effort to find acceptable design features to improve their tanks' performance. But here is where weaknesses appeared most often. Despite the numerous setbacks, much experience was gained in the realm of planning, design and production—the most important prerequisite for the next step in building up the Red Army's armored troops. The problem of creating a fast armored vehicle to support the cavalry, though, could not be solved. Large cavalry units had already played a significant role in the Tsar's armies. Their value in waging war was put to the test anew in the Revolution by both the red and white troops. On the broad plains of the southwestern Soviet Union, for example, the 1st Mounted Army, under its commander S. M. Budyoni, had been decisive in gaining victory. If these numerically strong troops were to be kept at a suitably high level, they had to be mechanized and armored.

As in the other countries with advanced military development, effective principles of action and forms of organization for motorized and armored troops were sought in the Soviet Union. In the second half of the combat directives for the infantry, written in 1927, the use of tanks in close cooperation with infantry was handled in detail. The tanks available at that time were, on the basis of their tactical-technical capabilities, not suited for handling individual tasks as did the combat cavalry in previous wars. With the introduction of the MS-1 light tank, the possibilities of tank use were improved. In the "provisional directive" for the use of tanks, issued in 1928, two forms of their use were explored:

1. Close cooperation with the infantry in penetrating enemy defenses,

2. Handling individual tasks in the enemy's hinterland, such as attacking artillery, interrupting supplying, breaking the communications and command of the enemy troops.

In the military press, there appeared at that time a whole series of articles, of which the works of K. B. Kalinovski, a Soviet Army commander, deserve special notice. He explored the various possible uses of tanks. The articles "The use of tanks and their cooperation with the infantry" and "The tank in defense" appeared in 1927, "The tank in offensive action" in 1928 and "Fast tanks in mobile combat" in 1929.

Higher officers for the armored troops were trained at two schools: the "Special School for Armored Vehicles and towing Vehicles" and the "Motorization for Progress" school in Leningrad. In 1929 motorized units that were intended for independent operations began to be established. A motorized regiment that was formed consisted of a tank battalion (with up to 30 tanks), an armored vehicle unit, a motorized rifle battalion and a battery of artillery.

The T-28 medium tank design for the Red Army began with the British 16-ton tank built by Vickers-Armstrong Ltd. Common to both designs are the heavy armament divided among three turrets, and the thin armor.

The first motorized brigade that was established in May 1930 consisted of two tank battalions, two motorized rifle battalions, one reconnaissance battalion, one artillery unit and various special formations. For the first time, such a large body of troops was equipped exclusively with vehicles from Soviet armament production: The MS-1 (T-18) light tank, BA-27 armored vehicle, tractors and other vehicles. In all, the brigade had sixty light tanks, 32 tankettes, 264 trucks and 12 tractors. After reorganization and expansion in 1931, it was composed of the following:

1. Reconnaissance group at regimental strength (one tankette unit, one armored car unit, one motorized rifle battalion and one artillery unit),
2. Attack group at regimental strength (two tank battalions, two self-propelled gun units, one motorized rifle battalion),
3. Artillery support group (three 76.2 mm gun and 122 mm howitzer units, one anti-aircraft unit)

In all, the brigade consisted of only 4,700 men, 119 tanks, 100 tankettes, 15 armored cars, 63 AA machine guns on self-propelled mounts, 32 7.6-mm self-propelled guns, 16 122-mm howitzers, 32 37-mm self-propelled AA guns, 12 76.2-mm self-propelled AA guns, 270 trucks and 100 tractors.

In the course of training and large-scale maneuvers held in 1929 and 1930, experience in utilizing such large motorized and armored units could be gained for the first time. This contributed to the fast further development of theories about the use of armored troops. At this point it had already been shown that the MS-1 light tank and BA-27 armored car would not meet future requirements either technically or tactically. It was necessary to make basic improvements to tank technology in terms of their performance capability, mechanical reliability and useful characteristics. In the course of the first Five-year Plan, the necessary material prerequisites came into being in the Soviet Union.

2

The Development of Armored Troops in the Red Army, 1930-1939

1. The influence of foreign tank construction

Besides the already mentioned imitation of foreign tanks, in which Russia oriented itself to the presumed progress in designing, the Soviet government set out to buy armored vehicles for the purposes of evaluation and testing. In the latter half of the twenties, a KH-60 wheel/track tank had been bought (1927) from the Skoda works in Pilsen. A Fiat 3000 B light tank was bought in Italy.

The Soviet leadership did not delude itself into thinking that great numbers of their own tanks could be produced in a short time. And the hoped-for help from Germany through the cooperation of the Reichswehr with the Red Army did not bring the desired support in the field of tank development. Only when license rights to build the BMW M-6 aircraft engine were obtained, could an acceptable powerplant be available for medium and heavy tanks built as of 1932-1933. It was therefore decided, as a transitional solution, to buy tanks in Britain and the USA. On December 20, 1929, a special commission under the Director of the Institute for Mechanization and Motorization in the Central Command of the Armored Troops, I. A. Khalepski, went abroad. In the USA and Britain they had opportunities to examine tanks and armored vehicles. The firm of Vickers Armstrong Ltd. then ranked among the best-known manufacturers of tanks. The Soviet Union ordered 15 Mark II medium tanks, 26 Carden-Lloyd Mark VI tankettes, eight Carden-Lloyd amphibian tanks, 15 Vickers-Armstrong six-ton tanks and twelve halftrack trucks from them. On March 21, 1930, the British Ministry of Trade approved the sale of the ordered war materials to the Soviet Union, which also secured the license rights. In a German secret Service report of 1931 it can be seen that as of May 31, 1930, fifteen British Carden-Lloyd and Vickers-Armstrong six-ton tanks had been sent to Newcastle for shipping. A short time later, another thirty tanks had been delivered for shipping to the Soviet Union. In addition, several tanks were sent to Germany for evaluation and testing.

The tanks bought in Britain were very thoroughly examined by the Red Army in the vicinity of Voronesh. The same applies to the two Christie M.1931 (T-3) wheel/track tanks bought in the USA. All the models seemed to be suitable for use by the Soviet forces. Based on them and the acquired license rights, tanks with considerably better capabilities than those previously developed and manufactured in the Soviet Union could be produced. As before, the meager dependability of all mechanical parts drew most criticism. Now it had been decided to use well-designed and time-tested foreign tank models. They were to be adapted to meet Russian needs. The goal was to produce usable tanks to meet various combat needs in the Red Army as quickly as possible. The Soviet leadership wanted a modern, mechanized and armored army.

In the book "Outline of Tactics for the Tank Weapon" by A. Gromuitshenko, which appeared in Moscow in 1935, the Red Army's tanks are classified as:

1. Reconnaissance tanks,
2. Battle tanks,
3. Penetration tanks,
4. Special tanks.

In the *battle tank* group there were two different models: light tanks (T-26) for direct support of the infantry, and fast wheel/track tanks (BT) for long-range battle groups in the mechanized and armored units. In the *penetration tank* group there were medium (T-28) and heavy tanks (T-35), which were gathered in special tank brigades to support other units.

As early as 1932, two mechanized brigades, one machine-gun brigade and one independent Flak artillery unit were combined to form the Red Army's first independent operative unit, a mechanized corps. It included over 500 tanks and 200 other vehicles. By the beginning of 1936 there were already four mechanized corps, six independent mechanized brigades, six independent tank regiments, 15 mechanized regiments of cavalry divisions, and 83 tank battalions and companies in rifle divisions.

A further effect of the policy being followed in tank organization was that the personnel of the newly created motor vehicle and tractor factories could gain the practical experience that was absolutely necessary for large-scale tank production. Several functionaries in the armament industry were trained as were the designers, so that they would be able in the future to carry out their own tank projects from the drawing board through production.

In a book published to mark the fiftieth anniversary of the founding of the Red Army, entitled "Fifty Years of Armed Forces in the USSR," it is stated: "The tank industry overcame the difficulties in the establishment of a Russian tank industry and increased its pro-

In 1931 production of the T-27 small tank began. The basis for this tankette was the Carden-Lloyd small tank, 26 of which had been bought. The combat value of this weakly armed and only lightly armored tank was meager.

duction tempo steadily. Thus in the course of the first Five-year Plan more than 5,000 tanks were built. By the end of the second Five-year Plan, the Army already had over 15,000 tanks, including some 12,000 modern battle tanks. At the same time, the Leningrad and Kharkov factories developed new perspective tank models."

In fact, the standard tanks of the Red Army in the thirties were, without exception, tanks either bought abroad, made under license or built using adopted concepts. In the past, Soviet authors have done everything to keep this fact silent or play it down. Igor Shmelyov, for example, writes in "Tanks in Battle," a book published in Moscow in 1984, on the devlopment of the fast-moving BT tank: In 1931 Soviet designers created a wheel/track tank . . . and concentrated on its technical perfection." It is not noted that the ancestor of this successful tank development came from the USA. The already often-quoted candidate of the technical sciences, Engineer Colonel V. D. Mostovenkov, expressed himself as follows: "In the foreign press, it is often mentioned that in 1931 the Soviet Union had acquired the six-ton tank from Vickers, the wheel/track Christie tank and the Carden-Lloyd small tank from foreign countries, and they formed the basis for the T-26, the BT-2, and the T-27 small tank."

From here on, "deep-digging" conclusions that the Soviet tank designs depended on those of foreign countries are brushed off.

The T-27 small tank and cavalry, seen during Red Army maneuvers. In the background is a two-turret T-26 light tank. In the early thirties, T-27 tanks appeared in battle against the Basmatchen.

It is purposeless to polemicize about this question. The practice of Soviet tank construction, which created the best tanks in the world before World War II, inspires more than one answer to this assertion. At this point, let us look at the following:

1. The tanks bought abroad were not those that had gained general admiration and used to equip armies, but rather models that the military leadership of those countries had declined. The Vickers six-ton tank and the small Carden-Lloyd tank were not used to equip the British Army, and the Christie tanks were not accepted by the U.S. Army.

2. Such tanks could have been developed in the USSR, too, but with greater time expenditure, since the country had as yet no sufficiently trained cadre of designers and skilled workers. The international situation at the time, though, compelled the Soviet industry to build up the production of urgently needed tanks for the army as fast as possible.

3. The designs of all these tanks, and especially the Christie tank, were modified considerably. The turrets were newly developed and included new armament, turret turning mechanism, ball mantlet, main friction clutch, and other features.

As for the installation of tank armament, the Soviet designers could learn nothing from the Americans. When some Soviet tank soldiers got acquainted with the American M 3 light tank, they were surprised by the primitive installation of the weapons, the turret turning mechanism, turret mounting, etc.

In contemporary evaluations, the armored troops of the Red Army were seen as follows:

"In a comparatively short time, using foreign armies as models, Russia developed new types of armored vehicles at a high technical level, produced masses of them and introduced them into the Red Army. It can be seen in numerous press reports that Soviet Russia was believed to have more than 10,000 tanks.

More specifically, the number of available tanks is estimated as follows:

6000 light reconnaissance and amphibian tanks,
4000 light battle tanks
1000 medium battle tanks,
300 heavy battle tanks."[2]

As for the number of tanks actually available in the Red Army, very contradictory data appeared up to 1941. In Germany, where the subject was naturally being dealt with very intensively, the reported numbers of tanks were always rejected as being fantastic and corrected downward. For instance, it is said in a report on the estimation of the Soviet tank weapon by the General Staff of the Army Quartermaster General IV, Enemy Armies East, in 1939: "Among others, the stated number of 18,045 available tanks is estimated to be much too high. . . ." When the war between Germany and the Soviet Union began in 1941, the falseness of these corrections, some of them coming from the Commander-in-chief of the Wehrmacht, Adolf Hitler himself, had been proven. On the other hand, these figures make it very clear what tremendous achievements the Soviet government and its armament industry had made in just ten years.

2. From "Przeglad Voysk Panzernich", Vol. 3 & 4, Warsaw 1938, and "Die Panzertruppe", Vol. 6 & 7, Berlin 1939.

II. The Soviet Tanks, 1931 - 1939

1. Small and Amphibious Tanks

At first it seemed as if small tanks, so-called tankettes, would be given a special place in the framework of the Soviet tank-building program. This trend was based on a theory that, like the tank itself, came from Britain. The small tanks were actually nothing but armored machine-gun carriers, made in part by utilizing standard motor vehicle components, and a reaction to the costs, not regarded as being bearable, of the creation and maintenance of larger tanks. These "very light two-man tanks," as one of the first chroniclers of tank development, Fritz Heigl, wrote in May 1930, should "be created in the thousands, like the Carden Lloyd, and thus flood the battlefield." This idea fell on all too fertile soil in a country like the Soviet Union, whose leadership was obsessed with arming the proletarian masses.

The Carden-Lloyd small tank was tested thoroughly. In 1931 a prototype, essentially identical to the British original, was already built. Testing began before the end of the year. Like the British model, the small tank proved to be a highly simple and robust vehicle. The low center of gravity prevented it from turning over on steep slopes. The prototype was reworked in the design bureau under the leadership of N. Kosyrev, so that its hastily prepared series production could begin in the last quarter of 1931. The official designation of this small tank was T-27.

The crew of the T-27 consisted of the commander, who also operated the air-cooled 7.62 mm caliber DT machine gun, and the driver. The two sat side by side. The thickness of the front, side and rear armor was 10 mm, that of the top 6 mm, and that of the bottom 4 mm; this was to provide protection from light infantry weapon fire. It was shown years later that these qualitative requirements were not always fulfilled. At the major overhauling of a great number of T-27 tanks in February 1938 it was learned that those with chassis numbers 78, 90, and six others had armor plates of ordinary

The T-33 (MT-33) light amphibious tank was built as a test model at the AMO auto factory near Moscow in 1932. It weighed three tons, had armor 7 to 9 mm thick, and was armed with a 7.62 mm machine gun. The crew consisted of two men. In 1933 the vehicle went into series production under the designation of T-37.

cast steel instead of chrome-nickel steel. They could be penetrated by any machine gun.

While the first series of T-27 small tanks showed only slight differences from the British original, those built in 1932 and 1933 were given various modifications. First the fighting compartment was lengthened to the rear. The running gear had a pair of road wheels added on each side. The body was fitted with a shot deflector at the front.

Instead of the separate hatch cover for the driver and ocmmander/machine gunner, two connected hatches were used now; they opened together and extended across the full width of the vehicle. At the same time, the riveted armor plate was expanded so that it covered the tracks and offered more storage room for ammunition and equipment. The very short length of the vehicle was

Attempts to transport T-26 small tanks by air, so that the paratroops and airborne troops being organized by the Red Army could use them, extended over several years. This picture of a Tupolev TB-1 bomber with a small tank suspended under its fuselage was taken in 1936.

Type A of the T-37 light amphibious tank differed only slightly from the original model. The 7.62 mm DT 1929 mounted in a ball mantlet in the turret had an effective range of 800 meters. The (theoretical) rate of fire was 600 rounds per minute, the initial velocity of the bullets was given as 840 m/sec. There were 585 bullets on hand, carried in drum magazines.

A T-37 A at the motor vehicle test center building of the Army Weapons Office of the German Wehrmacht in Kummersdorf, near Berlin. Here captured weapons and vehicles were examined. The T 37 A shown here is a command tank, as shown by the antenna bracket on the body above the tracks. The armor thickness, measured by German specialists, is marked in white.

achieved by locating the engine between the driver and the commander. The fighting compartment was very narrow, the temperature very hot, and the ventilator, located in the rear behind the engine, could injure the crew. All in all, conditions were very bad for both men, who had to be very small in stature on account of the limited space.

The engine, gearbox, and differential drive of the T-27 were taken from the GAZ-AA truck. The top speed was 40 kph, the range on paved roads was 85 kilometers. Because of the low weight, a median specific ground pressure of only 0.75 kp/sq.cm. was attained.

The leadership of the Red Army gave much attention to their paratroops and airborne troops. For this purpose, T-27 small tanks were hung under the tails of two-engined TB-1 (ANT-4) bomber planes and landed by air in 1931.

It was soon obvious that the firepower of the T-27 was too meager. Attempts to strengthen the armament began as early as 1931. They led to a light self-propelled mount, weighing about three tons, with a 37 mm gun. A second variation also carried a 7.62 mm DT machine gun. The tank gun was mounted in a balcony-like projection on the right side of the vehicle. Naturally, the space inside grew even smaller, and only test models were ever built.

In 1933 the series production of the T-27 ended. The Red Army decided against the full use of the contract, originally for 5,000 vehicles of this type. In all, there were made:

Year	Number
1931	348
1932	1693
1933	500
Total	2541

In the mechanized and armored units of the Red Army, the T-27 was used for reconnaissance and securing. In addition, it was intended for use in breaking weak resistance during pursuit combat. Small numbers of these tanks were used in the early thirties against rebel bands on the border of Afghanistan. The actual value of the T-27 for the developing armored troops of the Red Army consisted of having a mechanically reliable and cheaply produced armored vehicle available in large numbers within a short time. It

The T-37 A was 150 mm higher than the later T-38. The balsa-wood floats above the tracks were a typical feature, as was the square armor-steel container on the engine hood. It held the ventilator that cooled the engine.

Because of the numerous lakes, the T-37 saw action in the 1939-40 war against Finland. This picture shows Finnish soldiers retrieving a captured tank of this type to make it usable for their own forces. In 1944 the Finnish Army had about thirty T-37 A light amphibious tanks.

In the summer months of 1941, the Red Army lost most of its light amphibious tanks during the war with the German Wehrmacht. Their combat value was regarded as very meager anyway, and the Red Army dug some of the light tanks in for use as fixed firing positions.

was capable of performing useful service individually and in formation. At the end of the thirties, the T-27 could also be used in premilitary training. Small numbers also saw service in the initial period of the 1941-1945 war, though there it was less a combat vehicle than a towing tractor for light guns. The T-27 was replaced in production by light amphibious tanks.

***Right Column*: The T-37 light amphibious tank had problems in making the riveted joints in the armor plate watertight; thus only 70 of them were built. Propulsion in the water was noteworthy: the three-bladed propeller allowed forward and reverse motion in water, enabling a top speed of 6 kph.**

The T-38 or T-28 M-2 light amphibious tank replaced the T-37 A in series production as of 1936. The new model was lower and had better suspension for its running gear. The turret with the 7.62 mm machine gun was moved to the left side.

Tactical - Technical Data

Crew: 2 men
Weight: 2.7 tons
Armament: 1 DT 7.62 mm caliber machine gun, with 2520 rounds
Armor plate:
Front: 10 mm
Sides: 10 mm
Rear: 10 mm
Top: 6 mm
Bottom: 4 mm
Powerplant: 4-cylinder 4-stroke GAZ-AA gasoline engine
Performance: 40 HP at 2200 rpm
Fuel capacity: 46 liters
Power to weight: 14.7 HP/ton
Length: 2600 mm
Width: 1630 mm
Height: 1440 mm
Ground clearance: 240 mm
Top speed: 40 kph
Range: 80 km, finally 120 km
Climbing angle: 40 degrees
Spanning ability: 1200 mm
Climbing ability: 500 mm
Wading ability: 500 mm
Specific ground pressure: 0,75 kp/sq. cm.

Rear view of a T-38 M-2, photographed on the German-Russian front in July 1941. The T-38 lacked the additional balsa floats over the running gear.

A few T-38 M-2s were armed with a 20 mm SchWak aircraft gun. This had already been tested in the mid-thirties, when a vehicle had been armed with this gun, operated by the driver. Because of the cramped conditions in the turret, this attempt to use the gun went no farther.

On this T-38 M-2 light amphibious tank captured by German troops in the summer of 1941, the long flat hull can be seen clearly. The tracks were also wider than those of the T-37 A.

The T-26 light tank was based on the British 6-ton tank made by Vickers-Armstrong Ltd. Housing the guns in two separate turrets was also taken from this design. [p. 6] The Red Army's armored troops' requests concentrated from the start on arming the tank with an effective gun for use against armored and other targets.

This picture was taken during Red Army maneuvers in the early thirties. In the foreground is a T-26 light tank, 1931 model, always armed with two 7.62 mm DT machine guns. In the background is a BT fast wheel/track tank.

What with the geographical conditions existing in the Soviet Union, the vast open lands with few developed routes and numerous water obstacles, amphibious tanks had to attract particular attention from the military. Developmental work in other countries was followed with interest, with the designs developed in Britain making the best impression. Eight Vickers-Carden-Lloyd amphibian tanks had been bought in 1931. A prototype of the Soviet version appeared in 1932 at the AMO automobile factory near Moscow. It was designated "Morskoi 33," or "Malyi Tank 33" (MT-33). With its two-man crew, fully turning 7.62 mm DT machine gun mounted in a turning turret, and armor 7 to 9 mm thick, the tank weighed about three tons. The 63 HO gasoline engine gave it a speed of 45 kph. During testing, the running gear gave cause for criticism; thus the second prototype made use of running gear with a modified "Horstmann" shear-spring system. The designation of the amphibian tank had meanwhile been changed to T-33.

Simultaneously with the testing of the T-33 and its further development into the T-37, an alternative model, the T-41 amphibian tank, came into being at the design bureau of Kosyrev. In its tactical-technical data, it resembled the T-33, though it reached a speed of only 37 kph on land. What caused this design to be rejected, though, was its performance in the water, which was worse than that of the T-33. Further test models of small tanks, in both amphibious and other forms, were developed under the designation of T-34.

The further development of the T-33 led to series production in 1933 as the T-37 amphibian tank. Changes included the turret mounted on the right side, and the tracks. An interesting design feature of the T-37 was that it had a ship's propeller with adjustable blades for water travel, so that it could travel backward in the water. The engine, gearbox, and differential had again been taken from the GAZ-AA truck. Unlike the T-27 small tank, its specific ground

The T-26 light tank, 1931 model, before a parade. At first the mechanical rleiability of the Russian tanks had not been very high. There were numerous breakdowns in parades, a fact that left a bad impression on foreign observers and a worse one on the Red Army leadership. Thus in the thirties parades were often held in which up to 1000 specially prepared armored vehicles took part.

A T-26 1941 model captured by the German troops in the summer of 1941. The two cylindrical turrets, whose traverse field is listed as 265 degrees, can be seen clearly.

Rear view of a two-turret T-26 light tank, photographed on the eastern front in the summer of 1941.

pressure was only 0.55 kp/sq. cm. Thus its off-road capability was improved considerably.

The last T-37 amphibian tanks built were designated T-37 A. They had a slightly lengthened hull, floats attached on both sides of the track aprons, and a slightly higher weight (3.2 tons). In the command-tank version, the vehicle had one all-around antenna attached by special brackets. In 1935 there appeared a light self-propelled gun mount based on the T-37 and armed with a 37 mm 1931 tank gun and a 7.62 mm machine gun. The vehicle had a casemate body type, with the tank gun in the center and a ball mantlet to the left holding the machine gun. Only test models were built.

In the Red Army, amphibian tanks were to be gathered in companies and battalions and utilized for reconnaissance and securing of larger armored units. They were intended to make use of favorable situations and expand already gained positions through quick

Typical of the 1933 model T-26 was the angular, squarish upper body made of 15 mm armor plate. The turret contains the internal roller mantlet for the 45 mm tank gun, 1932 model, with a barrel length of 2072.5 mm (L/45) and a coaxial 7.62 mm DT machine gun. In a German report on the Russian T-26 tank in 1937, the quality of the vehicle and of its armor were highly evaluated.

A German collecting depot for captured Russian war materials. At right is a T-26 light tank, 1931 model. Captured tanks were used by the German Wehrmacht and numbered 737 (r) (= Russian) T-26 A, and used particularly for securing tasks in the hinterlands.

As of 1933 the T-26 light tank appeared with a completely new turret design. Now it was possible to mount the powerful 45 mm tank gun, 1932 model, and one or two 7.62 mm DT machine guns. In the rear extension of the turret the load of 100 shells and up to 4000 machine-gun bullets was stored.

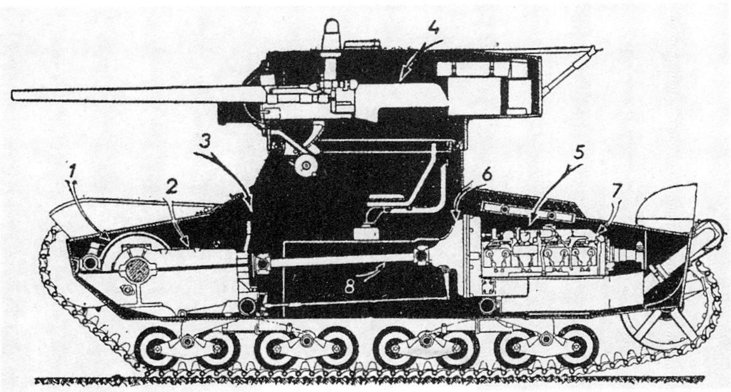

Cutaway drawing of the T-26 light tank, 1933 model. 1. Steering clutch, 2. Variable gears, 3. Driver's compartment, 4. Fighting compartment, 5. Engine room, 6. Main clutch, 7. Engine, 8. Crankshaft.

The T-26 TU command tank was used by platoon and company leaders. Their antennas made them easy to recognize and drew the fire of the enemy.

The T-26 light tank, 1933 model, as a command tank. These tanks, equipped with a radio, had an antenna in the form of a railing around the turret. They also had a microphone, a transformer, an extra battery, and a commutator. Thsu the command tanks had to carry less ammunition.

advances. They were to be used particularly in conjunction with the fast wheel/track tanks and the cavalry for fast crossing of water obstacles. Another important task for amphibian tanks was leading the Red Army in amphibian landing maneuvers. For this they were unloaded from ships off the coast in order to locate or capture suitable landing places on the shore. In the further development of action they were to secure the disembarking of the main forces and undertake advances into the enemy's flanks and rear. Particular demands were made on the crews of the amphibian tanks because their activities were planned to take place at night or under smoke screens.

In September 1936, Soviet Russia delivered the first 1933 model T-26 light tanks to the Spanish Republic. In all, 362 tanks arrived in Spain and saw action in the Civil War, which lasted until 1939. Most of those delivered were T-26es, though a few BT-5 fast wheel/track tanks were also sent the the Republican army.

Members of the Condor Legion, to which the German soldiers who fought on the Nationalist side belonged, examine a shot-down T-26 TU command tank. Because its armor was only safe from bullets and shell fragments, the Russian tank proved to be inferior to the well-organized antitank forces, who had small-caliber antitank weapons.

Between 1933 and 1936 there were 1,200 T-37 and T-37 A amphibian tanks built. Both types were utilized in the course of the war against Finland in the winter of 1939-1940 and in the war with Germany in 1941.

Tactical - Technical Data (T-37 A)

Crew: 2 men
Weight: 3.2 tons
Armament: 1 DT 7.62 mm caliber machine gun, with 585 rounds
Armor plate:
- Front: 9 mm
- Sides: 9 mm
- Rear: 9 mm
- Top: 6 mm
- Bottom: 6 mm

Turret armor:
- Front: 9 mm
- Sides: 9 mm
- Rear: 9 mm
- Top: 6 mm

Powerplant: 4-cylinder 4-stroke GAZ-AA gasoline engine
Performance: 40 HP at 2200 rpm
Fuel capacity: 100 liters
Power to weight: 12.5 HP/ton
- Length: 3750 mm
- Width: 2000 mm
- Height: 1820 mm

Ground clearance: 300 mm
Top speed: 36 kph on land, 4-6 kph in water
Maximum range: 230 km
Climbing angle: 40 degrees
Spanning ability: 1600 mm
Climbing ability: 500 mm
Wading ability: Amphibious
Specific ground pressure: 0.55 kp/sq. cm.

The 45 mm tank gun, 1932 model, with coaxial 7.62 mm DT machine gun. Of the total barrel length of 2072.5 mm, riflings covered 1650/2 mm. The breech was removable, and the vertical block worked automatically. The gun could fire armor-piercing and explosive shells.

A T-26 light tank, 1933 model, captured by the Germans in Spain. Before the end of 1936, the first two tanks of this type had been sent to Germany, where they were examined and tested by the Army Weapons Office.

In 1934 Turkey bought 64 T-26 tanks from the Soviet Union and organized the first tank battalion at Lueleburgaz in central Thrace. These pictures show tanks of this battalion during a drill in [p. 8] the second half of the thirties. In 1942 these tanks, then fully outmoded, were taken out of service.

During the 1939-40 winter war with Finland, the Red Army used large numbers of light tanks against the Finnish forces. Their combat did not have much success; large numbers of these tanks were destroyed or captured by Finnisn troops.

A Finnish collecting depot. In the foreground is a T-26 TU command tank, 1933 model, and behind it a "Komsomoletz" armored artillery tractor.

In 1934, studies and developmental work for completely new, modern light tanks were begun, with the T-37 at first serving as the starting point. Two projects are especially noteworthy: The amphibious T-43-1 of the AMO auto works near Moscow (Factory No. 37) and the non-amphibious T-43-2 from a Leningrad factory. The goal was light wheel/track tanks for reconnaissance purposes. Prototypes were tested, but no further work was done.

The further development of the T-37 at the AMO auto works led in 1936 to the prototype of a new amphibian tank, which was put into series production in the same year as the T-38. With a fighting weight of 3.3 tons, this tank was wider and lower than its forerunner. The turret was now on the left side and the driver on the right. Its shape resembled that of the later T-37 model. The GAZ AA motor, producing 40 HP, was still used. The design improvements included the introduction of friction couplings to transmit power to the tracks, in place of the differential used in motor vehicles. The new power train and steering worked more reliably. Further improvements included a new running-gear suspension, which allowed vibration-free driving.

There were renewed efforts to upgrade the armament of the amphibious tanks. For this purpose, a 20 mm SchWak aircraft gun was installed in at least the prototype and intended to be operated by the driver. Here, too, the cramped conditions inside the vehicle led the designers and the military to give up on these plans.

During the 1936 peace maneuvers, T-38s along with T-27 small tanks were transported as external loads under the tails of four-engined TB-3 (ANT-6) bombers and landed during the course of an air-landed operation. This attracted much attention outside the Soviet Union.

In 1938, series production of an improved model of this tank, the T-38 M-2, began. Its engine and gearbox, taken from the GAZ-

Finnish tank soldiers during a lull in battle in 1941. In the background is a T-26 light tank, 1933 model, captured from the Russians. In all, the Finnish forces obtained 67 tanks of this type (including flamethrowing tanks), which were used until 1961.

This July 1941 photo shows a T-26 light tank, 1933 model, that was immobilized by a mine. During the war with the Germans in the western part of the Soviet Union, the Red Army lost the majority of its T-26 tanks.

This 1933 model light tank, destroyed and abandoned after a German air raid, has a roller-mantlet cover on the turret, with angles rounded off.

Another form of the T-26 light tank, 1933 model. The turret has a roller-mantlet cover with the 15 mm front plate rising on either side. Also clear to see are the one-piece hatch for the two crewmen in the turret, the ventilator in the turret top, and the shape and arrangement of the vision slits. The round pistol loopholes under them are typical of Russian tanks.

N-1 truck, provided 50 HP at 2800 rpm, allowing considerably improved performance; speeds up to 46 kph could be attained.

Like the T-37, the T-38 or T-38 M-2 was used by infantry-tank battalions, with each unit having 38 of them. Airborne armored battalions were meant to have fifty of them apiece. Command vehicles could be recognized externally by the additional antenna for the radio set. One of the last special developments of the T-37/T-38 amphibian tank was the TM with lengthened hull and running gear.

In 1940, interesting experiments were carried out with the T-38 as the guide for a radio-controlled T-26 explosives carrier, capable of blowing up bunkers and other obstacles. The impetus for such projects came from the evaluation of combat experience gained in the 1939-1940 war with Finland. In the war with Germany in 1941, the T-38 and T-38 M-2 amphibian tanks played only a minor role, on account of their limited armor and firepower. Some of them were also dug in as immobile gun positions.

Despite its primary armament, still evaluated as sufficient in 1941, T-26 tanks had only scant chances of success in battle against German Panzer III and IV tanks. Their armor (15 mm) was too weak, their speed (28 kph) was no longer enough, and the three-man crew was overworked in battle. Lack of sufficient and powerful radio apparatus was also a disadvantage.

Most T-26 light tanks of all types were used in the tank battalions for direct support of the infantry. [p. 9] Such a battalion had 22 Type 26 tanks and 16 Type 37 or 38 amphibian tanks in 1941. There were also tank brigades with up to 267 light tanks. During the battles in June and July 1941, these units lost most of their combat vehicles within a short time.

Tactical - Technical Data

		T-38	T-38 M-2
Crew:		2 men	2 men
Weight:		3.3 tons	3.8 tons
Armament: 1 7.62 mm caliber DT machine gun with 1512 rounds			
Armor plate:			
Hull:	Front:	9 mm	9 mm
	Sides:	9 mm	9 mm
	Rear:	9 mm	9 mm
	Top:	6 mm	6 mm
	Bottom:	4 mm	4 mm
Turret:	Front:	9 mm	9 mm
	Sides:	9 mm	9 mm
	Rear:	9 mm	9 mm
	Top:	6 mm	6 mm
Powerplant:		4-cylinder 4-stroke gasoline engine	
	Type:	GAZ-AA	GAZ M 1
	Power:	40 HP at 2200 rpm	50 HP at 2800 rpm
Fuel capacity:		100 liters	100 liters
Power to weight:		12.1 HP/ton	13.2 HP/ton
	Length:	3750 mm	3750 mm
	Width:	2330 mm	2330 mm
	Height;	1630 MM	1630 MM
Grround clearance:		300 mm	300 mm
Top speed on land:		40 kph	46 kph
Top speed in water:		6 kph	6 kph
Range: 230 km		230 km	
Climbing degree:		40 degrees	40 degrees
Spanning ability:		1600 mm	1600 mm
Climbing ability:		500 mm	500 mm
Wading ability:		amphibious	amphibious
Specific ground pressure:		0.55 kp/sq. cm.	0.55 kp/sq. cm.

2. Light Tanks for Direct Infantry Support

In the thirties, the light tank for direct infantry support, designated T-26, was among the armored vehicles that had come to characterize the appearance of the armored troops in the Red Army. On the one hand, this was a result of characteristic external features. On the other, it was also the very large number of some 12,000 tanks of this type that made such an impression.

The development of the T-26 resulted from the request for a tank for direct infantry support. According to the thinking of Red Army military theorists, such a tank should be capable, thanks to its mobility, armor, and armament, of fighting successfully against enemy machine guns on the battlefield.

At the beginning of the thirties, the British Vickers-Armstrong six-ton tank best lived up to this conception. This type was not accepted by the Royal Tank Corps, but it was exported to or copied in numerous other countries. Its armament, consisting of two machine guns, was mounted in three turrets with limited traverse ranges. A second armament variant included a short-barreled 47 mm tank gun (QFSA) and a 7.71 mm machine gun. This version had only one turret. As already noted, the Soviet Union obtained several Vickers-Armstrong six-ton tanks in the spring of 1930. The first

A burned-out T-26, 1933 model. The effect of German defensive weapon fire on the 15 mm armor of the hull is easy to see. Note the pistol loopholes under the rear extension of the turret for defense against close-range tank attackers.

German soldiers examine two T-26 1933 model light tanks put out of action in July 1941. The Russian tanks could be equipped for night battles with up to three powerful spotlights (one in the middle of the hull, two on the roller mantlet of the tank gun).

During the fighting in the summer of 1941, numerous Russian tanks were abandoned because of minor mechanical damage or for lack of fuel, and lined the advance routes of the German troops.

tanks that arrived at Leningrad were examined and tested thoroughly by the faculty in mechanization and motorization at the "F. E. Dzerchinskiy" Academy of Artillery Weapons there. At the same time, the manufacture of prototypes began at the "Bolshevik" factory in Leningrad, as a license to build the tanks had been obtained from Vickers-Armstrong Ltd. The test vehicles were designated TMM-1 and TMM-2; externally they bore only slight differences from their British model. All further steps were taken in some haste. On February 13, 1931, the Revolutionary War Department of the Soviet Union gave orders to accept the T-26 light tank as armament for the Red Army without waiting for the conclusion of developmental work and testing.

Above all, the military required improvements in the two turrets, to allow the machine guns to be swung further to the sides for firing. Within a short time, characteristic shaped turrets with high cupolas at the rear appeared. Large visors were added in front for visibility. In order to avoid problems, the turning circles of the turrets had locks that limited their traverse range to 265 degrees. To improve the rate and accuracy of fire, the weapons were mounted in ball mantlets. In place of the water-cooled machine guns used in the prototypes, air-cooled 7.62 mm DT machine guns were used in the series production model. One disadvantage that appeared was that the seats of the two machine gunners (the commander sat in the left turret) were fastened in place between the engine room and gearbox and did not turn with the turrets.

The driver sat at the right, beside the gearbox. It was a multi-step mecnahical type with five forward speeds and one reverse. The engine was based on the British Armstrong-Siddeley powerplant

Infantry tanks of a German infantry regiment pass an abandoned T-26, 1933 model. The cylindrical turret set to the left and the opened driver's visor on the right side of the vehicle are easy to see.

A captured T-26, 1933 model, with a German crew. These vehicles were used by German troops and designated 738 (r) (+ Russian) T-26 B. Several were used to equip armored trains, while others were rebuilt into self-propelled gun mounts or towing tractors.

To improve the armor protection of the T-26 tank, it was fitted with a shot-deflecting conical turret from 1937 on. The armor plates were no longer riveted on, but were welded. At first the hull with the angular armor plate of the 1933 model T-26 had to be retained. The vehicle shown here came from an early production run. Note that on this T-26 TU the brackets for the radio antenna, which formed a rail around the turret, can still be seen. The mount for an anti-aircraft machine gun are also in place.

The number of Red Army armored vehicles lost in the western Soviet Union in the summer of 1941 was large. In the German Wehrmacht report of August 6, 1941, their numbers were listed as 13,145. The collecting commands were not capable of taking all of them away before winter began. These pictures of abandoned T-26 tanks were taken in November 1941.

This T-26 1937 model was shot down near Brody at the end of June 1941. It is an early-type tank with angular armor plates. Besides the 45 mm 1934 model tank gun, it had three 7.62 mm DT machine guns. One was coaxial and mounted with the tank gun, another in a ball mantlet in the rear of the turret, and the third in a bracket for anti-aircraft use. There were TN-9 panoramic scopes in front of the commander's and gunner's visors.

The last version of the T-26 light tank, 1937 model, had a newly formed turret with angled armor and similar armor on the hull. Command tanks for platoon and company chiefs (T-26 TU) were now fitted with the less noticeable rod antenna.

and was installed at the rear. It produced 91 HP. A firewall separated it from the fighting compartment. The armor plate of almost all first-series (1931-1933) T-26 tanks was riveted on and offered protection from infantry-weapon fire and splinters. The tank's hull was mounted on road wheels with four times four semi-elliptical leaf springs and swinging arms. On each side there were also four return rollers. The drive wheel was at the front.

In the autumn of 1931, series production of the T-26 commenced. By the end of the year, 120 two-turret light tanks of this type had been built.

The meager armament of the eight-ton tank, consisting of only two machine guns, was unsatisfactory. The Red Army's requirements concentrated from the start on increasing the firepower of the T-26. Thus a 12.7 mm caliber heavy machine gun was installed experimentally in the left, or commander's, turret. Another variant to appear was the T-26 TU command and support tank. In its right turret it carried a short-barreled 37 mm tank gun, while the usual 7.62 mm DT machine gun remained in the left turret.

In the version of the T-26 TU made in 1933, a radio set was also installed in the right turret. These tanks were externally recognizable by the antenna attached all around the hull by brackets. These tanks were reserved for platoon and company leaders. The company leaders in particular were overworked with the tasks of providing fire support and leading their companies as well as main-

Front view of a T-26 1937 model. The 45 mm 1937 model tank gun differed from the 1932 model in having electric firing, A goodly number of this type of tank also had a TOP tank targeting scope with stabilizer; the TO-D tank targeting scope had been used previously.

This T-26 1937 model tank got stuck in a bomb crater and was photographed by a German war correspondent in July 1941.

It could only be put out of action in the midst of a German marching column, after it had spread death and destruction there—a T-26 1937 model light tank.

Typical of a great number of 1937 model T-26 light tanks was the 7.62 mm DT machine gun movably mounted in a ball mantlet in the rear extension of the turret. Sometimes this machine-gun bracket was removed and the round opening covered with an armor plate (picture below).

taining communications to their battalions. And there was little space to spare in the small turrets.

The performance of the 37 mm gun in the T-26 TU was evaluated as insufficient. Meanwhile, various other countries were introducing special 2 cm and 3.7 cm antitank guns into their armies. They now became the most dangerous enemies of the tanks, which were now safe from ordinary bullets. As before, the tanks' most important task was destruction. This was a prerequisite for the success of their own attacks. For it, higher-performance tank guns were called for. They already existed in the form of the 37 mm PS-2 tank gun, 1930 model. This was a variant of the 37 mm tank gun of 1930 (made under license after being developed by Rheinmetall of Germany). The barrel, 1665 mm long, was able to fire 0.665 kg shells with a muzzle velocity of about 800 meters per second. The resulting stress was more than the turning circle of the right turret could stand; it tended to break. In addition, there was not enough space inside the turret to operate the tank gun.

It was obvious that a completely new turret had to be designed. In 1933 the T-26 was fitted with a new turret which extended over the hull's entire width, was armed with a 37 mm BS 3 (1930 model) tank gun, and had originally been developed for the BT wheel/track tank. The turret and the gun were not properly balanced, which made aiming in rough terrain difficult. Here too, the designers had made the mistake of attaching the loader's and gunner/commander's seats directly to the bottom of the hull. This made aiming the weapon difficult. Meanwhile, the designing of a new 45 mm tank gun had been completed. It was designated Model 1932. Along with a turret that had been reworked again, this gun was included in the series production of the T-26 as of August 1933. The new large, cylindrical turret with extended rear held the 1932 45 mm tnak gun in a roller mantlet, as well as a 7.62 mm DT machine gun. Some tanks had another machine gun of that type in a ball mantlet to the rear. A few of these T-26 tanks were fitted with an anti-aircraft machine gun. The command tank (T-26 TU) was equipped with a radio set, and was recognizable by the antenna, which took the form of a turret railing. The radio set had a sending power of 15 to 20 watts and a range of two kilometers. In this version a weight of 9.4 tons gave a median specific ground pressure of only 0.55 to 0.65 kp/sq. cm. In the course of series production, a number of improvements were made, including a new design for the armored covers of the visor and pistol loopholes, and the track aprons were fitted with storage chests. Finally, aluminum road wheels were introduced.

Production of the T-26 was expanded very quickly and reached 5,500 tanks by 1936. At this time the Red Army intended to have the T-46 wheel/track tank produced in its place; it resembled the T-26 externally but had wheel/track running gear with four driven road wheels. After the production of a small series of T-46 tanks, the design of which was complicated and not very dependable, production of this type was halted. There was no sense in building a tank that was meant to have characteristics similar to the BY wheel/track tank, was armed and armored like it, but did not have the stated purpose of replacing the BT tank. In 1936, production of an improved version of the T-26 was resumed. In all, some 12,000 T-26 light tanks were produced by 1940 at various Soviet tank factories. They were used in the tank battalions of infantry divisions,

In these pictures the form of the running gear, with eight small road wheels mounted on leaf springs, can be seen clearly. The engine-room cover is typified by the saddle-shaped air intake for ventilation; behind it on the left side are the braces for the exhaust and hot-air pipes.

which had 38 tanks each. Tank or mechanized brigades were to have 201 or 267 T-26 tanks.

The T-26 tanks saw their first action in 1934-1935 in the Manchurian border area and during conflict with Japanese troops in Mongolia. In February 1938, 82 T-26 tanks were delivered to the Chinese central government, all the vehicles having an additional machine gun at the rear and one anti-aircraft machine gun. A large number of tanks of this type gained some publicity during the Spanish Civil War of 1936-1939. In all, the Soviet Union delivered 362 tanks, mostly T-26 and a few BT, to the forces of the Spanish republic.

On the Spanish battlefields the T-26 made a lasting impression, especially thanks to its powerful tank gun, all the more so as the German and Italian tanks used there had only one machine gun. In the summer of 1937, two T-26 tanks captured by the Spanish Nationalists were sent to Germany and examined thoroughly. Here are several excerpts from the report of the 8th Unit of the Army General Staff, from August and September 1937: The armor of what was called the "Russian Vickers-Armstrong tank" was evaluated as secure against [SmK] shots. Literally: "The quality of the armor plate is good, . . . the Russian workmanship is well executed." The quality of the tracks was criticized; they tend to come off. On account of the layout of the running gear, "the tank swings very strongly on uneven terrain, so that it hold steady as a firing platform." The penetrating power of the 45 mm 1932 tank gun, which was a first-class piece of work, is given as 35 mm of armor plate at a distance of 500 meters. Just a year later, in July 1939, it was estimated that "the superior armament of the Soviet T-26 tank, compared to the German and Italian small tanks in Spain, made the mere design weaknesses fade into the background."

In Germany the experience gained from the Soviet T-26 in Spain was hurriedly put to use in the development of tanks with tank guns. Later it also influenced the organization, structure, tactical and operational conduct of armored units. The Soviet military experience led to the realization that "with the right organization of antitank defense and and sufficient combat readiness of the troops, . . . small-

The arrangement of the turret visors on the 1933 model T-26 was not satisfactory. In the vehicles made with a conical turret from 1937 on, separate visors were used, one round and the other angular.

These pictures were taken by a German soldier near Brody, a small city in the western Soviet Union, on June 26, 1941. The T-26 light tank, 1937 model, had belonged to the Red Army's 8th Mechanized Corps, which had tried here with its more than 1000 tanks to counterattack and stop the German armored divisions streaming eastward. There was heavy fighting, during which the corps was wiped out.

Production of the 1937 model t-26 and its variants had been halted during 1940. The tanks completed by then numbered 1549. In June 1941, when the war with Germany began, T-26 tanks of all types made up half the tanks (about 12,000) of the Red Army.

From the Russian standpoint, the simple design and easy maintenance of the T-26 were virtues. Among its chief faults were its not very great technical reliability and its low speed.

caliber (20 to 37 mm) antitank artillery makes the use of tanks with bulletproof armor senseless." This conclusion was based above all else on the use of the German 3.7 cm L/45 antitank gun in Spain, and it gave further impetus to the development of armor plate in the Soviet Union.

The experience that came from the Spanish Civil War influenced the production of T-26 tanks, which had been started again in 1937. They were fitted with shot-deflecting conical turrets, with armor plate the same thickness as before but no longer riveted together; they were now linked by electrical welding. There were two different types of roller mantlets for this turret type, one angular and one with rounded edges. A little later they began to build the hulls with diagonally located armor plates. Here too, electric welding was used.

The change in armament meant that numerous tanks were equipped not only with the machine gun beside the tank gun, but with another in the rear of the turret; some had brackets to hold anti-aircraft machine guns. Like the BT-7 tank, the T-26 had also had a vertical stabilizer built in as of 1937. Command vehicles (T-26 TU) for company and platoon leaders, previously easy to recognize with their all-around antennas, now received radio sets with rod antennas. Naturally, the installation of the radio set reduced the amount of ammunition that could be carried. With the enlargement of the fuel tank, the range could be extended from 160 to 225 kilometers. Although the armor thickness of the 1933 T-26 was maintained, the last T-26 version had a fighting weight of some 10.3 tons.

Experience gained in the 1939-1940 winter war against Finland, especially the costly combat along the Mannerheim Line, made it clear once again that even the armor of the most recent T-26 gave no protection against antitank weapons. The following comes from a report by a finnish Army member:

1. The armor of the Russian tanks is poor.
2. Antitank guns made in Sweden penetrate the armor of the Russian 15-ton tank smoothly.

These two 1937 model T-26 light tanks were hit during a mobile battle with German tanks in July 1941 and burned out. The penetrated armor on the tank in front is easy to see.

Based on experience from the 1939-40 winter war with Finland, some 1937 model T-26 light tanks were fitted with added armor 15 to 30 mm thick. The weight gain and loss of mobility were accepted for the sake of better protection. The tanks thus modernized appeared in the summer of 1941 in battle against the German Wehrmacht.

The T-26 TU command tank was an early version of the 1937 model. Despite the severe damage caused by an artillery shell that hit the hull, a number of features can be seen: the roller-mantlet cover shows angular lines (as on the 1933 model T-26), two firing lights are attached to the roller mantlet, and the bracket for a 7.62 mm anti-aircraft machine gun is also worthy of note. The older ring antenna for the radio, forming a railing around the turret, is still present. Typical of these hybrids are the vertically mounted armor plates that form the upper body.

This picture was taken on an advance route of the 24th Armored Division of the German Army in southern Russia in June 1942. At this time, T-26 light tanks (this is the 1937 model) were already seen less often.

After the combat on the Karelian isthmus in December 1939, additional armor plate began to be applied to a goodly number of T-26 tanks, as well as T-28 medium tanks. This modernization, to be sure, was carried out only on the T-26 tanks made since 1937, as well as on the OT-130 flamethrowing tanks. It brought a considerable gain in weight and a loss in driving characteristics. In 1940 the production of the T-26 and its variants came to an end. In that year 1,549 of the vehicles were produced. Along with the BT tanks, the T-26 was the main type of Soviet tank in the thirties. Its design was uncomplicated. The tank was easy to steer, easy to service, and did not require much maintenance. Through the use of an engine with horizontal cylinders, the height of the hull could be kept low. Many design features were tested in the T-26 that became common in Soviet tank construction in the following years. The tank's weaknesses could be said to include its insufficient speed (30 kph), its not very well-balanced weight distribution, and its inadequate technical reliability. In the first months of the war between Germany and the Soviet Union, the T-26 again appeared in large numbers, but despite numerous attempts to increase its combat value, it showed that it could not compete with German tanks or antitank defenses. Most of the T-26 tanks were lost by the autumn of 1941.

Various tracked and armored vehicles of the Red Army at a German collection depot. In the middle is a T-26 light tank, 1937 model.

The OT-26 light flamethrowing tank was based on the T-26 light tank, 1931 model. Its production began in 1933. It was used in the armored flamethrower brigade of the Red Army, which had been set up in the mid-thirties.

Tactical - Technical Data (T-26, 1931 model)

Crew:		3 men
Weight:		8.6 tons
Armament: 2 7.62 mm caliber DT machine guns, with 6000 rounds		
Armor plate:		
Hull:	Front:	15 mm
	Sides:	15 mm
	Rear:	15 mm
	Top:	10 mm
	Bottom:	6 mm
Turret:	Front:	15 mm
	Sides:	15 mm
	Rear:	15 mm
	Top:	10 mm
Powerplant: 4-cylinder, 4-stroke horizontal T-26 gasoline engine		
Performance:		91 HP at 2200 rpm
Fuel capacity:		182 liters
Power to weight:		10.4 HP/ton
	Length:	4880 mm
	Width:	2410 mm
	Height:	2080 mm
Ground clearance:		380 mm
Top speed:		30-32 kph
Range:		160 km
Climbing degree:		32 degrees
Spanning ability:		1800-2000 mm
Climbing ability:		750 mm
Wading ability:		900 mm
Specific ground pressure:		0.55 kp/sq. cm

In the T-26 TU command and support tank, the right turret held a 37 mm 1928 model tank gun (with 180 rounds). The ammunition for the 7.62 mm DT machine gun in the left turret was reduced to 3,000 rounds.

The OT-26 had a fighting weight of 9 tons and a top speed of 30 kph. The two-man crew (driver and commander/flamethrower operator) were protected by 15 mm armor. The 7.62 mm DT machine gun and the flamethrower were coupled together.

The faults of the OT-26 light flamethrowing tanks led to the development of the OT-130, which was produced as of 1930. Along with the flamethrower (various statements of the amount of oil it carried) it was armed with a 7.62 mm DT machine gun with 2898 rounds.

This close-up photo clearly shows the 1938 model flamethrower, which was powered by compressed air and could fire up to 70 flames of burning oil up to 50 meters.

The improved version of the OT-130 light flamethrowing tank, 1938 model, weighed 10.3 tons, had a two-man crew, and was also armed with a 7.62 mm DT machine gun and a flamethrower. The most important difference was the improve armor protection for the two weapons.

An interesting comparison: Both pictures were taken at the same place, but at different times. The upper picture was taken in the Ukraine in July 1941, the lower one in November of the same year. Vehicles of an armored flamethrower unit of the Red Army can be seen, still standing where they were put out of action by the Germans during the summer battles. In the center is an OT-130 light flamethrowing tank, 1938 model, the older type, at left is a T-26 light tank, 1933 model, and in the background and at right are other flamethrowing tanks.

Tactical - Technical Data (T-26, 1933 model)

Crew:		3 men
Weight:		9.4 tons
Armament:	1 45 mm caliber 1932 tank gun, with 100 rounds; 1 or 2 7.62 mm caliber DT machine guns, with 4000 rounds	
Armor plate:		
Hull:	Front:	15 mm
	Sides:	15 mm
	Rear:	15 mm
	Top:	10 mm
	Bottom:	6 mm
Turret:	Front:	15 mm
	Sides:	15 mm
	Rear:	15 mm
	Top:	10 mm
Powerplant:	4-cylinder, 4-stroke horizontal T-26 gasoline engine	
Performance:		91 HP at 2200 rpm
Fuel capacity:		285 liters
Power to weight:		9.2 HP/ton
	Length:	4880 mm
	Width:	2410 mm
	Height:	2410 mm
\Ground clearance:		380 mm
Top speed:		28 kph
Range:		375 km
Climbing degree:		32 degrees
Spanning ability:		1800 mm
Climbing ability:		750 mm
Wading ability:		900 mm
Specific ground pressure:		0.65 kp/sq. cm.

The T-26 TU command tank had an all-around frame antenna. The radio set was mounted in the rear extension of the turret, which reduced the amount of ammunition carried for the guns.

Tactical-Technical Data (T-26, 1937 model)

Crew:		3 men
Weight:		10.3 tons
Armament:	1 45 mm caliber 1934 tank gun, with 165 rounds; 1 to 3 7.62 mm caliber DT machine guns, with 3654 rounds	
Armor plate:		
Hull:	Front:	15 mm
	Sides:	15 mm
	Rear:	15 mm
	Top:	10 mm
	Bottom:	6 mm
Turret:	Front:	15 mm
	Sides:	15 mm
	Rear:	15 mm
	Top:	10 mm
Powerplant:	4-cylinder, 4-stroke horizontal T-26 gasoline engine	
Performance:		91 HP at 2200 rpm
Fuel capacity:		292 liters
Power to weight:		8.7 HP/ton
	Length:	4620 mm
	Width:	2440 mm
	Height:	2330 to 2410 mm
Ground clearance:		380 mm
Top speed:		30 kph
Range:		150 to 225 km
Climbing degree:		32 degrees
Spanning ability:		1800 mm
Climbing ability:		750 mm
Wading ability:		900 mm
Specific ground pressure:		0.65 kp/sq. cm.

The T-26 TU command tank had a rod antenna. The radio set was housed in the rear extension of the turret, thus the ammunition for the guns was decreased.

A close-up view of the weapon hatch of an OT-130, 1938 model. Behind a fixed armor plate the machine gun and flamethrower were mounted movable. The flame pipe at the left was protected by another armored cover. For the commander and flamethrower operator there was a panoramic scope available (atop the turret on the right side).

An OT-130 flamethrowing tank, 1938 model. Here too the armored hatch on the turret front can be seen. Also note the headlight, to the left of the opened driver's visor. It could be swung completely forward with the armored cover when not in use and thus protected from fire.

Since 1932, the T-26 light tank served as the basis for the development of numerous special tanks, self-propelled mounts and other tracked vehicles. To have a vehicle available for artillery support tasks, several T-26 tanks were fitted with a turret that could hold a 76.2 mm 1927/32 tank howitzer and a 7.62 mm DT machine gun. This armament, though, proved to be unsuitable for a light tank. Except for a small series of T-26 artillery tanks built in 1934, this variant did not go into production.

Two other special tanks were built to fulfill combat tasks that belonged to the broad spectrum of the Engineer troops. First the ST-26 (Saperskiy Tank = engineer tank) must be mentioned. There were several variations made as bridgelayers. A type based on the 1931 model T-26 and already tested in 1934 carried a seven-meter wheel-channel bridge. Its load limit is stated at 14 tons. In a German Secret Police (Gestapo) report on November 9, 1935, another variant of the T-26-based bridgelaying tank was mentioned. This was a bridge-carrying tank that was driven into a ditch and could then extend its 3.5-meter bridge 1.5 meters at each end through the use of gears. It was electrically powered. Its equipment included a radio set. Every bridgelaying tank had to be followed by a tractor that could tow the tank back out of the ditch after use. Test models of this bridgelayer were built in Leningrad in 1934.

In addition, old T-26 tanks were used as mine-removal vehicles. To clear a track barely one meter wide ahead of each track, a mine-removal device ("Thresher") was used. The operating speed was 5 to 6 kph.

The flamethrowing tank based on the T-26 gained significance in the Red Army. Increasingly large numbers were taken from the

This OT-130, 1938 model, was shot down by the crew of a German 3.7 cm AA gun during the winter combat on 1941-42. Even at long range, the 15 mm armor offered no protection from the fire of that guns' armor-piercing shells.

In 1939 the last version of the light flamethrowing tank based on the T-26 was put into production: the OT-133. It was somewhat lighter than its predecessor, carried an improved 1939 model flamethrower and two 7.62 mm DT machine guns, and its turret and hull much resembled the 1937 model T-26 light tank. The vehicle shown here was shot down during fighting in the Ukraine in August 1941.

Burned-out OT-133 light flamethrowers line the advance routes of the motorized German attack columns. They differ considerably from the T-26 light tanks armed with tank guns, and thus could be recognized quickly and be knocked out very quickly because of their weak armor.

An indefinite number of OT-133 light flamethrowing tanks were equipped with 20 to 30 mm added armor in the spring of 1941. This close-up shows clearly the arrangement and attachment of the armor plates.

production of all series of the light tank for equipping as flamethrowing tanks.

First came the T-26 1931 model. It stood out because it had only one turret, on the right side of the vehicle, in which a 1933 model flamethrower (left) and the 7.62 mm DT machine gun in the usual ball mantlet on the right side. The oil tank and compressed-air bottles were in the hull to the left. The supply of oil allowed giving up to seventy one-second bursts of flame at distances up to 35 meters. The crew consisted of two men, the driver and the flamethrower-machine-gun operator, who was also the commander. All other data corresponded to the 1931 model T-26. It was designated OT-26 Ognemetnig Tank (flamethrower tank). The OT-26 was built from 1933 on. Some 500 of them in all were built. Some of the tanks were used to form a flamethrower brigade in the mid-thirties.

Since the OT-26 flamethrowing tank was not satisfactory in every way, production of the OT-130 was begun in 1938. The basis of the design was the 1933 model T-26. Instead of a 45 mm 1932 tank gun, a 1938 model flamethrower, operated by compressed air and reaching targets up to 50 meters, was installed. The improved model could also give 70 bursts of fire, but widely differing statistics as to the amount of oil carried exist (135 to 400 liters). During production of the OT-130 the turret mantlet was modified; the vehicles built last were recognizable by their box-shaped mantlet. Along with the 7.62 mm DT machine gun mounted in the turret, many OT-130 flamethrowing tanks had a second machine gun in a ball mantlet at the back of the turret. The crew of the tank consisted of two men, and the weight is stated as 9.3 tons.

The OT-130 saw action against the Japanese in Manchuria and against the Finns in Karelia in 1939-1940. At this time the Red Army received the final version of the OT-130 flamethrowing tank based on the T-26: the OT-133. It weighed 9.5 tons and carried a 1939 model flamethrower in its turret, along with one or two machine guns. Its performance was substantially like the 1938 model of the OT-130. Four hundred liters of oil were carried, plus four flasks of compressed air. After the winter war against Finland, some

A test model of a mine-removal tank with its impact removal device. This vehicle was based on the T-26 light tank, 1931 model, and in one hour it could clear 5000 to 6000 meters of mined terrain in a path 0.9 meters wide.

Also tested was a T-26 mine-removal tank with a blade mine removal device. This apparatus, rather complicated and easy to damage, was not used further.

OT-133s were given complete added armor for the upper hull and the turret (similar to the 1937 model of the T-26 light tank). Flamethrower units with OT-26, OT-130 and OT-133 saw action against German forces in the summer of 1941. They suffered severe losses. A few flamethrowing tanks of the T-26 series still saw action in the winter of 1941-1942.

Along with these T-26-based special tanks, there were numerous experiments and special developments that were based on this tank. Experiments were made as early as 1935 with an amphibian T-26 TU, 1931 model. Floats on both sides of the vehicle kept it afloat. It was able to attain 3.5 kph in the water. One year later a wading T-26-Pch light tank was tested. With an air duct, it was able to wade up to five meters deep. The riveted armor of the 1933 model T-26 caused problems, as water penetrated into the tank sooner or later.

In 1936 deep-wading tests were carried out with the 1933 model T-26 light tank, in up to five meters of water. The project was designated T-26 Pch. While underwater, the tank received air through a snorkel mounted on the turret.

Another 1933 model T-26 was used for tests with the AT-1 tank glider from the design bureau of O. K. Antonov. It had two tailfins at the rear and double wings on the sides. Special flaps were meant to decrease the landing speed of the flying tank.

Older T-26 tanks were rebuilt as DT-26 (Dunimovaya Tank: foglaying tank) foglaying tanks. As a rule, these tanks retained their turrets, though without weapons. Containers of fog and a blowing apparatus were located either in the right turret or on the rear of the tank.

After the 1939-1940 winter war in Karelia, the Red Army tested turretless T-26 tanks as explosives carriers. They were meant to blow breaches in defensive lines. The T-38 amphibian tank was used as a guiding vehicle, and steering was done by radio.

Let us now look at the development of self-propelled gun mounts (Samochodnaya Ustankovka: SU) on the chassis of the T-

The Red Army's armored troops worked hard to use the capabilities of their tank technology to allow tanks to overcome water obstacles by themselves. This was the purpose of amphibious tests carried out with a 1931 model T-26 light tank in 1935. Added floats kept the vehicle up; the marching speed in the water was stated as 3.5 kph.

The ST-26 was developed for use by the armored engineers. It carried a seven-meter vehicle bridge that could be laid ahead of the tank and support vehicles weighing up to 15 tons. Test models were built in 1933, and a small series was produced in the mid-thirties.

The SU-5 light self-propelled artillery mount of 1934: This one is armed with a 122 mm divisional howitzer (SU-5-2). The heavily armored upper body was open to the rear. The top speed for these support vehicles was listed at 30 kph.

In 1935 tests were made with the SU-6 self-propelled anti-aircraft mount. The 11.3-ton vehicle carried a 76.2 mm 1931 anti-aircraft gun; its 6.5-kilogram shells were suitable for firing on air tragets up to 9200 meters in altitude. The vehicle's top speed was 21 kph.

The T-26 light tank was produced in 1935. It represented an attempt to blend the combat abilities of the T-26 light tank and the BT fast wheel/track tank into a unified tank technology for the Red Army, but only a small series resulted. The weight of the tank is listed as 15 tons, and the three-man crew had a 45 mm tank gun, three 7.62 mm DT machine guns and a flamethrower as weapons. The armor was 15 mm thick. The tank could reach 58 kph on tracks and 80 kph on wheels.

The first series of BT wheel/track tanks were still very similar to the American Christie fact tank. The separate mounting of the weapons in cylindrical turrets can be seen. The 37 mm tank gun had a barrel 1665 mm long (L/45), which was aimed with the shoulder. At its right is the 7.62 mm DT machine gun in a ball mantlet.

The BT wheel/track tank had noticeably large links making up its tracks. Their durability was limited by the high speeds possible with this tank.

The BT-2 wheel/track tanks that were armed with the DA-2 7.62 mm twin machine gun, although outmoded in every sense by that time, still saw action in the battles against the German troops in the summer of 1941. Next to the twin machine guns is the ball mantlet for a third DT machine gun.

Another BT-2 with DA-2 twin machine gun, shot down by German defensive weapons and photographed in July 1941.

26. In the Red Army, self-propelled mounts were regarded as tanks with artillery armament having higher calibers than those of the tank guns in ordinary tanks. In order to keep the weight of the self-propelled mounts low, a turning turret was usually dispensed with, and the armor was made thinner or done away with entirely. In the thirties, much work was done in the Soviet Union on the development of test models of the most varied types of self-propelled mounts. Among them were various vehicles based on the T-26. One of the first prpjects was already underway in 1932 at the Kirov works in Leningrad, under the direction of Engineer S. Ginzburg: the AT-1 (Artilleriskiy Tank) artillery tank. In 1935, test models of a self-propelled mount with closed casemate body and a 76.2 mm PS-3 gun were built. In the body, built of rigid 15 mm armor plate, the gun had a traverse range of 20 degrees, and an elevation range from -1.5 to +43 degrees. The vehicle was 1950 mm high and weighed 9.5 tons. The crew consisted of three or four men.

The Kirov works also developed a whole family of light self-propelled mounts, designated SU-5. The three versions were based on the T-26 chassis, had a raised section at the rear armored only to the front, and carried regimental or divisional artillery guns.

1. SU-5-1, a 76.2 mm 1927 regimental cannon or 76.2 mm 1902/30 divisional cannon. Traverse 15 degrees, elevation -3 to +60 degrees; ranges of 8,500 to 10,000 meters were possible.

2. SU-5-2, a 122 mm 1910/30 divisional howitzer. Shells weighing 21.76 to 23.05 kg could be fired up to 8,875 meters.

3. SU-5-3, a 152.4 mm 1931 mortar with a maximum range of 5,000 meters; shot weight 40.25 kg.

The weight of the self-propelled mounts varied from 10.3 to 11.0 tons; the armor was 6 to 15 mm thick. Depending on the gun type, crews consisted of three or four men. Between 1935 and 1937 a series of fifteen vehicles was built for testing purposes. Another test model of a light self-propelled mount appeared in 1941. It was

Captured BT-2 wheel/track tanks were rarely put to use in the German Army. They proved to be too complicated and liable to break down. Most of them were scrapped.

Tank units equipped with fast wheel/track tanks made a lasting impression on foreign military officials in the course of numerous large-scale Red Army maneuvers in the thirties. They were used in tank brigades of 278 tanks and in cavalry regiments that had 64 of these tanks. There were also BT tanks in heavy tank brigades and some tank battalions.

a very simple solution. On the T-26 chassis a platform was set up. Mounted on it was a fully turnable 76.2 mm 1927 regimental cannon with a shield, as had been used until then on the SU-12 self-propelled mount. The SU-12 was based on the GAZ-AAA 1.5 ton (6x4) truck.

Self-propelled mounts for anti-aircraft guns were also developed in the Soviet Union between 1934 and 1936. A design bureau, under the direction of Professor F. L. Klystova of the Leningrad Academy of Artillery Weapons, was responsible for this project. Another test vehicle was designated SU-8 and was armed with a 76.2 mm 1931 anti-aircraft gun. The gun had no armor protection, and thus had a 360-degree traverse and an elevation range from -5 to +85 degrees. With a crew of five or six men, it had a fighting weight of 11.3 tons; its speed was only 23 kph. At the left side of the front a swingable 7.62 mm DT machine gun was installed in a ball mantlet.

Single models of light self-propelled mounts on T-26 chassis saw action against German troops in the summer of 1941.

3. Fast Wheel/Track Tanks for Long-range Battle Groups

In a land with such great distances as the Soviet Union, there was almost necessarily a need for a tank that could move at high speeds on wheels or tracks. Thus the invention of a wheel/track tank by the American W. J. Christie had to be of interest to the Soviet military. Two examples of the Christie M-1931 (T-3) tank were bought in the USA and tested very carefully at the tank test center in Voronesh in 1931. In great haste, a new tank was designed on the basis of these. The Kharkov "Comintern" factory produced the prototypes. Even before they were finished, the Revolutionary War Council of the Soviet Union decided on May 23, 1931, that the production of another new tank, designated BT-2, should begin. Series production began in September 1931. At the military parade in Red Square on November 7 of that year, three BT tanks participated.

The fast wheel/track tanks were intended for use in the mechanized and armored units of the Red Army, and in cavalry units. Their task was to be advancing into the enemy's hinterlands, after a successful breakthrough of his defenses, to break supply lines, roll

At the end of 1932 the BT-5 wheel/track tank was put into production. The most important innivation was the cylindrical turret with rear extension; it held a 1932 model 45 mm tank gun, a 7.62 mm DT machine gun, and a two-man crew. The version shown here, a BT-5 TU, can be recognized by its antenna in the form of a railing on the turret.

Contemporaries regarded the "Russian Christie" as a useful battle tank with poor armor, good weapons, total off-road ability and a high top speed. (See Wehrtechnische Monatshefte, No. 8, Berlin 1936, p. 354.)

Only small numbers of the BT-5 wheel/track tank appeared on the Republican side in the Spanish Civil War between 1936 and 1939.

over command posts and capture important defensive positions. The BT tank was best suited to this. In the contemporary press it was characterized as follows: "Christie fast tanks are, because of their high speed and full off-road capability, the new-age mechanized combat cavalry, whose use in open terrain is foreseen, where they can develop their speed fully, in order to come at the enemy quickly from effective shot ranges." Like its model, the Christie tank, this tank could run either on wheels or tracks. Off the road, it moved forward on tracks, while on paved roads it ran on wheels. The rear road wheel on either side was the drive wheel; the power was transmitted from the gearbox to the drive wheels by a chain drive. Changing from wheel to track drive took about half an hour. When it ran on wheels, the tracks were stored on special racks above the running gear, so that a change was possible at any time. On wheels, a third of the vehicle's entire weight rested on the rear pair of road wheels. This gave considerably worse towing ability than when it ran on tracks. If the crew neglected to switch back to tracks after leaving paved roads, the drive wheels sank into the soft ground and tended to spin. The use of the wheels was thus limited. Another characteristic of the BT tank was the individual suspension of the road wheels. Every wheel had twin hard-rubber tires and was linked via an axle arm with a large coil spring. This was mounted vertically inside the side hull armor. With this suspension, spring movements up to 350 mm were possible, which kept the chassis steady

In the vicinity of Minsk the Germans captured a whole trainload of damaged BT-5 wheel/track tanks. Aside from the impression that these tanks made with their high speed, they no longer played any role in the combat between the German Wehrmacht and the Red Army in 1941.

The power of inner detonations has blown the turret of this bT-5 tank off its hull and flung it aside. The turret was identical to that of the 1933 model T-26 light tank (this is the version with upright [p. 16] roller-mantlet covering). Among its typical features were the big, angular folding turret hatch and the lateral vision slits with pistol loopholes below them, visible here.

A BT-5 wheel/track tank, abandoned but almost undamaged, gives the German soldiers a motif for a souvenir photo in July 1941.

The weak armor of the BT-5 often resulted in direct hits setting the fuel supply (396 liters of gasoline) on fire and burning the tank out completely, as in this July 1941 photo.

This rear view of a totally burned-out BT-7 shows the conical shape of the turret and the different hatches.

The BT-7 wheel/track tank was supplied to the armored troops of the Red Army as of 1935. It featured a better powerplant and a new armored hull design, with armor plates no longer riveted but welded together. At first the turret of the predecessor BT-5 was retained.

In this early BT-7 the difference between the welded hull and the riveted turret, which was already used on the BT-5 wheel/track tank and the 1933 model T-26 light tank, can be seen clearly. The driver's hatch in the front hull is made in two parts which open upward and downward.

On the advance route to Luck in July 1941, armor-piercing shells have easily penetrated the 13 mm armor of this early-type BT-7's turret. The ventilator between the hatches is open; the openings for the panoramic scope on top of the turret are covered with armor plates.

The 45 mm 1932 or 1934 model tank gun installed in the BT-7 had a barrel 2072.5 mm long (L/46) and a semi-automatic vertical breech. It could fire twelve shots per minute. According to German data, armor-piercing shells from this gun could penetrate 22 mm of armor at 1500 meters.

A BT-7 wheel/track tank of the early type, with a firing light attached to the roller mantlet. The panoramic scope on the top of the turret is easy to see. The plug for the pistol loophole under the side sighting slit was put in from inside.

even when moving fast on uneven terrain. Servicing them in the field was laborious. Still, this form of suspension, combined with the advantageous power-to-weight ratio (in the BT-2 33, 6 HP/ton), provided an important prerequisite for the tank's good handling qualities. The main advantage of the fast BT wheel/track tank was not that it could be utilized with its wheel/track running gear, but first of all that, even when running on tracks, it could move at high speed (62 kph).

The original powerplant was an American aircraft engine of the "Liberty" type that produced 400 horsepower. In later variants of the BT tank, this powerplant was replaced by the Russian-built 12-cylinder M-5 aircraft engine. For those times, the range of the first wheel/track tank was a noteworthy 150 to 200 kilometers on tracks and 250 to 300 km on wheels.

The tank was guided by a steering wheel. The driver sat forward in the center, and the turret was right over the center of the hull. Unlike the American model, which had welded armor, the Soviet BT was completely riveted. A further shortcoming of the BT-2 was seen in its insufficient armament. The reason was the shortage of space in the small cylindrical turret. At first only a 1931 model 37 mm BS-3 tank gun was installed. In this version there was no machine gun. In addition, the observation capability from the turret was not sufficient. This problem was solved by vision slits on the sides. The first sixty BT-2s were delivered in that state. Another 350 tanks had a 7.62 mm caliber DA-2 twin machine gun and a separate 7.62 mm DT machine gun in a ball mantlet. The twin machine gun had an elevation range from -25 to +22 degrees. The most important version of the BT-2 was surely that with a 1931

Just before World War II began, the Red Army had disbanded its mechanized corps, which had existed since 1933. By mid-1940 this was seen as a mistake. The new formation of nine mechanized corps began, and they were supplied with over 1000 tanks. In the first phase of the war with Germany they lost most of their tanks, including many of the BT-7 type.

The final appearance of the BT-7 wheel/track tank was recognizable by the conically shaped welded turret. The roller mantlet inside held a 45 mm 1934 or 1938 model tank gun, which was joined by a 7.62 mm DT machine gun. Some tanks had a movable machine gun in the rear extension of the turret; others were armed with an anti-aircraft machine gun instead. Typical features include the two round hatches in the turret top and the NT-9 panoramic scope.

This BT-7 wheel/track tank was a total loss because of burning fuel and exploding ammunition. Note the bracket for the 7.62 mm anti-aircraft machine gun.

model 37 mm BS-3 tank gun, plus one DT machine gun in a ball mantlet. The two weapons were not coupled; the tank gun was aimed by means of a shoulder brace (elevation -8 to +25 degrees). The fighting compartment for the two crewmen in the turret was very cramped. There was no room for a radio set. The ammunition consisted of 92 to 96 armor-piercing or explosive shells for the 37 mm tank gun and 2,709 rounds for the machine gun.

In various works on Soviet tank technology, two other variations of the fast wheel/track tank besides the BT-2 are noted, the BT-3 and BT-4, which differed in terms of their armament. The BT-4 with its two machine-gun turrets, as in the 1931 model T-26, is of interest and was intended for infantry support. A self-propelled mount for a 76.2 mm SU-1 regimental cannon was also projected. And in 1934 a design bureau at the "Red Proletarian" factory in Moscow worked on a BT-2 artillery tank with a 76 mm gun and a 7.62 mm DT machine gun. It too remained only a project. Production of the BT-2 lasted till the start of 1933. Although this type formed only a small part of all the BT tanks that were built, it still saw action in the 1939-1940 winter war against Finland and the combat against German troops in 1941.

The insufficient firepower of the BT-2 very quickly resulted in new military requirements, including:

-stronger armament;

-coaxial mounting of tank guns and machine guns;

-more space in the tank, especially from a new turret design;

-space to install a radio set;

-improved mobility by using a reliable high-powered engine made in the USSR.

Smaller improvements concerned the suspension and the installation of targeting and observation equipment.

At the end of 1932, production of the fast BT-5 wheel/track tank began. The turret of the first series built differed only slightly from that of the BT-2. Its armor was riveted, except for the rear extension of the turret, which was welded. In the gun mount there was now the new 1932 model 45 mm tank gun, coupled with a 7.62 mm DT machine gun. The gun, also installed in the 1933 model T-

The sometimes insufficient training of the Russian tank soldiers resulted in many tanks having to be abandoned because of bad terrain conditions, minor technical damage, or often only a lack of fuel. This BT-7 wheel-track tank got stuck and was photographed in July 1941.

Heavy German air raids put this BT-7 wheel/track tank out of action. On the turret, torn loose from the hull, the ball mentlet for a 7.62 mm DT machine gun in the rear extension can be seen.

26, had a maximum range of 4,800 meters. The initial velocity of the 1.43 kilogram tank shell was given as 760 meters per second. At 100 meters, 42 mm of armor plate could be penetrated. The explosive shell weighed more than two kilograms. Along with the TOP tank aiming scope with twofold magnification and a 15-degree field of vision, a PTK panoramic scope, projecting from the turret top, was used. The two rectangular escape hatches in the turret were new (the BT-2 had only one on the right side). During the 1933 production year, the old cylindrical turret with an added rear extension was replaced by the turret including a rear extension, also used on the 1933 model T-26. Some of the ammunition, which consisted of 115 shells and 2,394 machine-gun rounds, was carried in the latter. The BT-5 TU command tank, 1934 model, carried only 72 shells for the tank gun, to leave room for the radio set. This version was recognizable by the radio antenna around the turret.

A BT-7 wheel/track tank in the streets of Grodno, photographed in the first half of July 1941. The fire of enemy weapons tore the whole rear extension off the turret.

BT-7 tanks were fitted with turrets of varying types. Along with two round hatches (above), there were turrets with one round and one oval hatch (center) and also those with two oval hatches (below).

A BT-7 wheel/track tank captured by the Germans, seen in the driving test center of the Army Weapons Office in Kummersdorf near Berlin. Here it was designated Light Tank 74 (r) BT-. The German forces very rarely used tanks of this type.

With the new, larger turret and the more powerful weapons, the BT-5, while keeping the armor of the BT-2, attained a fighting weight of 11.5 tons. Among its other characteristics were strengthened components for the running gear and the use of a Soviet-made M-5 aircraft engine. The motor produced 350 HP, and the power-to-weight ratio sank to 30.4 HP/ton.

A small number of the BT-5 tanks carried a 76.2 mm 1927/32 tank gun with L/16.5 barrel length. With this gun, 6.2 kg explosive shells could be fired up to 7,125 meters. There was also a 7.62 mm DT machine gun. The task of this type, designated (BT-5) Artillery Tank, was to attack the first line of attacking tanks with fire from its large-caliber gun.

Along with the BT-5 artillery tank, the Red Army tested a number of special tanks based on the wheel/track tank in the mid-thirties. They included engineer tanks to lay fascine mats, mine-removal tanks and bridgelaying tanks. In March 1935 the BT bridgelaying tank, still equipped with a wooden vehicle bridge, was first tested. An improved model had a metal bridge and was equipped for self-defense with the machine-gun turret of the T-38 amphibian tank.

For the fast BT tanks, which were often supposed to operate in combat far from their own troops and thus be cut off from support forces, the ability to overcome water obstacles quickly was of decisive importance. Thus from 1934 to 1936, at first with the BT-2 and later with the BT-5, wading tests were carried out. The vehicles were given added equipment like that of the T-26 Pch, with which they could wade through water obstacles up to five meters deep. They were designated T-5 Pch. A further means of overcoming water obstacles, by making the BT-5 amphibious through the addition of floats or Faltwende, was tested in various forms in 1935. Finally, a variant of the fast wheel/track tank appeared in 1936 as a flamethrowing tank, using the turret of the OT-133.

In the mid-thirties the BT-IS wheel/track tank was developed, utilizing components of the BT-5. This tank, developed under the

A BT-7 wheel/track tank on the battlefield at Grodno. Bitter fighting took place here on Jule 24 and 25, 1941 between armored units of the German Army and the Red Army. The Russian counterattacks were badly organized and failed to achieve their purpose. Many tanks were lost.

Close-up of a BT-7 turret as used since 1937. The PTK panoramoc scopes stuck up like horns from the turret top. They had twofold megnification and a field of vision stated as 22 degrees. Also recognizable is the bracket for the anti-aircraft machine gun. The barrel of the tank gun was destroyed by explosion.

Captured BT-7 wheel/track tanks were disposed of on orders from the Army Weapons Office and their armor scrapped. This example was photographed in the spring of 1942.

direction of designer N. F. Zygankovich, had an important new feature in the form of three pairs of road wheels, all driven when the tank ran on them. In 1937 five vehicles were delivered for testing purposes. They were recognizable by the angled hull armor. Its purpose was to deflect direct hits. In a test model of the BT-IS developed further in this way, this form of armor was improved on; the running gear received angled side armor and the turret shape was also changed.

International attention was attracted by the BT tank, often called the "Russian Christie Fast Tank" at the time, after it appeared in the Red Army's large-scale military maneuvers in the Kiev Military District. Among other things practiced there was the concerted action of a mechanized corps and a cavalry division to surround and destroy an enemy force. 1,040 tanks, which had to cover up to 650 kilometers at a quick marching speed in a short time, took part in this maneuver. Similar large maneuvers took place in White Russia a year later.

In April 1937 the Soviet Union delivered the first twenty BT-5 tanks to the Spanish Republican forces. In all, 64 wheel/track tanks of this type saw action in the Spanish Civil War from 1936 to 1939. In 1938 the Spanish Nationalists were able to capture or knock out six of these tanks, unfamiliar to them until then, in the combat on the Ebro front. From then on they were used by the Nationalist forces. The Red Army used BT-5 tanks in battle against the Japanese at the Chalchin-Gol in July 1939, in the occupation of the western areas of White Russia and the Ukraine in September 1939, in the Finnish winter war of 1939-1940, and in combat against the German forces in the summer of 1941.

Work continued intensely on the further development of the BT-5. The BT-6 project, though, never got beyond the design stage. As of 1935, the new BT-7 tank model was in production. Among its major features were a modern engine, an improved gearbox with three forward speeds in place of the previous four, new Saslavsky system brakes, and a new main clutch. The motor, based on a BMW aircraft engine, produced 450 HP at 1750 rpm. It was designated M-17 T and was also used in M-17 L form in the T-28 medium tank. The front armor of the hull was increased to 30 mm, that on the turret to 15 mm. The side armor remained as on the BT-5. A new feature was that the armor plates on the hull and turret were no longer riveted on but welded together. This process increased the stiffness and resistance of the armor and the strength of the joints between the steel plates.

Very typical features of the BT-7 wheel/track tank were the two large exhaust pipes for the twelve-cylinder M-15 T engine, which produced 450 horsepower and used 790 liters of fuel to cover 375 kilometers on tracks.

Again and again, almost undamaged tanks fell into the hands of German troops. These are BT-7 wheel/track tanks that got stuck. Many crews paniced and fled. In other situations they fought against all attacks in their hopeless positions and died in their tanks.

A Red Army light tank brigade's BT-7 after a battle. Such a unit was composed of staff, staff units, an armored reconnaissance battalion, and four tank battalions with a total of 295 wheel/track tanks of this type, plus other armored vehicles.

At first, BT-7 tanks were built with the cylindrical turret of the BT-5. Soon after production began, though, a conically shaped turret that gave more protection from infantry weapon and machine-gun fire was introduced. It was typified by two round hatches on top, which later won the BT-7 the nickname of "Mickey Mouse" among German soldiers. An improved 45 mm 1934 tank gun was installed, and was later fitted with an electric firing system.

In 1938 the aiming system was improved again. It was now characterized by a vertically stabilized sight line. The gun was given 1938 designation and was combined with a TOP-30 targeting scope (twofold magnification, 15-degree field of vision). The BT-7 also used a panoramic targeting scope (two as of 1938). The better targeting systems had made electric firing necessary.

Several BT-7 tanks had, in addition to a coaxial machine gun in a roller mantlet, another 7.62 mm DT machine gun in a ball mantlet at the back of the turret. Some were also equipped with an anti-aircraft machine gun. Tanks without radios carried 172 to 188 tank-gun shells. The BT-7 TU command tank could only carry 132 to 146 shells. For the machine gun, 2,394 rounds were carried. Older versions of the BT-7 TU with cylindrical turrets still carried the 71-TK radio set with all-around antenna. Command tanks with the conical turret had a rod antenna. As with the BT-5, small numbers of BT-7s were armed with the 1927/32 76.2 mm tank gun. This artillery tank version carried forty shells if it had a radio or 50 if it did not. In addition, the two-man turret crew could use a 7.62 mm DT machine gun in a separate ball mantlet. Because of the higher weight of the BT-7 A tank (14.5 tons), driving on wheels was generally not expected. An OP-7 flamethrowing tank based on the BT-7 was also built but did not reach the troops.

The BT-2 and BT-5 were typified by large-link tracks. On wet ground in particular, these tracks were inclined to slide. From the BT-7 on, smaller-link tracks were used, as they were more suitable for the running gear of these fast-moving tanks. Driving on wheels was almost completely eliminated. In place of the former wheel steering, a control stick was used.

Fighters and dive bombers of the German Luftwaffe often attacked Red Army armored units while marching or preparing for action, causing heavy losses. These two pictures were taken by German soldiers in July 1941.

Before production of the BT-7 began, tests were proceeding on the PT-1 amphibian tank (based on the BT-5). It was typified by a higher hull. Along with the usual turret weapons, it had another machine gun in a ball mantlet on the hull ahead of the driver. The project ended for the time being with the PT-1 A.

A further development had begun with the BT-5. In 1938 several vehicles of this type had a W-2 Diesel engine installed for testing. The engine was based on a 12-cylinder Hispano-Suiza aircraft powerplant. The desire to have a special Diesel tank motor grew out of the earlier problems in using aircraft engines in wheel/track tanks. The M-17 T in the BT-7 was not fully satisfactory either. After successful testing in the BT-5, the Diesel engine, designated W-2, was put into series production in 1939 and installed in the BT-7. This version was designated BT-7 M. The fighting weight increased to 14.65 tons. All the tanks were armed with the 1938 45 mm tank gun and three DT machine guns (one beside the tank gun, one in the rear of the turret, and one as an AA gun). The top speed on tracks was increased to 62 kph (86 kph on wheels), and the range was 600 to 700 kilometers.

Production of the last version of the BT fast wheel/track tank began in 1939. In place of the BT-7 M designation, it was also called BT-8. In the spring of 1940, the T-34 replaced the BT-7 M (BT-8). A year later, in 1941, the last BT-7 M/BT-8 tanks left the factories. A version called Artillery Tank BT-8 A, with a 76.2 mm 1927/32 tank gun, was built only as a test model. Note that this tank also had a 7.62 mm machine gun ahead of the driver.

These BT-7 tanks were put out of action in the central sector of the eastern front by tanks of the 7th Armored Division (Armored Group 3), and photographed in the first half of July 1941.

The large road wheels of the BT-7, equipped with rubber pads (as were those of the other wheel/track tanks), were suspended individually on large coil springs which provided adequate suspension even at high speeds.

In the BT-7 the 45 mm 1934 model tank gun was usually used. The gun was turned to the side with the turret (360 degrees), and its elevation range was from -8 to +25 degrees.

Some 6,000 tanks of all BT series were produced. The greatest numbers of them were BT-7s; the BT-7 M (BT-8) was merely a transitional model to the T-34, and 706 of them were built. The value of the BT tanks was their high speed on tracks, and their long range under the conditions existing in the Soviet Union (few and bad roads, insufficient railroad lines) was another advantage. The strong armament of these tanks must also be noted. The first motors used had technical problems; they were hard to start and were very prone to overheating. When started, they sometimes caught fire. The mechanical reliability of the BT tanks certainly left something to be desired. The tracks gave rise to constant criticism. Finally, experience with the BT-5 in the Spanish Civil War in 1936-1939 showed another weak point: the armor. Despite numerous improvements, this still could not be cured in the BT-7.

BT-7 tanks saw service against Japanese troops at the Chalchin-Gol River in the summer of 1939. The Soviet Marshal G. K. Zhukov wrote in his "Memories and Thoughts"[3] that the action of the 11th Armored Brigade, which had over 150 tanks, constituted the main strength of the Soviet troops in the coverless country. "We decided to put them into action at once, to drive the just-crossed Japanese troops out of action and give them no time to dig in and organize antitank defenses. . . . About 10:45 A.M. the main strength of the 11th Armored Brigade moved out and attacked the enemy on the march." A Japanese soldier who had been taken prisoner later reported to Zhukov: "A few dozen tanks suddenly attacked our troops. They caused terrible confusion among us. . . ."[4]

Less favorable conditions for this type of tank existed during the 1939-40 winter war with Finland. Many BT tanks were destroyed in the impenetrable Karelian woods or captured by Finnish troops. The Red Army's tank soldiers had to gather similarly bad experi-

3. Zhukov, G. K., Memories and Thoughts, Moscow 1969.
4. Some of the BT-2 tanks were armed only with a 37 mm tank gun.

After a Diesel ennige had been installed in a BT-5 wheel/track tank for testing in 1938, series production of the BT-7 M (also called BT-8) could begin in 1939. A notable innovation, the 12-cylinder Diesel engine produced 500 HP, which gave the 14.6-ton tank a top speed of 62 kph on tracks.

Production of the BT-7 M (BT-8) ended in after another 706 of the tanks had been built in 1940; they were replaced by the new T-34 medium tank. In the following year's battles, the BT-7 with the Diesel engine appeared fairly seldom.

A BT-7 TU command tank, presumably one from early (1937) production, as indicated by the antenna, which is still a railing around the turret. Command tanks built later had rod antennas. To make room for the radio, the ammunition was limited to a maximum of 146 tank-gun shells and 2394 7.62 mm machine-gun bullets.

Among the rarer versions of the BT-7 wheel/track tank was the BT-7 A artillery tank of 1938. It was used for second-line artillery support and held a 76.2 mm 1927/32 model tank gun in an enlarged turret, as well as a 7.62 mm DT machine gun.

ences in the summer of 1941. In the German technical journal "Wehrtechnische Monatshefte," no. 9, Summer 1942, it was estimated, "The BT was certainly quite a fast tank, but it had faulty steering and poor-quality tracks. . . . It was not equal to the German tanks." In Tank Recognition Chart 2 accompanying Army Service Directive 469/2a, "Tank Defense of All Weapons," published on February 1, 1943, the BT was mentioned as "a fast light tank with good mobility" and insufficient armor. By the summer of 1942, the Red Army's armored troops had lost the greater part of their BT fast wheel/track tanks.

The BT-7 light flamethrowing tank (first type) was also called OP-7 and weighed 11.5 tons. Besides its usual armament of a 45 mm 1934 model tank gun and a 7.62 mm DT machine gun, it carried a flamethrower on the left side of the bow of its hull. The supply of burning oil was limited.

Tactical - Technical Data (BT-2, 1931 model)

Crew: 2-3 men
Weight: 10.2 tons
Armament: 1 BS-3 37 mm caliber tank gun (1931 model), with 96 rounds;
1 DT4 7.62 mm caliber machine gun, with 2709 rounds;
or 1 twin DA-2 7.62 mm caliber machine gun, with ? rounds;
1 DT 7.62 mm caliber machine gun with ? rounds
Armor plate:
Hull: Front: 13 mm
Sides: 13 mm
Rear: 13 mm
Top: 10 mm
Bottom: 6-10 mm
Turret: Front: 13 mm
Sides: 13 mm
Rear: 13 mm
Top: 10 mm
Powerplant: 12-cylinder 4-stroke Liberty gasoline engine
Performance: 343 HP aat 2000 rpm
Fuel capacity: 400 liters
Power to weight: 33.6 HP/ton
Length: 5760 mm
Width: 2150 mm
Height: 2200 mm
Ground clearance: 350-380 mm
Top speed: Tracks: 62 kph; wheels: 110 kph
Range: Tracks: 150-200 km; wheels: 250-300 km
Climbing degree: 40 degrees
Spanning ability: 2100 mm
Climbing ability: 750 mm
Wading ability: 1000-1200 mm
Specific ground pressure: 0.63 kp/sq. cm. on tracks

A second variant of the BT-7-based flamethrowing tank already had the conical turret with the 45 mm 1934 model tank gun and 7.62 mm coaxial DT machine gun. Because of the enlarged and armored oil containers on both sides of the hull (above the track aprons), its fighting weight (13.8 tons) was higher. The flamethrower pipe was mounted on the left side of the hull here.

Tactical - Technical Data (BT-5, 1933 model)

Crew: 3 men
Weight: 11.5 tons
Armament: 1 45 mm caliber 1932 tank gun, with 72 to 115 rounds
1 or 2 DT 7.62 mm caliber machine guns, with 2709 rounds
Armor plate:
Hull: Front: 13 mm
Sides: 13 mm
Rear: 13 mm
Top: 10 mm
Bottom: 6-10 mm
Turret: Front: 13 mm
Sides: 13 mm
Rear: 13 mm
Top: 10 mm
Powerplant: 12-cylinder 4-stroke M-5 gasoline engine
Performance: 350 HP at 2300 rpm
Fuel capacity: 400 liters
Power to weight: 30.4 HP/ton
Length: 5760 mm
Width: 2150 mm
Height: 2250 mm
Ground clearance: 350 mm
Top speed: Tracks: 52 kph; wheels: 72 kph
Range: Tracks: 200 km; wheels: 300 km
Climbing degree: 37 degrees
Spanning ability: 2000 mm
Climbing ability: 550 mm
Wading ability: 900 mm
Specific ground pressure: 0.65 kp/sq. cm.

***Right*: In 1935 five of the BT-IS wheel/track tank were built. The experimental vehicle featured angled armor plate on all sides and shows the Russian military leaders' and designers' interest in finding new ways to make armor more effective.**

In 1936 diving tests in a maximun of five meters of water were made with the BT-5 wheel/track tank. As in similar tests with the T-26 light tank, air was provided by a snorkel. The propject was designated BT-5 Pch.

In 1935 the wheel/track tank was already tested with two metal floats attached to the sides of the chassis.

The load limit of the 10.5-meter vehicle bridge for the BT bridgelaying tank of 1937 is listed at 15 tons. This special tank could reach a top speed of 52 kph and carried 13 mm armor plate.

Medium tanks with multiple turrets were built, using British models, at the "Bolshevik" factory in Leningrad and tested in 1931-32. After the Red Army armored troops' requests for higher firepower had been met by the use of the 76.2 mm 1927/32 tank gun, series production of the T-28 began in 1933.

On this T-28 the twelve small road wheels, which allowed vibration-free driving along with the effective suspension, can be seen. Special armored aprons protected the suspension on both sides.

Tactical - Technical Data		**(BT-7, 1936 model)**
Crew:		3 men
Weight:		13.8 tons
Armament:		1 45 mm caliber 1934 tank gun, with 132-188 rounds 2 or 3 7.62 mm caliber DT machine guns, with 2394 rounds
Armor plate:		
Hull:	Front:	22 mm
	Sides:	13 mm
	Rear:	13 mm
	Top:	10 mm
	Bottom:	6-10 mm
Turret:[5]	Front:	15 mm
	Sides:	15 mm
	Rear:	15 mm
	Top:	15 mm
Powerplant:		12-cylinder 4-stroke M-15 T gasoline engine
Performance:		450 HP at 1750 rpm
Fuel capacity:		790 liters
Power to weight:		32.6 HP/ton
	Length:	5660 mm
	Width:	2290 mm
	Height:	2420 mm
Ground clearance:		400-420 mm
Top speed:		Tracks: 53 kph; wheels: 73 kph
Range:		Tracks: 375 km; wheels: 500 km
Climbing degree:		32 degrees
Spanning ability:		2000 mm
Climbing ability:		550 mm
Wading ability:		1200 mm
Specific ground pressure:		0.75 kp/sq. cm.

During the battles with German troops in the summer of 1941, the T-28 tanks assembled in the Red Army's heavy tank brigades were impressive for their size and firepower, but their weak armor let them be put out of action very quickly by defensive weapons.

Each of the two turrets to the right and left of the driver held a 7.62 mm DT machine gun, and one or two more of the same weapon were in the main turret, one in a separate ball mantlet to the right of the 76.2 mm tank gun. Some tanks had another machine gun in the rear of the turret. At the end of the thirties they were also fitted with a bracket for an anti-aircraft machine gun on top of the turret.

5. Some still fitted with the old cylindrical turret, then 13 mm armor on front, sides and rear, 10 mm on top.

Both pictures were taken by German soldiers to remember "Stalin's Giants" by, as they formed a striking motif. The exhaust pipes and the radiator for the 12-cylinder M17 engine (which produced 450 to 500 HP) can be seen.

Tactical - Technical Data (BT-7, 1939 model, also BT-8)

Crew:		3 men
Weight:		14.4-14.5 tons; 14.65 tons
Armament:	1 45 mm caliber 1938 tank gun, with ? rounds (no data)	
	3 7.62 mm caliber DT machine guns, with 2394 rounds	
Armor plate:		
Hull:	Front:	22 mm
	Sides:	13 mm
	Rear:	13 mm
	Top:	10 mm
	Bottom:	6-10 mm
Turret:	Front:	15 mm
	Sides:	15 mm
	Rear:	15 mm
	Top:	15 mm
Powerplant:	V-12-cylinder 4-stroke W-2 Diesel engine	
Performance:		500 HP
Fuel capacity:		no data
Power to weight:		34.7 HP/ton
	Length:	5660 mm
	Width:	2290 mm
	Height:	2420 mm
Ground clearance:		350 mm
Top speed:		Tracks: 62 kph; wheels: 86 kph
Range:		Tracks: 600 km; wheels: 700 km
Climbing degree:		32 degrees
Spanning ability:		2000 mm
Climbing ability:		550 mm
Wading ability:		1200 mm
Specific ground pressure:		0.78 kp/sq. cm.

4. Medium Tanks

In the Soviet Union, the request for a medium tank with powerful armament had led to the TG-1 in 1929. Its powerplant, though, proved to be very unreliable, and its development was halted in 1931. The new development of a support and destroyer tank was

In 1938, 96 T-28 medium tanks were built. During the year the more powerful 76.2 mm L-10 tank gun with a longer barrel (L/26.5) was put into use. This picture, taken in July 1941, shows T-28s with the olf 1927/32 tank gun (left) and the new type (right).

This T-28 medium tank with 7.62 mm L-11 tank gun was captured by the Finns in the 1939-40 winter war. The Russians saw the weak armor as a major fault; it was soon increased to 50 to 80 mm.

A T-28 M medium tank at the driving test building of the Army Weapons Office on Kummersdorf, near Berlin. The armor, strengthened by added plates on the main turret and by the right machine gun, can be seen. This raised the fighting weight of the tank to 32 tons. Poorer handling was accepted.

Another photo from Kummersdorf. In the foreground is a T-28 M medium tank, in back is an older type without added armor. The antenna for the 71-TK-1 radio forms the turret railing.

urgently requested by the armored troops of the Red Army to support the units equipped with light tanks. They were to see action where strongly fortified and defended enemy positions could make the success of Russian attacks questionable. At the beginning of the thirties the general attitude was that a tank that could meet these requirements had to be strongly armed. Its guns were to be mounted in several turrets. Such concepts came from Britain, where the Vickers 16-ton tank (Medium Tank MK III, A 6) with its three turrets had attracted attention. The idea of a "land cruiser" was borrowed from the navy.

In the Soviet Union, too, this tank attracted attention. In 1931 the testing department for mechanical design at the Leningrad "Bolshevik" Machine Factory (as of 1932 Works No. 174, renamed "Kirov" in 1934) began to develop a medium tank. At that time the factory was busy with the production of the T-26 light tank. Under the direction of S. A. Ginsburg, the new multiturreted tank quickly took shape. Test models were finished by the end of the year. In 1932 extensive testing could be carried out. In the main turret a 45 mm tank gun was installed. In each of the two minor turrets, to the driver's left and right, was a 7.62 mm DT machine gun. The vehicle's armor was 20 to 30 mm thick, could go 60 kph, and weighed 17.3 tons. The basic design and fighting weight were very similar to the Vickers 16-ton tank, the model for this tank which was now designated T-28.

In the course of developmental work, many changes were made to the vehicle. The most important change concerned the armament. In place of the 45 mm 1932 tank gun, a 76.2 mm 1927/32 tank gun (a version of the same-caliber regimental cannon) was introduced. At the same time, the turret was enlarged to include a rear extension. With the new main armament, the tank came closer to meeting its task of providing artillery support as a medium tank. The 45 mm gun had fired a 2.15 kg shell; now the shell weighed 6.20 kg.

Specialists from the Army Weapons Office prepare to ship a T-28 medium tank and a T-35 heavy tank (left) to Germany. The tanks had been captured in June and July 1941.

Older-type T-28 medium tanks are seen in a military parade on Red Square in Moscow. The tank still appeared in this form in combat against the Germans in the summer of 1941.

The German designation for the captured T-28 medium tank was "Medium Tank 746 (r) (= Russian) T-28". Although most of the approximately 500 tanks of this type that were built fell into German hands, they were rarely put into service.

At +25-degree elevation, shot ranges up to 7,125 meters were possible. A tank targeting scope and a panoramic targeting scope were available for aiming. The shape of the two machine-gun turrets had also been changed. Their traverse range is stated as 220 degrees. In some tanks, another DT machine gun was mounted in a rear niche of the main turret. The ammunition included 64 to 70 76.2 mm shells and 7,938 to 8,320 rounds of machine-gun ammunition. The armor, 20 to 30 mm thick, offered protection from large-caliber infantry weapon fire and shell fragments. Each T-28 was equipped with a 71-TK-1 radio set (replaced in 1935 by the 71-TK-2 model) and also had a foglaying device. The tank's crew numbered six men.

The T-28 stood out for its steady handling and ability to overcome obstacles. The 12-cylinder, 4-stroke M-17 L gasoline engine was based on a BMW aircraft engine. It developed a maxmimum of 500 horsepower. The mechanical gearbox had five forward speeds and one reverse. A special lock prevented shifting gears without using the main clutch. The armored hull was carried by four coupled road wheels. An advantage was that the turret had a turning stage that made the turret crew's work considerably easier. The first T-28 tanks from series production were turned over to the Red Army in February 1933, and took part in the May Day parade in Moscow. After seven years, at the beginning of 1940, production was stopped. By then the Kirov Works in Leningrad had produced 503 T-28 tanks in all. They were divided by year as follows:

Year	Number	Year	Number	Total
1933	41	1937	39	503
1934	50	1938	96	
1935	32	1939	131	
1936	101	1940	13	

T-28 tanks belonged to the heavy armored brigades of the Red Army. They had 136 tanks of this type, as well as 47 BT tanks. One heavy tank brigade (the 5th) had a mixed assortment, 62 heavy T-35 tanks and 32 T-28 medium tanks. Several tank battalions for infantry support had both BT and T-28 tanks (35 per battalion).

The tank units equipped with T-28s belonged to the elite of the Red Army. The tanks were displayed proudly, along with T-35 heavy tanks, at the yearly parades on Red Square in Moscow, and in other large cities. The first combat in which the T-28 saw action took place during the occupation of the western areas of the Ukraine and White Russia in September 1939. During the winter war in Karelia in 1939-40, a serious fault of the T-28 made itself known: its weak armor. A number of T-28s were shot down by the Finns, and some were captured and used by the Finnish forces.

Tanks of this type built since 1938 had a more powerful 76.2 mm L-10 tank gun with L/26.5 barrel length. The shell, weighing

These two photos show older-type T-28 medium tanks that were captured by German troops in the western boundary areas of the Soviet Union.

This T-28 is already armed with the long-barreled 76.2 mm L-11 tank gun. A typical feature is the added armor over the edge of the turret. On the turret is a bracket for a 7.62 mm anti-aircraft machine gun.

A newer-type T-28 medium tank with added armor has been put out of action. Its gun could reach targets up[to 7300 meters away. For aiming, a targeting scope and two panoramic scopes were on hand.

This picture of a destroyed T-28 M with a 76.2 mm L-11 tank gun shows interesting details of the tank's rear end. The transverse muffler takes up the whole width of the hull. The gearbox can also be seen.

German soldiers remove fuel from a T-28 M medium tank captured from a supply train. The picture was taken at a railway depot in the Ukraine in August 1941.

This older-type T-28 was abandoned and burned by Red Army men.

A T-28 in the Moscow Military Museum.

6.2 kg, could be fired with an initial velocity of 555 m/sec. The separate 7.62 mm DT machine gun, mounted to the right of the tank gun, had an elevation range of -30 to +30 degrees and a traverse of 60 degrees (independently of the range of the main turret). At the beginning of 1940, attempts were made to strengthen the T-28 tank's armor plate. Through the addition of more armor, the front plates of the hull and turret were made 50 to 60 mm thick, while the side and rear armor were increased to 40 mm. The vehicle's weight increased to 31 to 32 tons. Vehicles with the longer tank gun and added armor were designated T-28 E or T-28 M. They saw action in 1940 when the Mannerheim Line was penetrated. Some T-28s, still armed with the 76.2 mm 1927/32 tank gun, were fitted with a conical main turret. The T-28 became the basis for a whole series of special tanks and other experimental and special vehicles. Among the best-known types was the T-29 medium wheel/track tank. The first plans for it were made in 1934 at the developmental office of the Kirov works in Leningrad. At that time a young engineer named M. I. Koshkin worked there. Several years later he played a major role in planning the T-34. The T-29 resulted from a military request for a tank that combined the firepower of the T-28 with the mobility of the fast BT wheel/track tanks. At first a version was developed that had four large road wheels on either side, driven by a special transmission. A variation built somewhat later was fitted with an aphonic transmission that allowed the same performance on tracks as on wheels. These tanks were designated T-29-4 and T-29-5. One of their most important features was their weight, which was stated as 28.5 tons. Their crews consisted of five or six men, they were armed like the T-28, with a 76.2 mm 1927/32 tank gun and four or five machine guns. On tracks the 1936 version reached 54 kph, on wheel 80 kph. The range was between 240 and 350 kilometers. The 1938 T-29s were armed with the 76.2 mm L-10 tank gun, and a modified variety carried a gun of the same caliber with the designation PS-3. In 1937-39 work was done on another medium wheel/track tank, designated "Article 115." Projected data included a weight of 32 to

In the spring of 1939 the T-28 medium tank was tested with a two-ton rolling mine remover. The width of each path was half a meter.

In 1935 the T-29 medium wheel/track tank had been built and tested. The first version, seen here, weighed 28.5 tons, had a five-man crew, and was armed with a 76.2 mm 1928/32 model tank gun, four 7.62 mm DT machine guns and one anti-aircraft machine gun. By 1939 further versions and projects appeared, to be halted only after the acceptance of the T-34 medium tank.

The II-28 bridgelaying tank was created in 1939-40 by using the chassis and hull of a T-28 medium tank. The vehicle carried a bridge that could carry fifty tons and was unloaded to the front.

33 tons, a six-man crew, armor up to 50 mm thick, a 76.2 mm L-10 tank gun, two 12.7 mm machine guns in separate turrets, and three 7.62 mm machine guns. The development of single-turret (T-34) medium tanks with shell-safe armor resulted in the end of developmental work on this possible successor model to the T-28.

Test models of the T-28 were made with an 85 mm F-39 tank gun, as well as running-gear components of the T-35 heavy tank (coil springs with swinging joints) and the KW heavy tank (torsion-bar suspension). In 1937 testing of a wading T-28 was begun; it had a standpipe for oxygen supply that allowed wading to depths of 4.5 meters. In May and June 1939 a T-28 mine-removal tank with a rolling mineseeking device was tested. This device, weighing more than two tons, was attached to the tank so that it could explode mines on the road ahead of the tank with its very heavy specific ground pressure. In one hour, ten to twelve kilometers of mined marching paths could be swept.

In 1938-39 the IT-28 bridgelaying tank appeared, using the chassis of a T-28 E production tank. In place of a turret, the tank

The new heavy tank was designated T-35 and was used by the 5th Heavy Tank Brigade of the army, which had 148 tanks in 1938. [p. 23] These included 62 T-35, 32 T-28 and 54 BT-5 or BT-7 tanks. This unit also had 25 other armored vehicles.

Testing of a heavy tank with five turrets began in 1932. It was armed with one 76.2 mm 1928/32 tank gun, two 37 mm tank guns and several machine guns. Series production of the model shown here ended a year later. Besides the 76.2 mm tank gun in the main turret, it carried two 45 mm 1932 model tank guns in turrets mounted diagonally. This huge firepower was completed by five or six machine guns.

This 45-ton colossus was given up by the Red Army after all attempts to tow it failed (note the broken towrope at the bow!). This picture shows the suspension of the road wheels in pairs.

Another T-35, which was damaged in a German air raid. The picture shows the locations of the various turrets. Because of their great size, these tanks were popular photo motifs for the German soldiers. Some joker wrote "So ends a love affair" on the tank's apron.

carried a metal grid bridge 13 meters long with a load limit of 50 tons. The bridge could be unloaded forward in three minutes. The tank had a five-man crew. The two machine-gun turrets were retained. After successful testing in the 1939-40 winter war against Finland series production began. Because of the events of the summer of 1941, the number of IT-28 bridgelaying tanks remained low.

Two self-propelled mounts on the T-28 chassis were projected. The SU-8 self-propelled mount was intended for a 152.4 mm coastal cannon or a 76.2 mm 1931 anti-aircraft gun. With a weight of 17.6 tons, it had a top speed of over 37 kph. Another self-propelled gun-mount project appeared under the direction of A. A. Tolochkov. He had found an original way of putting a 152.4 mm coastal cannon into position. A plate had to be lowered directly under the gun. When that was done, the self-propelled mount could be raised to protect it from pressure and possible damage when firing.

On September 15, 1940, there had been 443 T-28 medium tanks; their numbers in Red Army service decreased to 411 by June 1941. The majority of these tanks were lost on the battlefields in 1941. A large number were put out of action by German antitank weapons, and others broke down with technical problems and lined the advance routes of the German forces. In Tank Recognition Chart 2, "The Soviet Russian Tank Weapon," as of February 1943, the T-28 is described as follows: "Antiquated model with numerous technical shortcomings . . . slow and not very mobile, rather lightly armored for its size, easy to fight against. At this time it is usually used only as an armored towing tractor."

The armor of the T-35 heavy tank, 11 to 30 mm thick, could be penetrated easily by even the German 3.7 cm antitank guns. The vehicle shown here shows several holes made by armor-piercing shells. The ponderous nature of the tank, almost ten meters long, was also a problem.

The pictures shown in this series were taken at various times but show the same tank. Lost in early July 1941, it had belonged to the 5th Heavy Tank Brigade of the Red Army. In place of the frame antenna on the turret, this T-35 already has a rod antenna. Note also the bracket for the anti-aircraft machine gun. In the armor of the main turret top are three panoramic scopes. The two 45-mm gun turrets each had such an observation device.

Tactical - Technical Data (T-28, 1932 model)

Crew:		6 men
Weight:		25.2 tons; 27.5 to 28.5 tons
Armament:		1 76.2 mm caliber 1927/32 tank gun, with 64 to 70 rounds 3 or 4 7.62 mm caliber DT machine guns, with 7938 to 8320 rounds
Armor:		
Hull:	Front:	30 mm
	Sides:	20 mm
	Rear:	20 mm
	Top:	10-15 mm
	Bottom:	10-15 mm
Main turret:		
	Front:	30 mm
	Sides:	20 mm
	Rear:	20-30 mm
	Top:	15 mm
Machine-gun turrets:		
	Front:	20 mm
	Sides:	20 mm
	Rear:	20 mm
	Top:	10 mm
Powerplant:		12-cylinder 4-stroke M-17 or M-17 L gasoline engine
Performance:		450-500 HP at 1400-1450 rpm
Fuel capacity:		650 liters
Power to weight:		17.5-17.9 HP/ton
	Length:	7360-7440 mm
	Width:	2810-2870 mm
	Height:	2620-2820 mm
Ground clearance:		500-560 mm
Top speed:		37-40 kph
Range:		140-220 km
Climbing degree:		43 degrees
Spanning ability:		2700-3300 mm
Climbing ability:		960 mm
Wading ability:		800 mm
Specific ground pressure:		0.72 kp/sq. cm.

Tactical - Technical Data (T-28 E or T-28 M)

Crew:		6 men
Weight:		31-32 tons
Armament:[6]		1 76.2 mm caliber L-10 tank gun, with 69 rounds 3 or 4 7.62 mm caliber DT machine guns, with 7939 mm
Armor:		
Hull:	Front:	58-80 mm
	Sides:	40 mm
	Rear:	40 mm
	Top:	23 mm
	Bottom:	23 mm
Main turret:		
	Front:	80 mm
	Sides:	40 mm
	Rear:	40 mm
	Top:	15 mm
Machine-gun turrets:		
	Front:	20 mm
	Sides:	20 mm
	Rear:	20 mm
	Top:	10 mm
Powerplant:		12-cylinder 4-stroke M-17 or M-17 L gasoline engine
Performance:		450-500 HP at 1400-1450 rpm
Fuel capacity:		no data
Power to weight:		15.6-16.1 HP/ton
	Length:	7360-7440 mm
	Width:	2810-1870 mm
	Height:	2620-2820 mm
Ground clearance:		500-560 mm
Top speed:		23 kph
Range:		140-180 km
Climbing degree:		43 degrees
Spanning ability:		2700-3300 mm
Climbing ability:		960 mm
Wading ability:		800 mm
Specific ground pressure:		0.77 kp/sq. cm.

6. Modernized T-28s were armed with either the 76.2 mm 1927/32 tank gun or the 76.2 mm L-10 tank gun.

This T-35 heavy tank was hit and destroyed by a bomb. In the background are two early-type BT-7 tanks with cylindrical turrets.

Tactical - Technical Data (T-29)

Crew:		5 men
Weight:		24.0-28.8 tons
Armament:[7]		1 76.2 mm caliber 1927/32 tank gun, with ? rounds 3 or 4 7.62 mm caliber DT machine guns, with ? rounds
Armor:		
Hull:	Front:	30 mm
	Sides:	20 mm
	Rear:	20 mm
	Top:	10-15 mm
	Bottom:	10-15 mm
Main turret:		
	Front:	30 mm
	Sides:	20 mm
	Rear:	20-30 mm
	Top:	15 mm
Machine-gun turrets:		
	Front:	20 mm
	Sides:	20mm
	Rear:	20 mm
	Top:	10 mm
Powerplant:		12-cylinder 4-stroke M-17 L gasoline engine
Performance:		450-500 HP at 1400-1450 rpm
Fuel capacity:		no data
Power to weight:		17.4-20.8 HP/ton
	Length:	7374 mm
	Width:	3180 mm
	Height:	2825-2850 mm[8]
Ground clearance:		450-475 mm
Top speed:		On tracks: 54 kph;[9] on wheels: 80 kph
Range:		On tracks: 230 km; on wheels: 328 km
Climbing degree:		35 degrees
Spanning ability:		3300 mm
Climbing ability:		1000-1200 mm
Wading ability:		1100 mm
Specific ground pressure:		0.76 kp/sq. cm.

5. Heavy Tanks

At the end of the twenties, various Soviet heavy and ultra-heavy tank projects attracted attention. Other countries had learned of them through secret-service sources. There was talk of 100-ton and even 1,000-ton tanks. When the reader recalls from the problems described in the first chapter that the Red Army's armored troops had grown out of the mechanical unreliability of the tanks it used, it becomes clear that such reports lacked any basis in fact. Design bureaus and workshops were only able to create test models of considerably smaller tanks with difficulty, let alone tanks of such sizes. And yet the Revolutionary War Council of the Soviet Union regarded a heavy tank as necessary. Similarly to the medium tank that later became known as the T-28, it was to provide additional reinforcement to army units breaking into fortified defensive zones. Corresponding to the tank philosophy common at that time, such a

The 45-mm gun turrets of the T-35 heavy tank were identical to those of the T-26 1933 model light tank and the bT-5 wheel/track tank except for their lack of rear extensions. Here too, both versions (projecting angular and rounded roller-mantlet covering) were used. The gun was a 45 mm 1932 model tank gun with a 2072.5 mm barrel.

tank had to be heavily armed and at the same time be able to lead a firefight on several sides. Thus its guns were supposed to be in several turrets. For this too there was a model, the heavy Vickers "Independent" tank. Two examples had been purchased in Britain in 1925-26 and tested by the Royal Tank Corps. The 32-ton type had five turrets, in which a 47 mm tank gun and five machine guns were mounted. Only test models were built. In the Soviet Union, though, the idea caught on and a heavy battle tank was conceived that even put the British model in the shade. The first prototypes of this "land battleship" were ready for testing as of July 1932. Unlike the "Independent" tank, they were more heavily armed. In the main turret, which was rounded at the top, a 76.2 mm 1927/32 tank gun was installed. Four small turrets (taken from the BT-2 fast wheel/track tank) were grouped before and behind the main turret. Two of

Several shells have damaged the barrel and mount of the 76.2 mm 1927/32 model tank gun in the main turret of this T-35. Unlike the two 45 mm guns, this weapon was mainly supposed to attack unarmored targets. The explosive shell weighed 6.5 kg, and its maximum range was 6763 meters.

7. Armed in 1938 with the 76 mm L-10 tank gun.
8. Differences result from use of tracks or wheels.
9. For the T-29s: 57 or 55 kph.

A noticeable direct hit has badly damaged the barrel of the left rear 45 mm 1932 model tank gun. Notine the unusually large jack attached to the side armor of the upper body.

them (right front and left rear) had 37 mm 1930 tank guns; two others (left front and right rear) had 7.62 mm DT machine guns in ball mantlets. Along with the machine gun mounted to the right of the gun in the main turret and the two other guns, this giant, almost ten meters long, had five machine guns, giving it the firepower of a whole platoon of light tanks. The machine gun mounted at the right in the bow was later omitted.

The prototype was first shown to the public at the May Day parade in Moscow in 1933. One year later, in a parade on the 17th Party Day of the Communist Party of the Soviet Union, an entire company of heavy tanks of this type rolled past the reviewing stand. At least a report of the Defense Department (T-3) in the Reich War Ministry in Berlin, dated March 8, 1934, says so. With a degree of astonishment the German technicians realized that the tank carried three tank guns plus machine guns. Truly: "The T-2 tank is thus more heavily armed than the French S-2 tank, and its speed is considerably higher."

Series production began at the Kharkov Locomotive Factory. As of 1935 new turrets replaced the BT-2 turrets for the secondary weapons. The tank-gun turrets resembled those of the BT-5 fast wheel/track tanks but had no rear extensions. In place of the 37 mm guns, 45 mm 1932 tank guns were installed. The machine-gun turrets at the left front and right rear were also new. They came from the T-37 amphibian tank. The main turret now had a cylindrical shape with a rear extension. The antenna for the radio set formed a railing around the turret. The ammunition was plentiful. In all, 96 76.2 mm shells, 220 45 mm shells, and some 10,000 rounds of machine-gun ammunition were carried. A ten-man crew operated the weapons and machines and drove the tank. They were linked with each other by telephone.

The tank had an M-17 engine that produced 500 HP; the gearbox had five forward speeds plus reverse. In the running gear, a suspension member was used for each pair of linked road wheels. The road wheels had rubber tires and were quite large. There were six on each side of the prototype, and production tanks had eight pairs.

The heavy "penetration tank" was designated T-35. The T-32 designation for the prototypes has not been confirmed to date in any Soviet source. W. D. Mostovenko writes in his book "Tanki" that only a few dozen of the T-35 heavy tanks were built. To be precise, there were 62. After another six T-35s were delivered with conical turrets in 1938-39, no further work was done. The tanks were used only in the 5th Heavy Tank Brigade, which also had 32 T-28 and 54 BT tanks in its fleet. Both types, the T-35 and the T-28, took part in the yearly parade on Red Square in Moscow. For this reason the brigade was stationed in the Soviet capital.

There were only a few variants of the T-35. For testing purposes, a turret with a flamethrower from the OT 130 was installed in place of one 45 mm tank gun turret. The development of self-propelled mounts that were projected or built experimentally on the basis of the T-35 are of interest. The intended weapons were the 254 mm cannon, 305 mm howitzer and 400 mm mortar. Despite the weight of up to 106 tons, speeds up to 26 kph are said to have been possible. The model was designated SU-7.

Tank experts of the Red Army particularly criticized the weak armor of the T-35, plus its big dimensions and insufficient mobility. With the advent of small-caliber armor-piercing guns, the purpose of heavy tanks with multiple turrets was put in question.

An interesting size comparison! The height of the T-35 heavy tank is ltsted as over 3.4 meters.

A further group of self-propelled mounts went by the designation of SU-14 and was intended for guns of 152.4 to 203 mm calibers. Leading the design work was the Kirov factory in Leningrad. In 1935 a prototype SU-14 with a 203 mm howitzer could be introduced, followed by a vehicle with the 152.4 mm (B-10) 1935 naval cannon. It was designated SU-14-1 or SU-BU-10, weighed 47.9 tons, and could reach 31 kph. Its armor was 20 to 30 mm thick. A crew of eight to ten men was needed to operate it. The SU-14 self-propelled mount with the 203 mm 1931 howitzer weighed about 50 tons and reached 20 kph; in terms of the other parameters it resembled the vehicle with the naval gun. Finally, in 1939 the "Barikady" works in Stalingrad produced a prototype of the SU-14-2 (also SU-14-Br-2) heavy self-propelled mount. Armed with a 152.4 mm (Br-2) 1935 gun, this vehicle, because of its heavier armor (50 mm), which also enclosed the running gear and the space for the gun crew, weighed some 65 tons. The prototype was taken to Moscow in 1941 and exhibited there. No further developments of heavy armored vehicles based on the T-35 are known.

The 12-cylinder M-17-M engine produced 500 HP and was located in the rear of the T-35 along with the five-speed gearbox.

The old-type T-35 could be recognized by the antenna for the 71-TK-1 radio in the form of a railing around the main turret. The radio equipment of some turrets was modernized; the vehicles were given less noticeable and less easily damaged antennas.

Workers from the Army Weapons Office load a T-35 heavy tank. Great steering power had to be used when moving the vehicle, which did not make it easy to get the tank onto the heavy-load cars of the German Railways.

Tanks of this type once joined the parading troops of the Red Army in the annual parade on Red Square in Moscow. After just a few days of war in 1941 their hulks lined the advance routes of the German troops.

In June and July 1941, T-35 tanks of the 5th Heavy Tank Brigade of the Red Army saw action against German forces in the Lemberg (Lvov) area. Many of the weakly armored giants broke down with technical faults, and others were easy prey for the German Luftwaffe, so that few could actually take part in combat.

From the German side, the T-35 was regarded as an obsolete model; the tank was too big, too ponderous and not mobile enough. Despite its striking size and number of turrets, it had only meager combat value. In a contemporary periodical it was even written that although the T-35 "with its mammoth size . . . appeared gigantic, it was actually a bogeyman." During the winter combat of 1941 before Moscow, a few specimens of the T-35 made an appearance. There is no information about the fate of these vehicles other than the presence of one in the Kubinka Tank Museum.

Tactical - Technical Data (T-35, 1935 model)

Crew:		10 men
Weight:		45 tons
Armament:		1 76.2 mm caliber 1927/32 tank gun, with 96-100 rounds
		2 45 mm caliber 1934 tank guns, with 220-226 rounds
		5-6 7.62 mm caliber DT machine guns, with 8230-10,000 rounds
Armor plate:		
Hull:	Front:	30 mm
	Sides:	20 mm
	Rear:	20 mm
	Top:	11-14 mm
	Bottom:	11-14 mm
Main turret:		
	Front:	20 mm
	Sides:	20 mm
	Rear:	20 mm
	Top:	11 mm
Tank-gun turrets (2):		
	Front:	20 mm
	Sides:	20 mm
	Rear:	20 mm
	Top:	11 mm
Machine-gun turrets (2):		
	Front:	20 mm
	Sides:	20 mm
	Rear:	20 mm
	Top:	11 mm
Powerplant:		12-cylinder 4-stroke M-17 M gasoline engine
Performance:		500 HP at 1450 rpm
Fuel capacity:		910 liters
	Length:	9720 mm
	Width:	3200 mm
	Height:	3430 mm
Ground clearance:		530 mm
Top speed:		30 kph
Range:		150 km
Climbing degree:		20 degrees
Spanning ability:		3500-4000 mm
Climbing ability:		1200 mm
Wading ability:		1200 mm
Specific ground pressure:		0.78 kp/sq. cm.

Note: The last-produced T-35 tanks are said to have had armor up to 50 mm thick and a weight of about 50 tons (T-35, 1938 model).

The same vehicle at the driving test center of the Army Weapons Office in Kummersdorf near Berlin. Here the tank was thoroughly examined and tested. The only known reuse of the armored giant by the Germans saw it listed as "Heavy Tank 751 (r) Russian T-35 A".

Six T-35 heavy tanks were built in 1938-39 that differed from the older tanks of this type by the shape of their turrets. After that, production was halted in favor of the KW single-turret heavy tank.

Front view of a T-35 of the last series. The ball mantlet for the movable 7.62 mm DT machine gun in the rear of the turret is easy to see.

The SU-14-1 heavy self-propelled artillery mount of 1936 carried a 152.4 mm B-10 (also called 1935 model) ship's cannon which could fire 43.5-kilogram shells to distances up to 20,000 meters. Its armor was 20 to 30 mm thick.

In 1939 the SU-14-2, likewise a heavy self-propelled artillery mount, appeared. It had an enclosed armored body with a thickness of 50 mm and was armed with a 152.4 mm gun. The 65-ton vehicle reached a top speed of 25 kph.

The first Red Army vehicle with shell-safe armor had already been built and tested in 1937. It had a fighting weight of 32 tons, a three-man crew, and was armed with a 45 mm tank gun and two 7.62 mm machine guns. The 60 mm armor offered protection from the fire of 37 mm antitank guns. Because of its low speed (30 kph), no further work was done on this model.

On July 9, 1941 the Chief of the General Staff of the German Army, Generaloberst Franz Halder, noted in his war diary: "Army Group Center submits a final report on the double battle of Bialystok-Minsk". The list of captured materials from this battle included 2585 captured or destroyed tanks. At this collecting depot near Minsk, Russian tanks and armored vehicles were gathered in great numbers. The photo was taken in August 1941.

3

The Development of Soviet Tank Technology, 1939-1945

The theoretical basis for the development of the armored troops in the Red Army already existed by the end of the twenties. Their role in modern warfare had been described by the Deputy Chief of Staff of the Red Army, V. K. Triandafilov, in his work "The Character of Operations of Modern Armies," first published in 1929: "No one has any doubt any more about the tremendous tactical significance of tanks in a future war. The present stage of development of automatic weapons in the infantry, the tendency to further growth and qualitative improvement of these weapons, the great spread of artificial obstacles in defense and the placing of means of holding back the enemy (artillery) behind the means of defense make the tank one of the mightiest means of attack in a future war." Working out the theory of deep offensive operations by the Soviet military formed the basis of command training in the Red Army in the thirties. In the current field service instructions of 1936, the prerequisites for achieving victory in modern warfare were formulated. The most important point was the creation of superiority in the main direction. Great significance was also given to "surprise and speed of action in conjunction with organization, skilled maneuvering, and the ability to make use of the terrain." Tanks were very well suited to fulfilling these requirements. Through their strong penetration and firepower, they gave direct support to the infantry. They could overcome obstacles of various types, were capable of destroying masses of opposition and opening a path through the enemy defenses for the infantry following them. In addition, large bands of tanks could carry out independent tasks and expand tactical success into operative success. The People's Commission for Defense undertook everything needed to establish armored troops that were capable of fulfilling these tasks. One quickly notices their tremendous quantitative development. The Soviet tank industry had overcome initial difficulties in the production of tanks. By making good use of experience and experimental designing gained in other countries it was possible, during the course of two five-year plans, to deliver more than 15,000 tanks to the Red Army. With them, the Soviet armed forces had the strongest armored troops in the world during the latter half of the thirties.

To be sure, the armored troops of the Red Army found themselves in a complicated situation at the end of the thirties. The weakening of the officer corps resulting from Stalin's 1937-38 personnel changes had led to false evaluation of the experience gained in

The successor to the T-38 M-2 amphibian tank, the T-40 amphibian tank, appeared as of 1940. Its shot-deflecting armor offered protection from infantry-weapon fire and shell fragments. The armament had been upgraded; the 12.7 mm DSchK 1938 model machine gun could be used against armored targets up to 300 and others up to 3500 meters. The two-man crew also had a 7.62 DT machine gun at hand.

The two machine guns of the T-40 light amphibian tank were coupled and mounted in an external mantlet.

The T-40 light amphibian tank was used for reconnaissance, support of infantry attacks against weak enemy forces, and particularly for combat around bodies of water. Its combat values was not rated very highly.

Very similar to the T-40 was the T-30 light amphibian tank, also produced in 1940. Little information about this tank is available.

the 1936-39 Spanish Civil War. As a result, the mechanized corps that had existed since 1933 were disbanded. The campaigns of the German Wehrmacht in Poland and Western Europe very soon made it clear that this decision had been wrong. Thus in 1940 nine mechanized corps were organized. In February and March 1940, twenty more mechanized corps were established, each of them with one mechanized and two armored divisions. Naturally the overly hasty new organization brought a multitude of problems, which could no longer be solved when the war with Germany began.

The development of armored troops in the thirties was dominated by the Command for Mechanization and Motorization in the Red Army. In particular, Chief I. A. Chalepski (until 1936) played a major role in the training of commanders for armored troops, as well as the education of talented tank designers in the armament industry. Within a short time the designers were able to develop a series of tank models that showed very characteristic features and differed from their foreign models within the tactical-technical parameters.

Without wanting to denigrate the accomplishments of the military cadre responsible for the ahcievements of the armored troops, it is still correct to evaluate the new tank designs created until the end of the thirties, which were also to be guides for international tank construction, as an important achievement of the officials and designers in the Soviet armament industry. The tendency to find their own constructive solutions, which emerged more and more clearly in Soviet tankbuilding since the mid-thirties, took on its decisive change, toward single-turret tanks with armor impervious to shells, from the experience gained in the Spanish Civil War. What were the causes? In the theory of tank warfare, tank-versus-tank combat typified the future concept of military conflict more and more strongly. A certain Alexandrov (perhaps a pseudonym) wrote on that subject in the journal "Motorisstsiya I Mechanisatsiya" at the end of the thirties: "In 'tank versus tank' combat, the decision

***Left*: A Red Army armored unit with T-40 light amphibian tanks prepares to march to the front late in the summer of 1941. The turrets offset to the left and engine-room covers on the right can be seen.**

In 1941 there were 41 of the T-40 light amphibian tank produced; in 1942 another 181.

In the T-40 S (Sychopytnui: dry land) light amphibian tank, its amphibian ability was sacrificed for the sake of slightly improved armor protection. Its production began in 1941.

This picture was taken during the battles in the spring of 1942 and shows a T-40 S that tipped over as a result of a driving error. The tunnel originally made for the water propeller can be seen. The opening for the propeller shaft was closed with an armor plate.

depends on the armament, speed and armor thickness of the two sides' tanks. A fast tank will be superior in maneuvering by using its high speed, but with heavy armor it will be inferior against fire by the enemy tanks. The greater chance of success will go to the faster but more heavily armed tank." Basically, these statements were proved true in Spain, but they were expanded in one important point: It was important to increase the armor protection. The losses of Soviet tanks during the 1939-40 winter war in Karelia merely added more evidence to experience already gained. At this time the development of a new generation of tanks with shell-safe armor had already made progress in the Soviet Union. The first test models (T-100 "Sotka") were tested by the heavy tank brigade in the Finnish war.

The first Soviet tanks with shell-safe armor had already been built in the spring of 1937. It was designated T-46-5 (T-111). Its sixty-millimeter armor offered protection from fire by antitank guns with a caliber of 37 mm, and at distances above 1,200 meters also from 76.2 mm ammunition. The weight increased to 28 tons, and

The T-50 light tank of 1941: By the end of that year, 48 tanks of this type had been completed. At the beginning of 1942 production ended. Despite its modern concept, the T-50 turned out to be too weakly armed and armored.

During the fighting in the spring of 1942, numbers of the T-60 light tank appeared. Despite its meager offensive power, it was produced in large numbers and complemented or replaced the medium and heavy tanks, which were often not available, in the independent tank battalions of the Red Army. This is an early-type tank, recognizable by its spoked steel wheels.

Snow and mud limited the mobility of the T-60 light tank, as this tank, photographed in March 1942, shows. A typical feature was the armor projecting from the roller mantlet of the 20 mm 1941 model (SchWak) tank gun, which was able to penetrate 24 mm of armor at 100 meters with its armor-piercing shells.

despite the 300 HP engine, a speed of only 30 kph could be attained. The armament consisted of the usual 45 mm tank gun and two machine guns. Aside from the armor and the suspension, the tank showed no important changes compared to earlier models.

Aside from the heavier armor, though, the firepower also had to be upgraded. In medium tanks, the Soviet military discarded, more quickly than was the case with heavy tanks, the concept of having to equip such a vehicle with multiple turrets. For that reason, the three-turret tank developed in 1938 ("Article 115") as a successor to the T-28 remained only a project.

In 1937 M. I. Koshkin had been appointed chief designer at the tank factory in Kharkov, which produced the BT fast wheel/track tank. Soon the job of modernizing this tank was replaced by the task of developing a new shell-safe tank. In 1938 the design bureau worked on the A-20 tank project. In the course of its development, Koshkin and the chief developmental engineer A. A. Morosov came to realize that the new medium tank with shell-safe

The first T-60 tanks were finished and turned over to the Red Army in mid-December 1941. In fewer than six weeks the Foreign Armies East Department of the German Army's General Staff reported that a large number of these tanks had been spotted facing the Army Group South.

These T-60 light tanks were put out of action in the combat of April 1942. The armor, angled on all sides, was at first up to 20 mm thick, but was increased to 35 mm on tanks produced since the spring of 1942. It still did not offer sufficient protection and could be penetrated by the German 3.7 cm antitank guns.

This T-60 light tank was put out of action near Cholm in the northern sector of the eastern front by close-range antitank fighters on February 23, 1942 (Red Army Day).

In the second half of May 1942 there was heavy fighting between units of the German Army Group South and strong Red Army forces under the command of Marshal S. K. Timochenko. By May 22, 1942 575 Russian tanks had been lost, including this T-60, which was painted olive green with a red star on the turret hatch.

armor absolutely had to be a pure tracked vehicle. For that reason the A-32 (or T-32) project was also worked out. In the summer of 1939, test models of both tanks were tested. The strongly angled arrangement of the armor plate on both tanks, by which considerable protection could be achieved with only 30 mm armor, attracted attention.

Both models used the W-2 Diesel engine as their powerplant. The A-20 still had a 45 mm tank gun, while the A-32 had a 76.2 mm gun installed. The further tests showed clear superiority for a pure tracked tank. A further strengthening of the armor to 45 mm resulted in the T-34 medium tank, which was put into large-series production. For a time, problems were caused by the efforts of the Armored Troop Command in the Red Army, which favored a considerably longer tank (like the old T-26) and contracted for the development of the T-50. But only 63 of these were built. With the introduction of the T-34, the simplification of tank production advanced along with the uniformization of tank equipping and training in the troops. It took over the tasks that had previously been met by the T-26 (infantry support), BT (long-range battle groups) and T-28 (fire support).

Something more complicated was the development of heavy tanks with shell-safe armor to replace the T-35. The tanks of this type developed since 1938 were originally to have three turrets, but in the course of developmental work, the number had been cut to two. The long loyalty to tanks with multiple turrets shows how strong the link with old concepts still was at that time. The two-turret tanks (T-100 and SMK) were each armed with one 76.2 mm and one 45 mm tank gun. With a maximum armor strength of 60 mm, the fighting weight was 56 to 58 tons. What was wanted, though, was a weight like that of the T-35 (45 tons) with simultaneous upgrading of armor and firepower, without influencing the maneuverability negatively.

The German designation for the captured T-60 was "Tank T-60-743 (r) - Russian T-60". It was regarded as a weakly armored vehicle of little combat value, for reconnaissance. These pictures were taken in the driving test center of the Army Weapons Office in Kummersdorf near Berlin in the summer of 1942.

In the second half of 1942, large numbers of T-60 light tanks appeared without turrets. In its place a launcher for 24 fin-stabilized 80 mm rockets (BM-8-24) had been mounted. Their range is stated as 5500 meters.

During the developmental work on the heavy tank, the design bureau, led by S. J. Kotin, came to realize that a heavy tank with shell-safe armor also should have just one turret with high-performance armament. The project for such a single-turret tank was approved by the Defense Committee of the People's Commissariat. Only by reducing the number of turrets and crewmen and making the interior space smaller could the necessary prerequisites for a heavy tank with heavy armor be attained without making it heavier than the T-35. In December 1939, the first plans were completed for the new heavy tank, with the designation KV (Kliment Voroshilov, Marshal of the Soviet Union and People's Commissar for Defense). They came directly from the Kirov works in Leningrad to the Karelian front for testing.

The W-2 Diesel engine installed in the T-34 was also used with minor modifications in the KV. After testing several suspension types, torsion bars were chosen for the heavy tank. The simple running gear no longer needed any special armor protection. New in both the T-34 and KV were wide tracks, to keep the specific ground

The line of light tank development in the Red Army was continued in 1942 with the T-70. It had stronger armor and higher firepower. The 45 mm 1938 model tank gun had electric firing and could penetrate 35 mm of armor at 500 meters with armor-piercing shells. A coaxial 7.62 mm DT machine gun was also installed.

Shot-down Russian tanks are seen on a battlefield south of the Kursk Bogen. At this time the T-70 (right) was still very numerous in the tank battalions of the Red Army. This picture was taken by a German war correspondent early in July 1943.

Russian and German tank experts regarded the combat value of the T-70 light tank as not particularly high. Weaknesses became apparent, especially in battle against tanks. In addition, the two-man crew was overworked with driving the tank, observing the battlefield and operating the weapons.

This picture shows a German collecting depot for captured Russian tanks and other vehicles in the summer of 1942. In the foreground are a T-34 medium tank and several T-70 light tanks.

Tank units of the Red Army that used T-70 tanks suffered large losses within a short time. This picture was taken in the summer of 1944.

The 45 mm 1938 model tank gun was removed. Seen in the Finnish Tank Museum in Parola in 1993.

This T-70 (r) light tank captured by the Germans was used by Assault Gun Brigade 276 in the autumn of 1944. The picture was taken near Schlossberg in East Prussia on November 26, 1944.

A further development of the T-70, the T-80 light tank appeared in the autumn of 1943. There were 120 built. Besides a more powerful powerplant (2 x 85 HP), these tanks had improved armor protection and a larger turret, with room for two men.

The SU-76 light self-propelled artillery mount in its original form, with a separate engine for each track, was built from December 1942 to May 1943. It was recognizable externally by its 76.2 mm ZIS-3 (1942 model) divisional cannon mounted exactly in the middle; in vehicles built later, it was moved to the left.

The two big servicing hatches flanking the driver's hatch can be seen clearly here.

From May 1943 on, the SU-76 M light self-propelled artillery mount was produced. Important changes had been made in the powerplant, where the motors were mounted on the right side, one behind the other. The armament with the ZIS-3 76.2 mm divisional cannon (1942 model) remained unchanged and could be completed with a 7.62 mm DT machine gun, two machine pistols and 20 hand grenades.

SU-76 light self-propelled artillery mounts in the streets of Berlin, photographed in the last days of April 1945. Each mount could carry a maximum of 60 shells (40 explosive, 15 armor-piercing and five undercaliber shells). At the beginning of 1944 new 12 RT radios, with a range between 15 and 20 kilometers, were introduced.

pressure as low as possible. The main components had been improved; their simple construction made training, servicing and maintenance easier. On the basis of the progress in electric welding of hulls and turrets for tanks by 1939, welded designs for medium and heavy tanks were developed.

In order to be able to equip the armored troops completely with the new T-34 and KV tanks, more than 15,000 tanks were needed, but in 1941 the Soviet armament industry could not produce more than 5,500 tanks, including numerous light ones. In addition, the building of new light armored vehicles meant for reconnaissance and special uses (such as air-landing) had begun. "The mobility of modern tanks is so great today that all combat action takes place quickly. Successful attacks by our own . . . tanks thus requires thorough reconnaissance, in order to spot enemy tanks early." At first the idea of amphibious tanks was retained, but it had to be given up with the last run of T-40s in favor of heavier armor. In the successor model, the T-60 light tank, the Armored Troop Command gave up from the start on amphibians. The same applied to the T-70, which went into production in 1942. All light tanks, because of their weak

When SU-76 light self-propelled artillery mounts began to be built in December 1942, the Artillery Administration of the Red Army formed thirty regiments of self-propelled artillery. Each was supposed to have 17 SU-76 and eight SU-122 at first. Later the Red Army changed to regiments with just one type of gun mount.

In the summer of 1944 several artillery brigades were formedn consisting of three regiments with a total of 60 SU-76 and five T-70 light tanks. Self-propelled artillery was intended for use in penetrating the enemy's tactical defense zone.

For the SU-76 i light self-propelled artillery mount, chassis of captured German Panzer III tanks were used. The fighting compartment with the 76.2 mm ZIS-3 (1942 model) divisional cannon was forward. The hull armor was at most 50 mm thick, that of the upper body up to 30 mm.

Like the SU-76, the SU-76 i was used in the regiments of the self-propelled artillery for direct support of the infantry in attacks and for defense against tank attacks.

armor and armament, played only a subordinate role in combat. Their manufacture at automobile factories, though, helped the Red Army make up for its tank losses in the summer of 1941.

An overview of the development of the Soviet armored troops to the beginning of the war shows that in terms of military technology, correct decisions of far-reaching significance have been made in the Soviet Union. The important feature was the development of tanks with shell-safe armor. Wrong decisions were made about the operative use of tanks and the structure of armored and mechanized units. The disbanding of the mechanized corps in 1939 was, as noted, a mistake, and their overly hasty new formation in 1940 and 1941 did not help to correct the mistake. But it is not correct to explain the great personal and material losses of the Soviet armored troops in the summer of 1941 on that alone. For example, V. D. Mostovenko writes: "The war began at a point when party and government were beginning to take steps to increase the combat strength and readiness of the Soviet forces, to reorganize and rearm them. It must be kept in mind that a goodly number of the old tanks were no longer fully operable then, while the new weapons had just been introduced into the army and were not yet fully mastered. Many units were being retrained. . . . For the USSR the war began at an extraordinarily unfavorable time, and this explains the great misfortunes and defeats. . . ." What Marshal G. K. Zhukov said after the war about the reasons for the 1941 defeat was much more real-

A variant of the SU-76 light self-propelled artillery mount was the ZSU-37 self-propelled anti-aircraft gun mount, which was delivered in 1945. In a turning turret, open at the top, a 37 mm Anti-aircraft Gun 39 was mounted. The rate of fire is stated as 160 rounds per minute and the maximum range as 6700 meters. The weight of the self-propelled mount was between 10.5 and 11.5 tons, the armor was 15 to 35 mm thick. The vehicle carried a six-man crew.

The A-20 medium wheel/track tank of 1939 had a four-man crew and a fighting weight of 18 tons. The armor protection was much improved by mounting the 20- to 25 mm plates at angles. The armament included a 45 mm 1938 model tank gun and two 7.62 mm DT machine guns. The A-20 was very fast, reaching a top speed of 65 kph.

The A-32 test tank was based on the A-20 but could drive only on tracks (top speed 65 kph). The armor was increased slightly to 30 mm. The firepower was much increased; in place of the 45 mm gun, a 76.2 mm 1938-39 tank gun (L-10) was installed. The two machine guns were retained. The A-32 had a four-man crew and was renamed T-32 during its testing.

The T-34 1939 model was developed from the T-32 test tank and had 45 mm armor made to deflect shots. The weight went up to 25.3 tons; the top speed was listed as 53 to 55 kph. For the 76.2 mm 1938/39 tank gun (L-10) there were 76 shells carried, plus 4725 rounds for the two 7.62 mm DT machine guns.

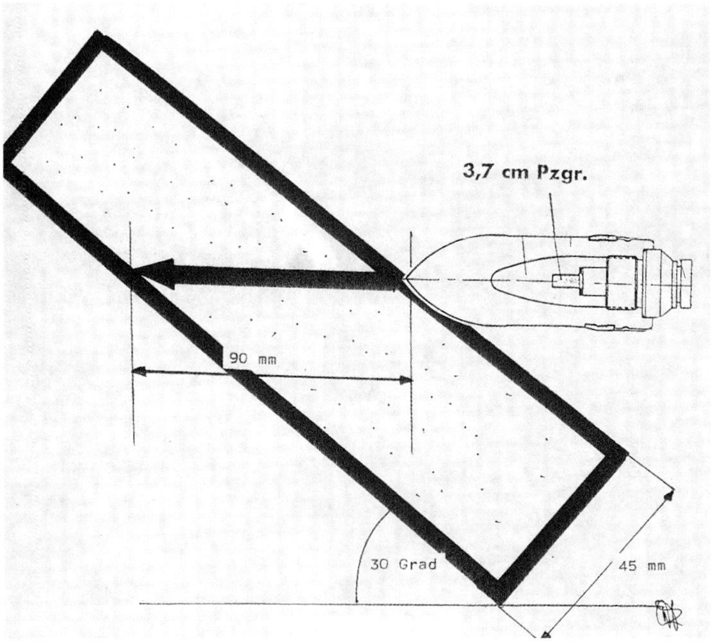

A schematic drawing of the lengthening of the penetration path of an antitank shell when it hits a 45 mm armor plate at a 30-degree angle.

istic. He said: "The main danger was that we were not aware of the striking power of the German Army."

Two things really astounded the Germans in the summer of 1941:

First: The great numbers of Soviet tanks. On June 22, 1941, the Red Army had a total of 23,637 tanks, including 967 T-34 and 508 KV. By August 6, 1941, 13,145 of them had been lost. At this point a comparison with the German side is interesting. The Wehrmacht began the war against the Soviet Union with about 3,300 tanks (1,404 of them Panzerkampfwagen III and IV).

Second: Amazement, indeed horror, was inspired by the superior combat strength of the modern Soviet T-34 and KV tanks. In a report about experiences in antitank action by Army Tank Destroyer Unit 561 it was stated that the 3.7 cm antitank gun "was powerless

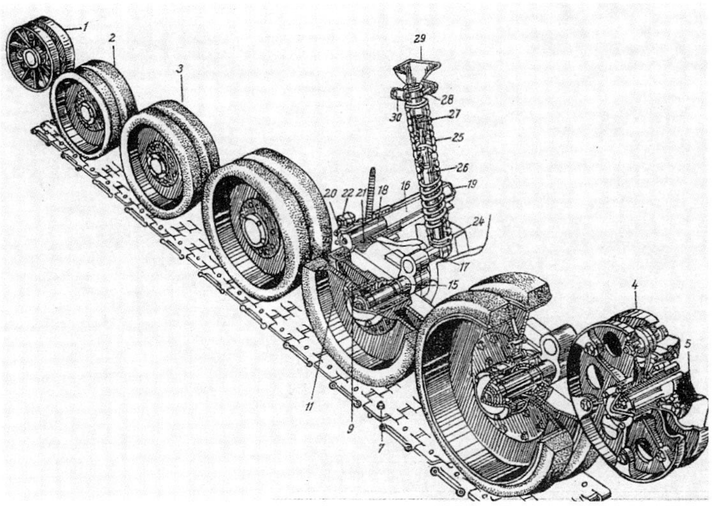

The running gear of the T-34 medium tank. The suspension used large coil springs and was tested sufficiently on the BT-series fast wheel/track tanks. In the T-34, along with the powerful Diesel engine, it made for steadiness of the body even at high speeds off the road. A disadvantage was the need for much space for the suspension in the already cramped hull.

The high combat value of the T-34 medium tank resulted from its firepower, mobility and armor protection being combined in what was then a nearly ideal manner. Thus the tank was a big problem for the antitank forces of the German Army in 1941. This T-34, made in 1939, still shows the laboriously curved front plate on the turret. The cast gun mount and side visors with pistol loopholes below are also typical. The tank driver had three periscopes for his use, two of them for side vision.

These two T-34 tanks stuck in a swamp also show signs of early production. The T-34 in the background is already fitted with the longer 76.2 mm 1940 model tank gun (F-34). It has a box mount in place of the cast type.

Here the crew has lost control of their tank during a German air raid and run into a house. The picture was taken early in July 1941.

Right: After the tank battle in the Grodno-Brody area at the end of July 1941. The 8th Mechanized Corps of the Red Army had about 1000 tanks and armored vehicles at the beginning of the battle, including modern T-34 tanks. The picture shows a T-34, 1939 model, and in the foreground a 45 mm 1937 model antitank gun.

The hull of the T-34 was made of welded armor plates 40 to 45 mm thick. The driver sat to the left, with the gunner of the movably mounted 7.62 mm DT machine gun at his right. In the cast steel turret were two crewmen, who had to carry out the tasks of the commander, aiming gunner and loader.

Rear view of a T-34 medium tank, 1939 model. In the 40 mm rear plate were two openings for the two exhaust pipes. The entire rear plate could be taken off to service the engine.

The same tank (pictured below) in a photo on a directive about fighting Russian tanks. Note the angled armor all around.

Arms Weapons Office staff transport a 1939 model T-34 medium tank. It was examined and tested at the driving test center in Kummersdorf near Berlin in order to find ways to attack it.

The German Minister for Armament and War Production, Albert Speer, examining the Russian T-34. He wanted to get a conception of the outstanding handling qualities of this tank.

A 1941 model T-34 medium tank put out of action. It can be recognized by the 76.2 mm 1938/39 model tank gun (F-34). This gun had a longer barrel (3170 mm = L/41.5) and a boxlike mount shield. Its armor-piercing shells could penetrate 69 mm of armor at 500 meters.

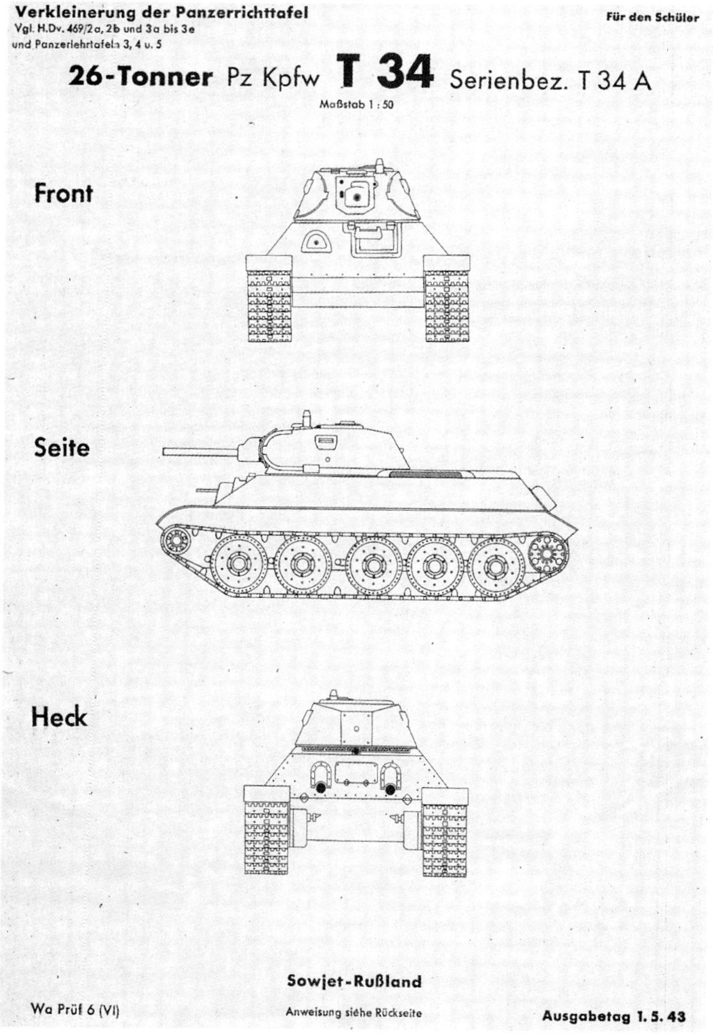

A picture of a 1939 model T-34 in a 1943 instruction table for tank recognition.

against the T-34, for the antitank shells slid off the angled surfaces. . . . The KV tanks, to be sure, did not have such an advantageous shape, but were armored so heavily (80 to 120 mm) that no shell penetrated."

The off-road superiority of the T-34 also made for surprises. The effectiveness of the German armored and antitank forces in battle against the two Soviet tanks was very limited. Their modernization and new weapons became urgently necessary. Within a short time there developed a competition of the engineers and technicians in the armament industries of both sides to create effective armor and armor-piercing ammunition with more destructive power. During the war, both the German and Russian armored troops received improved tanks with stronger armor and more effective tank guns.

As already noted, the Soviet light tanks lost importance during the course of the war. The T-34 became the most important type of tank, and its production process underwent constant simplification for the sake of increasing productivity. By 1943 the frontal armor of this tank reached a thickness of 60 to 75 mm. In the first half of 1942, the Soviet Union produced 11,177 tanks, so that the heavy losses of the previous year could gradually be replaced. The organization of the mechanized and armored troops was essentially changed. Along with the independent tank brigades and battalions, independent tank regiments were established, with two companies of medium tanks (23 T-34s) and one company of light tanks (16 T-70s). The experience of the 1941-42 winter war showed that it was necessary to create strong armored units that were capable of expanding successful operations in terms of depth. The achievements of the tank factories made it possible in 1942 to start forming armored corps with two tank brigades and one motorized rifle brigade. In April of that year, a third tank brigade was added to every corps. As of September 1942, mechanized corps with one tank brigade, three mechanized brigades and support troops were estab-

Rear view of T 1941 model T-34. Note the panoramoc targeting scope on top of the turret just ahead of the opened hatch. The large road wheels with their hard rubber pads can also be seen. Tanks of this type that were built at the end of 1941 had steel road wheels and rubber pads to save materials.

lished. In May 1942 the establishment of the 3rd and 5th Armored Armies was already begun; in July came the 1st and 4th Armored Armies. Every army had two armored corps, one independent tank brigade, one rifle division, one light artillery regiment, one guard launcher regiment, and its anti-aircraft unit.

In 1943 the Soviet armament industry delivered 24,000 armored vehicles, of which 16,500 were T-34 and KV tanks. At the beginning of July 1943, just before the battle of the Kursker Bogen, the Red Army's field forces had 9,580 tanks, the greatest number of them (6,223) being medium and heavy tanks. In this year, the Germans first had large numbers of modernized and newly developed tanks and assault guns to use. It had thus become necessary to arm the T-34 with a more powerful 85 mm tank gun. The first T-34/85 tanks reached the troops at the end of the year. During the year of

A close-up of the turret of a T-34 medium tank, showing the seats of the commander/gunner and loader on either side of the 76.2 mm tank gun, as seen through the open one-piece turret hatch.

Stuck, shot down and burned out—the fate of the majority of T-34 tanks on hand in the Red Army on June 22, 1941. They were lost in battles with German troops in the border areas and could only gradually be replaced by newly produced vehicles.

In a German directive on antitank fighting, the Russian T-34 was described as follows: "Of the tanks on the eastern front, the 26-ton T 34 is the most important. With its speed and mobility it can make good use . . . of its heavy armament. Because of its sloped armor plates it is hard to fight against."

The high combat value of the T-34, from the German point of view, was limited by the short lifetime of the W-2 Diesel engine, the poor observation conditions for the tank's crew, the not very good division of tasks among the four-man crew and the frequent lack of a radio. Many tank crews had to go into battle with brand new tanks without sufficient practical training. This made fighting the T-34 easier for the German soldiers.

This destroyed T-34 was used by the 8th Mechanized Corps of the Red Army during the heavy tank battles in the Brody area at the end of July 194.

The T-34 medium tank with its 76.2 mm tank gun could put German Panzer III and IV tanks out of action at a range of 1500 meters. On the other hand, the German tank crews had little chance of success in firing on the well-armored Russian tanks with their short-barreled guns.

1944 this model replaced the old T-34 with its 76.2 mm tank gun. The further development of the T-34/85, the T-44, achieved nothing of significance in World War II.

In 1944 the Red Army had, in all, six armored armies. In addition, there were independent mechanized and armored corps, tank brigades, and regiments. An armored corps consisted of 209 tanks and 49 self-propelled guns. In a mechanized corps there were 246 tanks and self-propelled guns.

In 1943 the KV heavy tanks in the tank brigades were already being exchanged for T-34s. Heavy tank penetration regiments were formed and equipped with this type of tank. All in all, the KV tank was not satisfactory in troop service, although numerous improvements had been made. It was less mobile than the T-34, but it too had only a 76.2 mm tank gun. Efforts to upgrade the firepower of the heavy tank led in 1943 to the KV-85, which was a transitional model to the IS (Iosef Vissarionovich Stalin, Chairman of the Council and People's Commissar) heavy tank. It reached the troops in the spring of 1944, and by that November, guard tank brigades of three regiments, each with 65 IS-2 heavy tanks, were being formed.

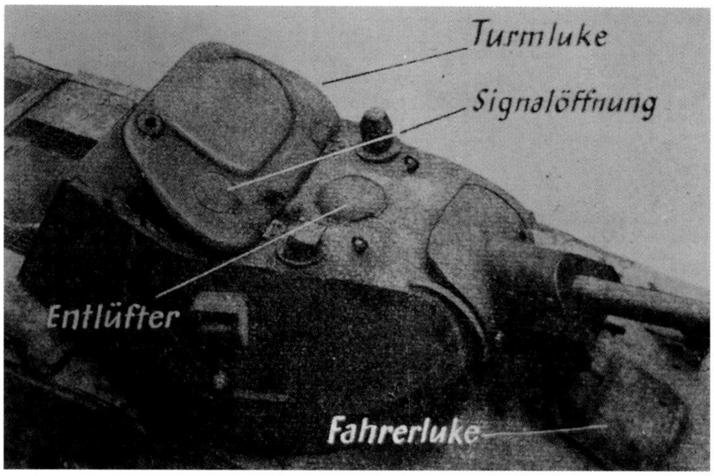

A close-up view of the turret of a T-34 medium tank, 1941 model. In back is the one-piece turret hatch with a signaling opening. In front of it are the ventilator (center), a turning periscope (right), and the turret panoramic targeting scope. Usually these devices had twofold magnification and a field of over 22 degrees. Linked with the tank gun was a TOD-1 targeting scope with twofold magnification and a 15-degree field of vision.

The effect of a German dive-bomber attack on a marching tank unit of the 8th Mechanized Corps of the Red Army. The 26-ton T-34s were apparently shoved into each other or thrown over with ease by the force of exploding bombs. Because of the meager effect of the ground antitank forces against the modern Russian tanks, the Luftwaffe was used more and more against them. This picture was taken at the end of June 1941.

During heavy fighting between the German 7th Armored Division and the 5th Armored Division of the Red Army, the Russian tank unit lost over eighty tanks on June 22 and 23, 1941, including numerous T-34s. The German losses were also high.

Various models of self-propelled mounts, armed with guns of 7.62, 85, 100, 122, and 152.4 mm calibers, were built on the basis of light, medium, and heavy tanks. There were 4,000 self-propelled mounts delivered in 1943, and 12,000 in 1944. The first self-propelled gun regiments had 17 light self-propelled guns (SU-76) and eight medium guns (SU-85). In 1944 the regiments were uniformly supplied with 21 self-propelled guns, which were divided into light, medium, and heavy units. In 1945, self-propelled gun brigades of three regiments were organized. These guns played an important role in supporting infantry and armored units.

The armored troops of the Red Army had to suffer severe losses during World War II from the ever-stronger German antitank defenses. All the same, they played the decisive role in the combat. The Chief of German Wehrmacht Equipment, General Buhle, had to admit with resignation in February 1945: "All battles in recent times made it clear that only the tank really made the difference." The great achievements of the Russian armament industry had a major part in making this impression on the German forces. Between 1940 and 1945, 87,200 tanks and 25,300 self-propelled mounts were produced. This not only made it possible to replace heavy losses on the front, but also to increase the numbers of available tanks constantly; by 1945 there were 105,383 tanks and 23,003 self-propelled mounts. The German industry had nothing comparable to use against them.

The war experiences of the Soviet armored troops had a decisive effect on their further technical and organizational development after World War II. They characterized their basis for action, even under the changed conditions of a possible rocket/nuclear weapon war.

1. Amphibian Tanks and Light Tanks

According to the Soviet tank philosophy, light tanks principally had three tasks to fulfill:

A light tank brigade of the Red Army included 64 light tanks of various types, 22 T-34 medium tanks, and seven KV heavy tanks as of August 1941.

An abandoned 1941 model T-34 after a battle on the Russian "Stalin Line" near Uman early in July 1941. The engine-room cover, 15 to 20 mm thick, was opened. Under it was the [p. 33] 12-cylinder, 4-stroke Diesel engine which produced 500 horsepower. Tanks holding 540 liters of fuel were located on both sides of the engine.

At a collecting depot for captured Russian tanks in November 1941, a T-34 medium tank, 1941 model, stands in the foreground, with 1933 and 1937 model T-26 light tanks.

A T-34 medium tank, 1941 model, with a German crew. Captured tanks of this type were used gladly by the Germans, though towing them in presented problems because of their weight and the lack of suitable recovery vehicles. They were designated "Tank T-34-747 (r)-Russian".

1. The pursuit of a beaten enemy and, for example, prevention of his holding his ground beyond a water obstacle.

2. Reconnaissance ahead and on the flanks of their own tank units while on the march.

3. Use in air-landed operations to support paratroops and airborne troops immediately after their landing.

Then as before, mobility of light tanks in the water took a high priority. From the search for a suitable successor to the T-38 M-2 there came, at the beginning of the forties, the T-30 amphibian tank. The chassis and hull were like those of the T-40 amphibian tank, which later went into series production, while the turret and armament were those of the T-60 light tank. Series production of the T-30 was ruled out in favor of the T-40. Because of the comparatively heavy turret, the handling characteristics of the tank in water did not live up to the requirements.

The T-40 amphibian tank was created during 1940. After testing had been completed successfully, the tank was introduced into the Red Army. As its powerplant, an engine from the auto industry was used. The six-cylinder GAZ 202 motor produced 85 HP and, along with a gearbox that also came from a motor vehicle, allowed a land speed of 44 kph; in water the maximum was 6.5 kph. Note that this 5.5-ton tank, like the KV, had a suspension using torsion bars. In the water it was moved by a four-bladed ship's propeller and steered by two rudder surfaces. The welded body of the hull resembled the hull of a boat. Float chambers were installed to improve its lift.

The turret, mounted to the left of center with external roller mantlets, carried a 12.7 mm DSchK 38 machine gun and a 7.62 mm DT machine gun. The large-caliber gun fired armor-piercing ammunition (BST) with a muzzle velocity of 895 m/sec. The tombac-plated steel-core bullet with tracer and incendiary additions could still pierce ten-millimeter armor at a distance of 100 meters. At 300 meters it could pierce 8 mm (at an angle of 60 degrees to the armor plate). At that time this was no longer sufficient for use against lightly armored targets, and the T-40 itself only had armor 13 mm thick at most. The insufficiency of the ammunition was already shown by the use of several T-40s in the 1939-40 winter war. In combat against German tanks in 1941, the T-40 scarcely had a

In the second half of 1941 the production of a turret, cast in two halves and them welded together, for the T-34 medium tank, 1941 model, began. The thickness of the armor reached 52 to 60 mm, and production could be greatly simplified. As of the end of 1941, road wheels without rubber pads were used.

The 76.2 mm 1940 model tank gun (F-34) is shown with part of its roller mantlet. The barrel and breech weighed 470 kilograms. The breech was a semi-automatic vertical type. The barrel had 32 riflings and was 3170 mm long, of which 2564 mm were rifled.

A T-34 medium tank built late in 1941, with its turret cast in two parts (upper and power) and easy to recognize. The shape of the hull front still shows the driver's hatch with three periscopes and the old-type machine-gun mount.

This picture was taken on the battlefield near Kharkov at the end of May 1942. The T-34 medium tank at the right has a driver's hatch in the hull with just two periscopes, but was fitted with an old-type turret. A typical feature is the curved front plate, an indication that production of the two turret types went on together for a long time.

chance. Therefore some of the tanks of this type produced in 1942 had strengthened armor at exposed places on the hull and turret. The added weight resulted in its loss of buoyancy.

Above all, it was the insufficient combat value of the T-40 (T-40 S) that resulted in its production being halted in 1942, after more than 220 vehicles had been completed. The German evaluation of this vehicle is interesting: "Weakly armored and armed, only limited combat value, easy to fight. The amphibiousness can be regarded as an advantage in carrying out operative reconnaissance in the bridge-poor East. . . ." (Tank Recognition Chart 2, "The Soviet Russian Tank Weapon", as of February 1, 1943, addendum to H.DV.469/2a)

No special tanks or self-propelled mounts based on the T-40 were developed or produced.

This T-34 medium tank, with chassis number 305 13 911, was built at Factory No. 112 in Gorki in 1942. It had a later-type armored hull. Note the improved armor protection on the machine-gun mount and the two periscopes on the driver's hatch. The cast two-piece turret is typical of the 1941 model. The vehicle is in the Warsaw Army Museum.

Tactical - Technical Data (T-40, 1941 Model)

Crew: 2 men
Weight: 5.5 tons
Armament: 1 12.7 mm caliber DSchK 38 machine gun, with 550 rounds
1 7.62 mm caliber DT machine gun, with 2,016 rounds
Armor plate:
Hull: Front: 10-13 mm
Sides: 13 mm
Rear: 10 mm
Top: 6 mm
Bottom: 6-10 mm
Turret:
Front: 14-15 mm
Sides: 10 mm
Rear: 10 mm
Top: 7 mm

Powerplant: 6-cylinder in line, 40stroke GAZ-202 gasoline engine
Performance: 85 HP at 3600 rpm
Fuel capacity: 206 liters
Power to weight: 15.4 HP/ton
Length: 4110 mm
Width: 2330-2350 mm
Height: 1950 mm
Ground clearance: 340 mm
Top speed: Land: 44-45 kph; water: 5-6 kph
Range: Land: 185-360 km (280)
Climbing degree: 34 degrees
Spanning ability: 1700 mm
Climbing ability: 600 mm
Wading ability: amphibious
Specific ground pressure: 0.46 kp/sq. cm.

A 1941 model T-34, with the rounded shape of the cast turret and the long-barreled 76.2 mm model F-34 tank gun easy to see.

A moving photo of a member of the German 18th Armored Division before the battle near Khvastovichi early in October 1941. Russian T-34 tanks carry infantrymen as they break out of the pocket south of Bryansk.

Turning to another light tank model of the Red Army, we find one that in a certain sense had a special position in Soviet tankbuilding: the T-50. The first experiences with the new T-34 medium tank were not positive either in production or troop use. This caused numerous complaints, which induced several representatives in the Armored Troop Administration to voice repeated objections, the purpose of which was to create a light tank, similar to the previous T-26, for infantry support. A development bureau under the direction of L. Troyanov and I. Bushnevov was empowered to create the prototype of such a tank. This development led to the T-50 light tank. At the end of 1940, two vehicles had been finished at Factory No. 174 in Leningrad. With a few improvements resulting from testing, this tank type was declared ready for introduction in April 1941.

The armor was 37 mm thick on all sides and thus offered (along with its favorable angles) protection from the fire of armor-piercing shells from 37 mm guns at ranges over 500 meters. Thus experience from the Spanish Civil War was considered for this comparatively light (13.5-ton) tank. The hull was welded, as was the turret, and had an angled form on all sides. The conically shaped turret had a commander's cupola with six angle seals, the visors of which could be closed with armored blinds. Three of the four crewmen worked in the turret. The armament with a 45 mm 1939 tank gun and a machine gun was sufficient for a light tank at that time. The tank shell, weighing 1.43 kilograms, could penetrate 35 mm of armor plate at 500 meters and 28 mm at 1,000 meters. The driver sat forward in the middle of the hull and could use a slit in the armor as well as a turning periscope for vision. Torsion-bar suspension had been chosen for the running gear. The six-cylinder W-4 Diesel engine produced 300 HP, allowing excellent performance. All the tanks were built to hold a radio set.

Because of a certain similarity with the KV heavy tank, the T-50 was nicknamed "Mali Klim," or "Little Klim(ent Voroshilov)," by the Soviet tank soldiers. In production, this simple tank type

The battlefield near Kharkov at the end of May 1942, with a T-60 light tank at the left and two T-34 1941 model medium tanks near it.

A dug-in T-34 Medium Tank, 1941 model. The Russian army dug in damaged tanks or those without engines as fixed firing positions. Thus they became important parts of Russian fighting power though without mobility.

proved to be rather complicated. The work required was about equal to that needed for a medium tank. It soon proved that it was not possible under the conditions of the war to to go on building such an expensive light tank. Thus production of the T-50 was halted at the beginning of 1942, after 65 tanks had been built. Some T-50 tanks were captured and used by the Finnish Army in 1942. There were no special vehicles based on it.

Tactical - Technical Data (T-50)

Crew:		4 men
Weight:		13.5-14.0 tons
Armament:		1 45 mm caliber 1938 tank gun, with 150 rounds
		1 7.62 mm caliber DT machine gun, with 400 rounds
Armor plate:		
Hull:	Front:	37 mm
	Sides:	37 mm
	Rear:	25-37 mm
	Top:	12-15 mm
	Bottom:	12-15 mm [page 53]
Turret:	Front:	37 mm
	Sides:	15 mm
	Rear:	15 mm
	Top:	12-15 mm
Powerplant:		12-cylinder in-line 4-stroke W-4 gasoline engine
Performance:		300 HP as 2000 rpm
Fuel capacity:		350 liters
Power to weight:		21.4 HP/ton
	Length:	5200 mm
	Width:	2470 mm
	Height:	2160 mm
Ground clearance:		350 mm
Top speed:		52-65 kph
Range:		350 km
Climbing degree:		35 degrees
Spanning ability:		2200 mm
Climbing ability:		700 mm
Wading ability:		1100 mm
Specific ground pressure:		0.57 kp/sq. cm.

From a German experience report of April 10, 1944, it can be seen that some T-50 tanks were fitted with heavier armor. The weight of that version is stated as 18 tons; its armament included a 7.62 mm DT anti-aircraft machine gun. All in all, the T-50 was just a brief episode in Soviet tankbuilding.

Tests with the T-40 and production of a small number of no longer amphibious T-40 S made the Red Army armored troops' interest in a light tank clear, as long as it had sufficient armor and a higher firepower. At the beginning of 1940, as already noted, the T-30 failed to give the desired results; in particular, it was not able to meet the request for sufficient mobility in the water. As for the armament of a light reconnaissance tank, the Soviet experts even thought of a gun with a caliber of 45 mm. This would mean a greater increase in weight.

The limited view for the crew of a Russian T-34 made fighting them with engineers' explosive charges, mines and incendiary bottles easier. This photo shows close-range German antitank fighters during a battle on the Volkov in the winter of 1941-42.

In the middle of 1941, completely different conditions prevailed for the forces of the Soviet Union. The Red Army had to draw back far to the east under the pressure of German advances. Important production facilities for tanks were lost, and the armored troops lost the majority of their tanks from prewar days on the battlefields between the Bug and the Volga. What they urgently needed were tanks and more tanks. In this complicated situation, light tanks offered the advantage that they could be produced in automobile factories, taking the burden off other branches of the armament industry. Of particular interest was the chassis of the T-40 amphibian tank. It was already designed and tested, and its powerplant consisted of automobile components. A design bureau in Moscow, under the leadership of N. A. Astrov, began to develop the T-40 further, so its armor and armament would meet the new requirements better. Its amphibious character was disregarded from the start. But

A fog cartridge exploded on the front plate of a 1941 model T-34 medium tank. Thus the crew's view could be limited even more, allowing close-range antitank fighters to get closer with their explosives.

This 1941 model T-34 medium tank was shot down during the winter battles of 1941-42. The weather washed off some of the white camouflage, and the olive green paint shows through.

the vehicle was too light to have a 45 mm tank gun installed. A radical new design would have taken too much time, so they turned to the 20 mm SchWak aircraft gun. This weapon had been developed for use in aircraft by the designers Spitalny and Komaritzky. It weighed only 45 kilograms. The incendiary tank shell weighed 0.096 kg (with electron cap) and could penetrate 24 mm of armor plate at 100 meters. The weapon was fully automatic.

In July 1941, the first T-60s were assembled at Factory No. 37 in Moscow. At the same time, production of the T-40 was going on in that factory. How did the new light tank differ from the T-40 amphibian tank, other than its heavier armament? The hull shape had been reworked to take larger armor plates at sharper angles. At first the armor plates were riveted; later they were welded together. In the front of the hull were the powerplant and power train, plus the controls at the driver's seat. The six-cylinder GAZ-202 engine was offset to the right in the middle of the hull. The fighting compartment was at the left, with the turret above. The fuel tanks were

T-34 tanks of various series were put out of action by the fire of heavy armor-piercing weapons. In the middle is a tank with rubberless running gear. The picture was taken in the spring of 1942.

This 1941 T-34 medium tank, with rubber-saving running gear, was captured in combat in the spring of 1942. Such economies had turned out to be necessary to reach the required production figures. Yet in the second half of 1941 only 62 percent of the planned production could be achieved (4177 tanks in all, including 1886 T-34s). Obergefreiter Alois Schlee stands beside the tank.

In 1942 a completely cast hexagonal turret for the medium tank was introduced. The side observation ports were eliminated, replaced by simple slits over the pistol loopholes. The armor was made thicker, with the turret front 60 mm, the sides and rear 52 mm thick.

The 1941 model T-34 medium tank compared with the light T-70 tank. Note the perforated road wheels without rubber pads but with sheet metal. The shorter lifetime of the road wheels and tracks was accepted in view of the ever-shorter life spans of the tanks.

This 1942 model T-34 medium tank is in the Military Museum of the Historical Institute of the Czech Army in Lesany. The main producer of T-34 tanks from July 1941 to September 1942 was the Stalingrad Tractor Works, which built 3600 tanks in that time period.

in the rear. The first series-produced T-60 left the assembly line on December 15, 1941. There had been delays. In the autumn of 1941, Factory No. 37, where the T-60 was being built, had been transferred from Moscow to behind the Urals. The auto factory in Gorki and Factory no. 138 in Kirov took over production of the tank. The armored body came from the Podolsk Machine Works. Meeting the planned daily production of seventy vehicles caused some trouble. Sometimes there were only forty built. The capacities of the suppliers were not sufficient. Yet the numbers completed were considerable. By the autumn of 1942, when T-60 production was halted, 6,292 tanks of this type had been built and delivered. They were largely used in independent tank battalions, which were supposed to have one heavy company (with KV tanks), one medium company (with T-34), and two light companies with T-60 tanks. The heavy tanks were actually lacking in many battalions. Light T-60 tanks took their place.

The Germans already had new tanks on the front at the end of January 1942. On January 26, 1942, the Army High Command, General Staff, Foreign Armies East Department (IIc)(No. 287/42) reported: "In the sector of Army Group South, large numbers of the new Russian T-60 tank have seen action recently. The T-60 is a

Typical features of the new cast steel turret, in addition to its rounded shape, were the ventilator at the rear and the two round hatches in its top. Ahead of the left hatch is the panoramic targeting scope. The opening for a turning periscope ahead of the right hatch has been covered with an armor plate.

Front and rear views of the T-34 medium tank, 1942 model. Its fighting weight had risen to about 30 tons, or even higher with added armor plate.

The 1942 model T-34 medium tank, seen from the front and back. The Red Army did not differentiate among the various production series (A, B, C, etc.), and dividing them by the year they were built has its problems. The reason is that improvements and simplifications were constantly being sought in tankbuilding, making a clear order of certain features difficult.

light tank. It can be handled effectively by the German 3.7 cm anti-tank gun. . . ."

Under normal weather conditions, the T-60 had shown satisfactory maneuverability and off-road capability, and was cheap and simple to produce, which was probably its greatest advantage. But the Soviet tank soldiers were not satisfied with its armor and armament, although these were upgraded in 1942. The commander of the 1st Armored Army, Generaloberst M. J. Katukov, did not speak very positively about it in a talk with Commander-in-chief Josef Stalin on September 17, 1942: "I can't find much good about the T-60. Of course it has automatic weapons, but only a 20 mm gun. It would not be up to a serious fight against tanks. Besides, it has too little ground clearance and is completely useless in mud or snow. In the fighting around Moscow we had to tow these tanks." The German evaluation was very similar: "Very small and light tank, very recently made. . . . Weak armor, little combat value. Technically of only limited use." The T-60 was replaced in production by the T-70.

In 1942 an interesting test was made with a T-60, its goal being the use of the 5.5-ton tank by the airborne troops. At first a vehicle—or just the empty body—was fitted with wings, a double tail with two horizontal fins and a vertical one, and was towed by a TB-3 bomber plane as a glider. It functioned in this form. Test flights with a complete tank failed, so the project was dropped. There are various designations for it: KT, A-T, or A-40.

During the war, the handholds on the hull and turret were among the identifying marks of T-34 series. They were there for machine-pistol soldiers to hang onto.

This tank was photographed in 1997 on the grounds of the Military History Museum of the Historical Institute of the Czech Army in Lesany.

Two noteworthy self-propelled mounts also arose on the chassis of the T-60. A design bureau at Factory No. 38 received a contract in 1942 to create a light self-propelled mount on T-60 basis for the new 76.2 mm ZIS-3 (1942 model) divisional cannon. Several prototypes were built and designated OSU-76. With the halt in T-60 production, this project was continued on the chassis of the T-70 light tank. The result was the SU-76 self-propelled mount.

Another self-propelled mount resulted during the building of the so-called BM-8-36 salvo launcher on the turretless T-60 tank. United in a package were 36 launching rails. It fired stabilized 82 mm explosive rockets with a weight of 8 kilograms to distances up to 5,500 meters. Tests for launching these rockets from tanks had already been carried out in the thirties with BT tanks. The 1942 version, using the T-60 tank, was an attempt to evaluate existing tank chassis.

A few T-60 tanks were used as towing tractors for 76.2 mm divisional cannons in the artillery regiments of several rifle divisions.

Tactical - Technical Data (T-60, 1941 model)

Crew: 2 men
Weight: 5.5-5.8 tons
Armament: 1 20 mm caliber SchWak 1941 tank gun, with 750-780 rounds,
1 7.62 mm caliber DT machine gun, with 945-1000 rounds
Armor plate:
Hull: Front: 14-20 mm
Sides: 15 mm
Rear: 10-13 mm
Top: 7-10 mm
Bottom: 7-10 mm
Turret: Front: 15 mm
Sides: 15 mm
Rear: 15 mm
Top: 7 mm
Powerplant: 6-cylinder in-line 4-stroke GAZ-202 gasoline engine
Performance: 70 HP at 3400 rpm
Fuel capacity: 320 liters
Power to weight: 12 HP/ton
Length: 4100 mm
Width: 2350 mm
Height: 1750 mm
Ground clearance: 300 mm
Top speed: 44 kph
Range: 315-614 km
Climbing degree: 28-29 degrees
Spanning ability: 1700 mm
Climbing ability: 600 mm
Wading ability: 870 mm
Specific ground pressure: 0.48 kp/sq. cm.

A 1942 model T-34 medium tank with a cast steel turret. In order to increase the already long range of this tank, the Red Army tank units used unarmored extra fuel tanks (literally "roll-tire barrels") carried on the track aprons.

A T-34 made in 1942, photographed on the battlefield in the south part of the Kursk Bogen early in July 1941. During the tank battle there, the Germans large numbers of new and modernized tanks, which could fire effectively on the T-34 from 2000 meters away. They caused the Russian tank units heavy losses.

Tactical - Technical Data (T-60, 1942 model)

Crew:		2 men
Weight:		6.4 tons
Armament:		1 20 mm caliber SchWak 1941 tank gun, with 780 rounds, 1 7.62 mm caliber DT machine gun, with 945-1000 rounds
Armor plate:		
Hull:	Front:	35 mm
	Sides:	25 mm
	Rear:	25 mm
	Top:	13 mm
	Bottom:	13 mm
Turret:	Front:	25 mm
	Sides:	25 mm
	Rear:	25 mm
	Top:	7 mm
Powerplant:		6-cylinder in-line 4-stroke GAZ-203 gasoline engine
Performance:		85 HP at 3400 rpm
Fuel capacity:		? liters
Power to weight:		10.9 HP/ton
	Length:	4160 mm
	Width:	2350 mm
	Height:	1780 mm
Ground clearance:		300 mm
Top speed:		42 kph
Range:		315-614 km
Climbing degree:		28-29 degrees
Spanning ability:		1700 mm
Climbing ability:		600 mm
Wading ability:		870 mm
Specific ground pressure:		0.46 kp/sq. cm.

A T-34 made in 1942, photographed on the battlefield in the south part of the Kursk Bogen early in July 1941. During the tank battle there, the Germans large numbers of new and modernized tanks, which could fire effectively on the T-34 from 2000 meters away. They caused the Russian tank units heavy losses.

In the winter of 1942-43, a more simplified hexagonal turret began to be built. It consisted of pressed and welded armor plates 52 to 75 mm thick. Tanks of this type appeared parallel to the 1942 model T-34 with cast steel turrets during the fighting around Kharkov in the spring of 1943 and in the tank battle at the Kursk Bogen.

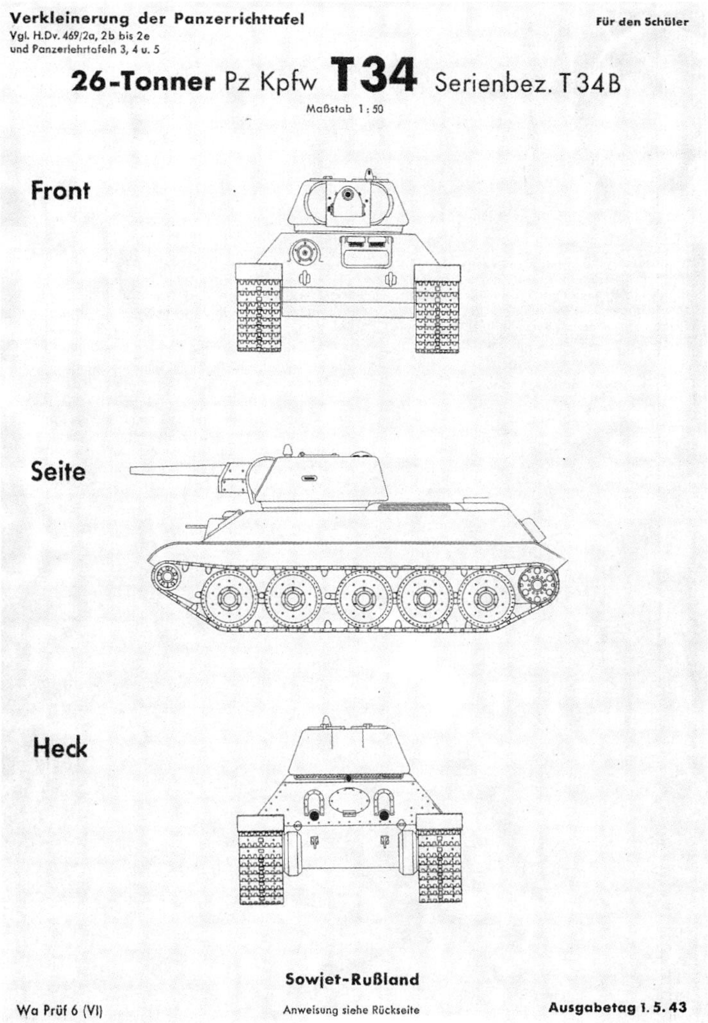

The T-34 1943 model as shown on a German tank recognition chart of 1943.

During the combat in the Kharkov-Byelgorod area on March 11-20, 1943, the Red Army, according to German data, lost 961 tanks. One was this T-34 1943 model with "Moskovskii Kolchosnik" (Moscow Kolchos-builder) lettering. Note the angled mount on the hull, only rounded above, for the bow machine gun.

Another T-34 with a hexagonal turret that fell victim to German tank defenses. The different road wheels are interesting. In the foreground is the track, 500 mm thick.

The reasons why the T-60 had to go into series production at the end of 1941 are known. The wish to arm light tanks with at least a 45 mm tank gun remained in force and led to a further devlopment of the T-60. At the end of 1941, the development bureau, under the leadership of A. A. Astrov, began the work. After testing, the T-70 was approved as a light tank for introduction into the armored troops of the Red Army. In April the conically shaped turret was changed again. Series production at Factories No. 37 and 38 sometimes ran parallel to that of the predecessor T-60.

In principle, the basic design of the T-60 was retained, with the driver's seat in front and the turret to the left. Two coupled 6-cylinder motor vehicle engines were installed (in tandem, along the right side). The differential and main clutch were united with the engines in one block.

T-70s built as of September 1942 had strengthened running gear, with parts not interchangeable with the old ones. The tracks were also widened from 260 to 300 mm. The road wheels and return rollers were made wider. The drive wheels and driveshafts were also made to new designs.

A basic problem and simultaneously the decisive weak point of the T-70 was the small turret, which now contained a 45 mm 1938 tank gun and a 7.62 mm DT machine gun, but only had space for one crewman. This was the commander, also loader and gunner. That overworked him. Attempts to fit the gun with automatic loading to increase its rate of fire did not succeed. In 1942, 4,883 T-70 tanks were built. In 1943 there were another 3,343 made until work was stopped that October. As of September 1943, T-70 tanks were fitted with new, more powerful engines (GAZ-203 producing 85 HP) and a more strongly armored turret. The light tank was used by the tank battalions in their tank brigades. For instance, the 143rd Nevel Tank Brigade of Tank Battalion 65 had two companies with ten T-34 tanks each. In Tank Battalion 259 there was, in addition to the two T-34 companies, one company with sixteen T-70 tanks. The third battalion consisted of motorized riflemen.

Although the T-70 offered higher firepower and better armor than its predecessor, its combat value was not rated highly by either the Soviet or German forces. Let us quote the armored leader, General M. J. Katukov, once again: "The light T-70, which was introduced just a short time ago, certainly has heavier armor, has a 45 mm tank gun and two auto engines, but does not stand out in any other features" Katukov ended his comments to Stalin on the Soviet tank on September 17, 1942, with the words: "One has nothing but annoyance with them. . . ." The judgment of the German tank experts was scarcely different: "Light tank, especially for combat reconnaissance, often used for communication and supplying on the battlefield. Fast, mobile armored vehicle with meager combat value, easy to fight against."

In the autumn of 1943, along with the upgraded final version of the T-70, the small number of 120 T-80 light tanks became avail-

As the "Tank T-34-747 (r) -Russian T-34-", the 1943 model T-34 was put to use in goodly numbers by some tank units of the German Army and Waffen-SS. On the rear of this vehicle's turret, the toolbox made for the Panzer III (Sd.Kfz. 141) and Panzer IV (Sd. Kfz. 161) is attached.

Pictures from the battlefield near Prochorovka, south of Kursk, where a tank battle took place on July 12, 1943 between the II. SS Armored Corps of the German attack force and the Russian 5th Guard Tank Army with its 850 tanks and self-propelled gun mounts. The Red Army men fought with great boldness and self-sacrifice against the enemy forces and their Tiger tanks, but could not break through the enemy lines. The 5th [p. 37] Guard Tank Army lost over 300 tanks and gun mounts on this one day, including those shown here.

During World War II the German antitank forces were able to increase their efficiency greatly. The results were growing numbers of tanks shot down, including T-34 tanks. Constantly increasing production figures of the Russian armament industry maintained the balance. Here another advantage of the T-34 is seen: it was especially suitable for large-series production.

able. From the start they were powered by two GAZ-203 engines producing 85 HP. But the most important innivation was the larger turret in which there was room for two men. The great elevation range of the 45 mm 1938 tank gun must be noted as unusual. With +60 degree elevation it was possible to fire on targets in the air or in upper stories of buildings. For this the tank had an added reflective visor.

As already indicated, production of the T-80 did not add up to high numbers. The whole problem in the production of light tanks was based on their too-light armament and armor, which was a noticeable weakness, above all in combat with the German tanks. Similarly, bad experiences fell on the Soviet tank soldiers with the "Valentine" light infantry tank and the M 3 "Stuart" light tank which were delivered to the Soviet Union through the lend-lease agreement.

A 1943 model T-34 that was put out of action by the German Assault Gun Unit 276 in East Prussia late in the summer of 1944.

Tactical - Technical Data (T-70, 1942 model)

Crew:		2 men
Weight:		9.2 tons
Armament:		1 45 mm caliber 1938 tank gun, with 70-90 rounds, 1 7.62 mm caliber DT machine gun, with 945 rounds
Armor plate:		
Hull:	Front:	35-45 mm
	Sides:	16 mm
	Rear:	15 mm
	Top:	10-15 mm
	Bottom:	10-15 mm
Turret:	Front:	35 mm
	Sides:	35 mm
	Rear:	35 mm
	Top:	10 mm
Powerplant:		2 6-cylinder in-line 4-stroke GAZ-202 gasoline engines
Performance:		2 x 70 = 140 HP at 3400 rpm
Fuel capacity:		440 liters
	Length:	4290 mm
	Width:	2420 mm
	Height:	2050 mm
Ground clearance:		300 mm
Top speed:		45 kph
Range:		350 km
Climbing degree:		35 degrees
Spanning ability:		1700 mm
Climbing ability:		650 mm
Wading ability:		900 mm
Specific ground pressure:		0.67 kp/sq. cm.

The hexagonal turrets of the 1943 model T-34 showed noticeable differences resulting from their production. The pistol loopholes on the turret sides were eliminated; those at the rear were kept, but without vision slits. There were also differences in the attachment for the panoramic targeting scope and the armor plate on top of the turret.

From the summer of 1943 on, the 1943 model T-34 medium tank was built with hexagonal turret and cylindrical commander's cupola. The tank was now 2650 mm high, a disadvantage more than made up for by the much improved all-around observation quality.

The turret of a 1943 model T-34 medium tank, with the commander's cupola and two-piece hatch easy to see. Just before the hatch is the panoramic targeting scope. The opening for a periscope in front of the loader's hatch (right side of the turret) was covered with an armor plate.

A 1943 model T-34 medium tank in the collection of the Military Technology Museum of the Historical Institute of the Czech Army in Lesany.

The wright of the 1943 model T-34 is given as, at most, 30.9 tons. The front armor of the hull was 60 mm thick, that of the turret 75 mm. The ammunition for the 76.2 mm 1942 model tank gun (F-34) numbered 100 shells, plus 3150 rounds for the two 7.62 mm DT machine guns.

Tactical - Technical Data (T-70, 1943 model)

Crew: 2 men
Weight: 9.8-10.0 tons
Armament: 1 45 mm caliber 1938 tank gun, with 70-90 rounds
1 7.62 mm caliber DT machine gun, with 945 rounds
Armor plate:
Hull: Front: 35-45 mm
Sides: 16 mm
Rear: 16 mm
Top: 10-15 mm
Bottom: 10-15 mm
Turret: Front: 60 mm
Sides: 35 mm
Rear: 35 mm
Top: 10 mm
Powerplant: 2 6-cylinder in-line 4-stroke GAZ-203 gasoline engines
Performance: 2 x 85 = 170 HP at 3600 rpm
Fuel capacity: 480 liters
Power to weight: 16-16.3 HP/ton
Length: 4420 mm
Width: 2470 mm
Height: 2080 mm
Ground clearance: 300 mm
Top speed: 45 kph
Range: 250-300 km
Climbing degree: 35 degrees
Spanning ability: 1700 mm
Climbing ability: 650 mm
Wading ability: 900 mm
Specific ground pressure: 0.51 kp/sq. cm.

Tactical - Technical Data (T-80)

Crew: 3 men
Weight: 11.6 tons
Armament: 1 45 mm caliber 1938 tank gun, with 94 rounds,
1 7.62 mm caliber DT machine gun, with 1008 rounds
Armor plate:
Hull: Front: to 50 mm
Sides: 16-25 mm
Rear: 16-25 mm
Top: 10-15 mm
Bottom: 10-15 mm
Turret: Front: 60 mm
Sides: 35 mm
Rear: 35 mm
Top: 10 mm
Powerplant: 2 6-cylinder in-line 4-stroke GAZ-203 gasoline engines
Performance: 2 x 85 = 170 HP
Fuel capacity: 480 liters
Length: 4420 mm
Width: 2500 mm
Height: 2180 mm
Ground clearance: 300 mm
Top speed: 45 kph
Range: 320 km
Climbing degree: 34 degrees
Spanning ability: 1800 mm
Climbing ability: 650 mm
Wading ability: 900 mm
Specific ground pressure: 0.83 kp/sq. cm.

This 1943 model T-34 medium tank is shown in the Military History museum in Dresden. It was one of over 100 tanks of this type that were sold to the East German People's Police in the early fifties. Later it was used as a recovery tank.

The T-70 and T-80 light tanks were of great importance during the war for their use in building self-propelled light artillery mounts, as well as in their intended function. In 1942 the OSU-76 self-propelled mount, based on the T-60, took form at Factory No. 38, and test models were built. A little later, a lengthened and widened version of the T-70 chassis was also developed as a self-propelled mount. It was at first designated SU-12. Factories No. 92 in Gorki and No. 38 in Kirov were involved in its development, working closely with the development bureau of Generals Petrov and Grabin. They were responsible for the artillery, in this case the 76.2 mm ZIS-3 divisional cannon (1942 model). In December 1942, a light self-propelled mount, designated SU-76, was declared ready for introduction. It was used above all in the self-propelled gun regiments of mechanized and armored corps. The first units of this kind had 17 SU-76 and eight SU-122 (see under medium tanks 1939-1945) in their six batteries. As of April 1943 there were single-type self-propelled gun regiments of four or five batteries which, if equipped with SU-76 guns, had five self-propelled mounts each. In 1944 several rifle and guard rifle divisions of the Red Army received their own self-propelled gun units.

Various views of the 1943 model T-34 at Dresden. This version has the vision slits and pistol loopholes in the turret sides and rear again; they had been omitted for a time. The camouflage light protected with a bow on the left side of the hull is one typical feature of the T-34 tanks used in East Germany after World War II.

The 1943 model T-34 medium tank compared with its successor, the T-34/85 of 1944.

A 1943 model T-34 before the Red Army monument at the Berlin Zoo. The T-34/76 designation came into use only with the introduction of the 85 mm tank gun (T-34/85).

By the end of 1942, 26 SU-76 had been delivered; in 1943 there came 1928 SU-76 and ZSU-37; in 1944 7,155 self-propelled guns of the two types, and in 1945 another 3,562. The ZSU-37 was a variation of the SU-76 as a light self-propelled AA mount carrying a 37 mm 1939 anti-aircraft gun.

A curious feature of the first-built SU-76 mounts was that the two GAZ-203 gasoline engines, along with a gearbox for each, were

installed at the right and left sides of the hull. This arrangement proved to be too complicated and sensitive. There were numerous technical breakdowns. In the spring of 1943 the development bureau of N. A. Astrov took on the job of thoroughly revising the SU-76. The principle of two motors in a row, originally used in the T-70, with a single gearbox, was used again. Later in May the self-propelled mount was put into series production with the designation of SU-76 M.

The construction was basically simple and resembled the T-70/T-80 light tanks in its fighting compartment, which was a rigid design, open above and moved to the rear. In front was the driver's seat with controls, linked to the fighting compartment by a passageway. The powerplant was installed on the right. The armor offered protection only from infantry weapons.

The 76.2 mm ZIS-3 (1942 model) divisional cannon could fire 6.2 kilogram explosive shells up to 8,600 meters (12 rounds per minute). Its use against heavily armored tanks had a chance of success only at ranges up to 900 meters. At these ranges, their tank shells could penetrate 49 to 62 mm of armor plate. With undercaliber shells the maximum was 90 mm.

The German forces first became aware of these light self-propelled guns in mid-July 1943, when one SU-76 was captured near Vechopanye on July 14 of that year. The Foreign Armies East De-

***Left, Above*: During the battles in the spring of 1944, these 1943 model T-34 medium tanks were shot down by German antitank forces. The holes made in the 45- or 52-mm hull and turret armor by 8.8 cm antitank shells can be seen clearly.**

The T-34/85 medium tank with the 85 mm D-5 T tank gun, which weighed 1530 kg, had a barrel 4386 mm long (L/51.6), and could fire four to seven shots per minute. Besides the primary armament, the five-man crew had two 7.62 mm DT machine guns to use. This tank was built in Factory No. 112.

The turret design of the T-34/85 was a compromise. Because of the 1944 model 85 mm tank gun (ZIS S-53) and the additional gunner located in the turret, it had more interior space. This resulted in particularly shot-sensitive areas in the lower part of the turret.

Cutaway drawing of the 1944 model T-34/85 medium tank.

The T-34/85 turrets built in 1944 and 1945 could be recognized by crude workmanship. A comparison of various turret shapes shows noticeable differences caused by production technology. This is also true of the arrangement of the doors or ventilators in the turret top, some before and some behind the turret top.

Loading a 1944 model T-34 medium tank that was sold to the East German People's Army after World War II. Typical features of this tank include the camouflage light on the left side of the hull and the tool chest on the rear of the turret.

partment of the Army High Command was astounded to learn at the beginning of 1944 that there was a type of SU-76 known as SU-76i, which had been produced at the Tank Repair Shop in Krasnoarmaisk by using captured German Panzer III tanks. In October 1943, such vehicles had appeared, and some captured, in the sector of the 16th Armored Grenadier Division. They had belonged to a self-propelled gun regiment of the 7th Mechanized Corps of the Red Army. There were some 200 of these 22-ton vehicles, and they were used as was the SU-76.

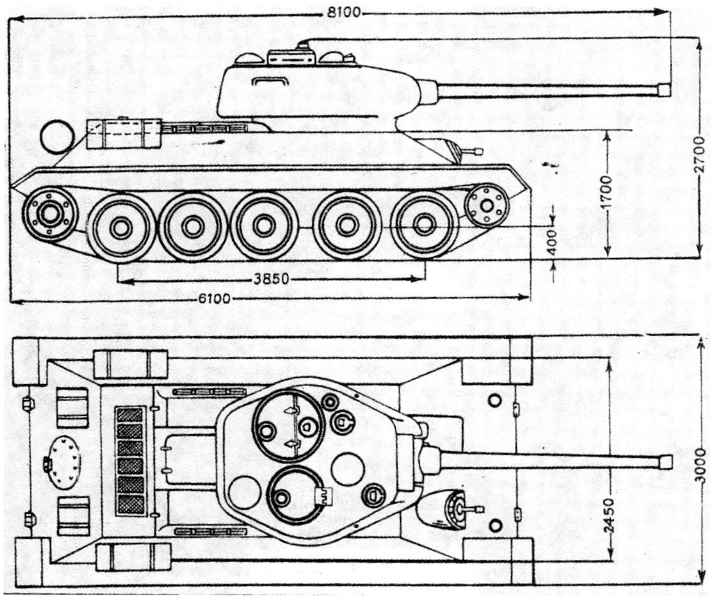

The most important dimensions of the 1944 model T-34/85 medium tank, with side and top views.

Tactical - Technical Data (SU-76, 1943 model)[10]

Crew:		4 men
Weight:		11.2 tons
Armament:		1 76.2 mm caliber ZIS-3 divisional cannon (1942 model), with 60 rounds, 1 7.62 mm PPSch-41 machine pistol
Armor Plate:		
Hull:	Front:	26-35 mm
	Sides:	10-16 mm
	Rear:	10-16 mm
	Top:	10 mm
	Bottom:	10 mm
Upper body:		
	Front:	35 mm
	Sides:	15 mm
	Rear (below):	15 mm
	Top:	no armor
Powerplant:		2 6-cylinder in-line 4-stroke GAZ-203 gasoline engines
Performance:		2 x 85 = 170 HP at 3600 rpm
Fuel capacity:		400-420 liters
	Length:	15.2 HP-ton
	Width:	2740 mm
	Height:	2200 mm
Ground clearance:		300 mm
Top speed:		45 kph
Range:		250 km
Climbing degree:		24 degrees
Spanning ability:		1600-2000 mm
Climbing ability:		650 mm
Wading ability:		900 mm
Specific ground pressure:		0.57 kp/sq. cm.

10. In the ZSU-37 anti-aircraft mount version, the vehicle carried a 37 mm AA Gun 39 with 320 rounds. The fighting weight is given as 10.5 tons. The turret armor was 6 to 16 mm thick.

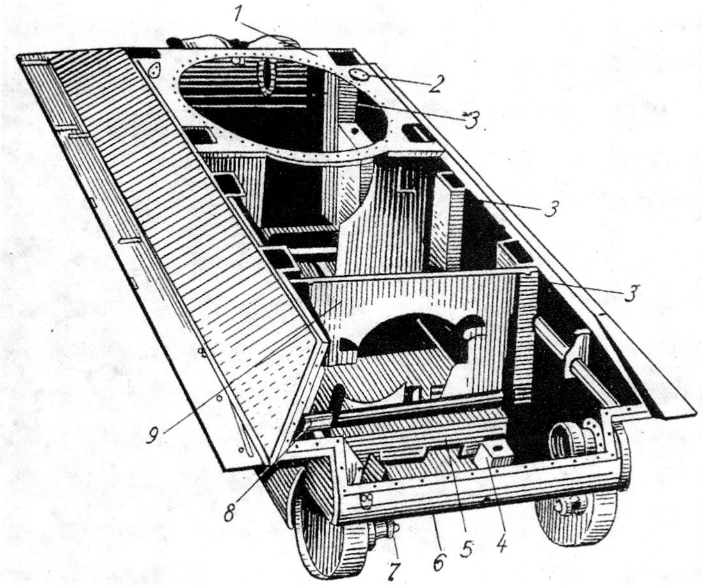

The armored hull of the T-34/85 medium tank, 1944 model (interior): 1. fighting compartment cover, 2. Closing lids for the openings over the fuel fillers, 3. Spring shafts, 4. Brake support, 5. Bulkhead for fastening the variable gears, 6. Lower rear armor plate, 7. Towing hook, 8. transverse support, 9. Dividing wall between engine room and gearbox.

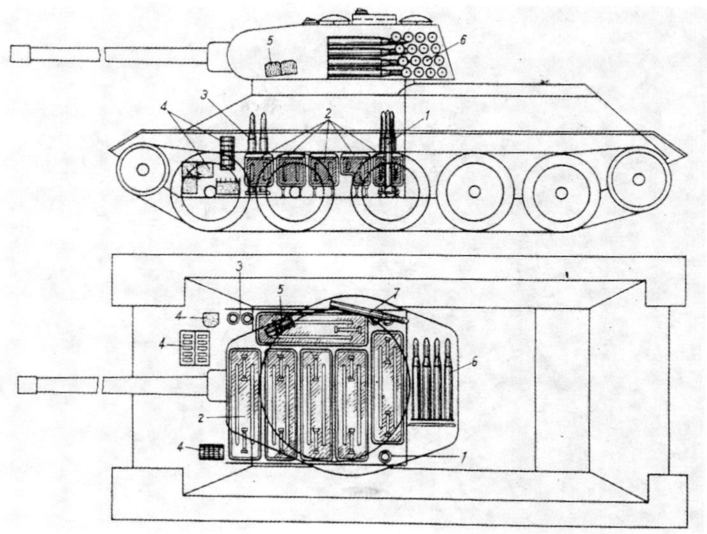

Ammunition storage in the 1944 model T-34/85 medium tank (56-60 shells and 1890 machine-gun rounds, 20 hand grenades and 36 signal flares).

Front and rear views of a badly damaged 1944 model T-34/85 medium tank with 85 mm 1944 model tank gun (ZIS S-53). It can be seen that the turret was made of an upper and a lower part welded together. The side vision slits and pistol loopholes are retained; the shutter is missing.

A tank regiment of the Red Army's armored troops had 35 T-34 tanks in February 1944. In general they were still armed with the 76.2 mm tank gun. T-34s with the more powerful 85 mm gun only reached the troops gradually despite intensely increased production. This 1944 model T-34/85 was shot down in Lithuania.

Amphibious light tanks for reconnaissance and security tasks had played a major role in the armored troops of the Red Army in the thirties. During the war years, there were various reasons why amphibious ability of light tanks had been downgraded in favor of higher firepower and effective armor protection. The T-60, T-70, and T-80 tank types resulted from this. In the course of the Red Army's advances toward the west, the armored units had to overcome numerous water barriers. Now they lacked light amphibious reconnaissance vehicles, for the available scout cars (BA-64) were neither amphibious nor sufficiently off-road capable. Their firepower equaled that of the amphibious tanks of the thirties. As a result, the Armored Troop Command requested an amphibious reconnaissance tank. The K-90 was built as a prototype with a 76.2 mm gun. Its running gear still showed elements of the T-70 light tank. The K-90 formed the foundation for a design that typified Soviet armored units of postwar times, the PT-76 amphibious tank.

2. Medium Tanks

Among the probably most important lessons learned from the combat between tanks and antitank weapons in the 1936-39 Spanish Civil War was, according to military experts in many lands, that the "tank . . . is inferior to well-organized antitank defense." If tanks were to maintain their justification as an effective and highly mobile means of combat, it was necessary to improve their armor protection. Further requests concerned their mobility and firepower, which likewise could not be neglected.

These experiences had also been evaluated thoroughly by the Soviet military leadership. They resulted in experimental designs like the BT-IS or the T-46-5 (T-11). They embodied a stage of experimental work in which the purpose was to learn how armor protection could be made more effective. Should the armor have a meager strength but be more angled? Shells striking it would slide off more readily. A further advantage of such a solution was that the weight of the tank could be kept down. That was good for mobility. Naturally, the production of an armored shell for such a tank was comparatively laborious. Another consequence was the cramped space inside.

In the T-46-5 (T-11), the first Soviet tank with shell-safe armor, the designers followed another path. The armor was strengthened. Now it offered protection from armor-piercing 37 mm shells. A result of this was the increase in weight to 28 tons; its mobility, at 30 kph, was just a trifle over that of the T-26. In terms of its shape, the T-46-5 (T-11) showed similarity with the most recent infantry escort tanks of that type.

In Soviet tankbuilding, a middle path was followed in the search for a medium tank with shell-safe armor. Armor plates of appropriate thickness were arranged to deflect shells. Thus the weight could be kept within reasonable limits and, if the tank were powered by a high-performance Diesel engine, its mobility could even be increased. On the basis of this concept there arose the T-34, whose developmental path to the higher stages will be followed below.

In November 1937, Engineer M. Koshkin took on his new duties as chief designer in the Kharkov Locomotive Factory. Almost at the same time, his development bureau was contracted to develop a modern wheel/track tank that was to have shell-safe armor and be armed with a 45 mm tank gun. The upper weight limit was set at 15 tons. N. A. Kutcherenko, a member of Koshkin's team, reported: "Our design bureau had been given the task of creating a medium tank with . . . wheel/track running gear. It was designated A-20. It turned out, though, that its fighting weight was three tons

Front view of a T-34/85 medium tank, 1944 model, with the weapon locations easy to see: The 85 mm 1944 model tank gun (ZIS S-53) and a coaxial 7.62 mm DT machine gun (at right in the roller mantlet). Left of the gun barrel is the viewing opening for the Tsch-16 targeting scope (fourfold magnification, 16-degree field of vision). In the hull on the right side was the second 7.62 mm ST (later DTM) machine gun, mounted in a ball mantlet, with a PPU-8 T targeting scope.

Burned-out tanks at a troop training camp in East Germany, photographed in the late sixties. Note the differing arrangement of the ventilators.

too great, which influenced its speed and maneuverability. We were all convinced that the tank, with that weight, had to have a pure track running gear. That would improve its off-road capability considerably without sacrificing speed. The loss of the reduction drive to the wheels would make it lighter and free space for other components."

Work on the A-20 continued in 1938. At the same time, the project of another medium tank with only track running gear originated, designated A-32, later T-32. It could be armed with a 76.2 mm tank gun, and its armor was thicker without going much over the specified weight. In August 1938 the High War Council of the Soviet Union occupied itself with the A-20 and T-32. The consultation was led by the People's Commissar for Defense, K. J. Voroshilov. Stalin was also present. It soon became obvious that the chances for the T-32 were bad. Koshkin, the chief designer, therefore spoke out in favor of the project: "I would like once more to repeat all the arguments, but am of the opinion that running on wheels makes sense to a certain degree for light tanks, but that the complicated power transfer is an unnecessary ballast for medium tanks, for we must equip the tank with heavier armor and armament and guarantee its maneuverability on the battlefield. . . . The project for the T-32 worked out by us stands out for the following features: In terms of its speed, it is not inferior to the light, fast-moving tanks, it has the armor of the earlier medium tanks and the

These two 1944 model T-34/85 medium tanks belong to the collection of the Military History Museum in Dresden. Note the differing turrets with the crudely welded joints.

In comparison, here is a T-34/85 M 2 built under license in the People's Republic of Poland after World War II. It shows considerably more careful workmanship, especially in the turret. This tank is in an open-air display in Kalawa, between Swiebodzin (Schwiebus) and Miezyrzecz (Meseritz) in Poland, and was photographed in April 1998.

This picture was taken in the central sector of the eastern front in August 1944. Close-combat antitank fighters have used Panzerfaust weapons to set several T-34/85 medium tanks afire.

Close-up of one of the T-34/85 tanks put out of action by several hits on the rear armor of the hull from German antitank weapons, seen in East Prussia in the autumn of 1944.

armament of the medium and heavy tanks. In this sense it is a kind of universal vehicle and is in no way worse than other tanks. It is superior to the light tanks in armor and armament, to the medium tanks in armament and the heavy tanks in speed and maneuverability. It appears that it can be used as a penetration and support tank for the infantry as well as for independent operative actions." How right Koshkin's observations were was to be shown several years later. A decision to build both tanks experimentally and test them, though, was made only after vigorous discussion, and after Stalin intervened in the discussion.

A few days later, likewise in August 1938, problems of tank armament were again taken up at a meeting of the Defense Committee. To replace the obsolete T-28 and T-35, it was decided to build a heavy penetration (destroyer) tank. In addition, it was decided to have a lighter tank that, in the sense of Koshkin's statement to the Defense Council, was a suitable universal tank to sup-

A burned-out T-34/85 1944 model of the 25th Guard Tank Brigade of the2nd Guard Armored Corps, shot down in battle in East Prussia at the beginning of January 1945. Along with this brigade, the 4th and 26th Guard Tank Brigades and the 4th Mechanized Guard Gun Brigade belonged to this corps, which had 207 T-34 tanks in all.

During combat in May 1945 in Bohemia and Moravia, these 1944 model T-34/85 medium tanks were destroyed. The losses of the Red Army's armored units were remarkably high until the end of World War II. Some armored armies lost up to 64 percent of their tanks in just a few days. On the other hand, the constant use of tanks helped to bring the war to an end quickly.

port the infantry and carry out operative tasks. The work on this took the form of the A-20 and T-32. In July 1939 the experimental department of the Kharkov Locomotive Factory had completed the prototypes of the A-20 and T-32. The A-20 had the same running gear as the BT, but three pairs of its road wheels were driven. Its fighting weight was 18 tons; its crew consisted of four men. The hull was armored up to 20 mm thick, with the armor plates mounted at large incline angles. This strengthened their resistance to shots. M. I. Tarshinov was responsible for the hull design. The A-20's armament consisted of a 45 mm tank gun and two 7.62 mm machine guns. The same speed, 65 kph, could be attained on wheels and tracks.

The T-32 was already armed with a 76.2 mm tank gun and two machine guns. The 19-ton vehicle had armor 30 mm thick, mounted in the same way as that of the A-20. It offered space for a four-man crew and likewise attained 65 kph, though only with track running gear. It had five large-diameter road wheels on each side.

The T-34 1942 and 1943 models and the T-34/85 1944 model were equipped with the PT-3 rolling mine removal device and used in armored engineer regiments with 22 T-34 and 18 PT-3 mine removal devices. Such units were formed as of June 1943. Their task was removing minefields or creating lanes through them so that armored units could move through.

The OT-34 medium flamethrowing tank was based on the T-34 1942 and 1943 models. In place of the 7.62 mm DT machine gun, the ball mantlet on the right side of the hull held an AT-41 or ATO-42 flamethrower. A special tank held 100 liters of oil. Otherwise the flamethrowing tank did not differ from an ordinary tank.

Similarly to the OT-34 medium flamethrowing tank, another such special tank was based on the T-34/85 medium tank, 1944 model. It was used in special flamethrowing tank units.

A T-34/85 1944 model mine remival tank during combat against the Japanese in the summer of 1945. The movable arm that holds the two rolling mine removal devices is easy to see.

By using older T-34 chassis, T-34-T medium armored towing tractors were created during the war and used to tow broken-down armored vehicles. The weight is listed as 25 tons, and the crew consisted of two men. Some vehicles had winches with 14-ton towing strength.

Only little information about the T-34-based armored bridge tested in 1943 is available.

In the summer of 1942, tests were made with a medium self-propelled mount based on the T-34. In December of that year the introduction of an armored vehicle armed with a 122 mm howitzer was decided on. It was designated SU-122.

In 1943, production of an improved version of the SU-122 medium self-propelled mount began. Externally it was recognizable by the new, better-armored gun mount. It was used in self-propelled gun regiments of four batteries, each with five guns. The original structure of five batteries turned out to be impractical.

This SU-122 medium self-propelled mount was captured unharmed by the Germans during the Kursk Bogen battles in July 1943 and sent to Germany.

This picture of the SU-122 medium self-propelled mount appeared on a 1944 German tank recognition chart; here it was designated Assault Gun T-34.

During 1943 another medium self-propelled mount appeared, designated SU-85. It was used in self-propelled gun regiments with four batteries of four guns each. They were supposed to support the T-34, which had only the 76.2 mm tank gun, and to attack heavy German tanks in particular.

The Testing Commission of the Armored Troop Command recognized a large number of improvements over the older tanks in both designs, including the W-2 Diesel engine. All further tests showed a clear superiority for the T-32. The experiences gained in the 1939-40 winter war in Karelia also spoke in its favor. The tank's great power reserves allowed the armor to be increased to a thickness of 45 mm. At the test commission's suggestion, the People's Commissariat for Defense decided on December 19, 1939, to introduce the T-32 tracked tank into the armored troops of the Red Army. It was designated T-34 from then on.

In February and March 1940, two of the first test models of the T-34 took part in a test drive from Kharkov to Moscow, where they were shown to members of the Soviet leadership. On the cobblestone pavement at the Kremlin, the drivers demonstrated the handling and maneuverability of the two tanks. After they had passed the hardest off-road tests, the government approved the tank for series production. The Kharkov factory that was producing the fast BT-7 wheel/track tank was converted to produce the T-34. Series production began in July 1940. 117 tanks of this type were completed by the end of 1940. This was, though, far from the planned production, which had been raised from 220 to 600 because of the tense international situation. The Kharkov Locomotive Factory (Factory No. 83) was to produce 500. The other 100 were to be built at the Stalingrad Tractor Factory.

All of this took place under the greatest secrecy. Not even the German secret service, which kept a sharp eye on Soviet military production at that time, knew anything of the new tank. This is all the more surprising, because an American photojournalist had seen the T-34 at the Stalin Tank School in Moscow in May 1941.

The progress of the T-34 was not free of difficulties. The production technology of the T-34, considerably more complex in comparison to the previously built tanks, was not mastered and caused much trouble. In a report of the Defense Committee it was said that reequipping the tank units with the T-34 was going at a "snail's pace." When the first T-34s saw action with the armored troops, many technical faults were found and drew harsh criticism. Meanwhile, the Armored Troop Command had even promoted a light tank, which had led to the already mentioned T-50.

The SU-85 medium self-propelled mount was first seen by German troops on the eastern front in October 1943, in use by self-propelled gun regiments. This picture shows a captured vehicle that was taken to the Army Weapons Office center in Kummersdorf near Berlin for testing.

A shot-down SU-85 medium self-propelled mount. As seen in German sources, the crew used a 10-T-15 targeting scope for direct firing on armored targets and a 1938 model panoramic scope for indirect firing.

The 1943 model 85 mm cannon (D-5 S) had a range of 950 meters in direct fire, and up to 13,700 meters could be reached in indirect fire. Along with antitank shells with tracers (BR-365), fragmenting O-365 K explosive shells with KTM-1 double fuses (785 m/sec) and similar O-365 shells with T-5 time fuses (792 m/sec) could be fired. The rate of fire was up to ten shots per minute.

Shot-down and burned-out SU-85 medium self-propelled mounts of a self-propelled gun regiment of the Red Army, photographed north of Jassy on June 27, 1944.

The faults resulted in the T-34 having to be examined again by the War Department. This resulted in a complete redesigning of the tank, which became known by the designation of T-34 M. The completion of this project would have taken another one and a half to two years. In this period the BT-7 M was to go back into production. This could not be accepted. On May 5, 1941, the Council of People's Commissars determined that 2,800 of the T-34 would be produced in the coming year, so the reequipping of the armored units could continue. At the same time, this council agreed to let the T-34 M project be continued. The building of prototypes was agreed on. It was planned to replace the previous tanks with that model in the future.

One of the first components to be changed was the armament. The designers at Factory No. 92 in Gorki began in July 1940 to develop a new tank gun. It was designated F-34. Early in 1941 this gun went into series production. Since the development of the T-34

The SU-100 medium self-propelled mount reached the self-propelled gun regiments of the Red Army in the latter half of 1944. It was similar to the SU-85, and its 100 mm cannon (D-10 S) was comparable to the German 8.8 cm Tank-destroyer Cannon 43 L/71 in performance. Besides the bigger gun, the SU-100 had a commander's cupola on the right side of the armored upper body, and a 10-RF-26 radio set.

Captured SU-85 medium self-propelled mounts were used occasionally by German tank-destroyer or assault-gun units, and were designated "Assault Gun SU-85 (r)".

During the battles near Chertkov in March and April 1944, these SU-85 medium self-propelled mounts were shot down in a duel with a German assault gun of Assault Gun Unit 276. The driver's hatch near the gun mount, somewhat to the left, can be seen.

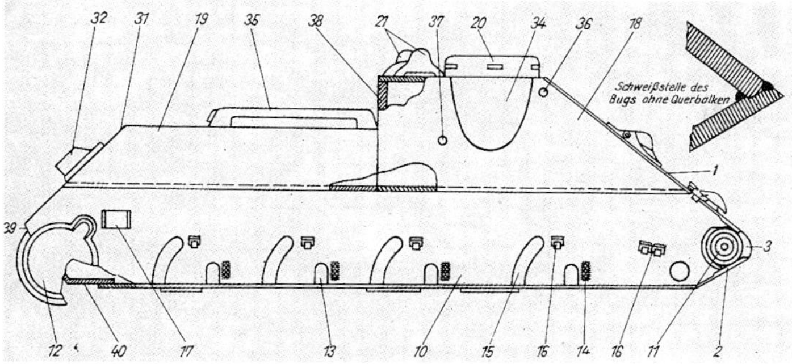

Side and top views of the armored body of the SU-100 medium self-propelled mount.

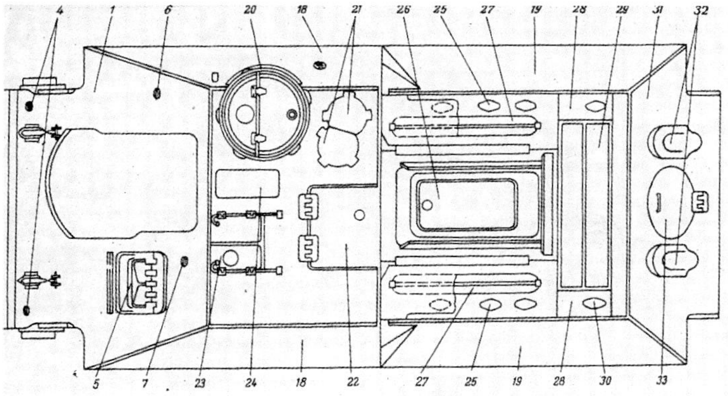

M had not continued yet, the gun, featuring a longer barrel and higher performance, was mounted in the old-type T-34. This was done as of February 1941. A second important improvement concerned turret production, which had proved to be too expensive. The attempts to develop a cast turret, which had failed until then, finally succeeded in June 1941. The new turret was cast in two halves, which were welded together. It replaced the old turret, made of rolled and cold-pressed armor plates, with a more complicated form. The new technology was introduced into production in mid-June. Because of a lack of rigidity in cast armor steel, this turret was somewhat thicker, 52 to 60 mm. Thus the innovations intended for the T-34 M were used in production of the old-type T-34. After the war with Germany created a whole new situation in June 1941, interest in the modernized T-34 M faded into the background. From then on the emphasis was on the maximum expansion of series production of the T-34.

The fighting weight of the T-34 1941 model had risen by 1.7 tons from that of the type made since 1939, to 28 tons. Linked with this was the increase in the specific ground pressure to 0.66 kp/sq. cm. This value equaled that of foreign tank models and was an important prerequisite of the T-34's superior off-road capability. This characteristic forced the German antitank defenses to be rethought. It was stated in an experience report: "The superior off-road capability of the T-34 required special tactical measures. . . ." In October 1942 the infantry regiment of a motorized infantry division reported: "The well-known off-road capability of the T-34 . . . was astounding. Through bog and swamp impassable for men, it drove through without trouble and destroyed our positions. . . ." The front armor of the hull was even increased to 60 mm in 1941.

Once again, let us hear German comments on it: "The main strength of the Russian tank is not so much in its *thickness* as in the angled bow plate." In fact, the tank's bow plate was tilted at 30 degrees. Theoretically, that meant that when the tank was on level ground, shells striking it had to break through 120 mm of armor actually 60 mm thick (30 degrees of tilt = an increase factor of 2). In practice, tank shells of the German 3.7 cm L/45 antitank cannon fired from 100 meters could only penetrate 35 to 64 mm of armor. The somewhat more powerful 5 cm Antitank Gun 38 was effective against the 1941 T-34's frontal armor at distances under 100 meters. That was not enough, since it was possible for the T-34, thanks to its higher speed (maximum 53 kph) to get out of range quickly.

The 1941 model T-34 was fitted with the 76.2 mm F-34 tank gun, which was superior to the somewhat shorter weapon of the L-11 type in terms of penetrating power. The former could penetrate 75 mm of armor plate at 500 meters, the latter 66 mm. With these values, both guns were capable of fighting the German tanks effectively at long range.

The tank gun was accompanied by two 7.62 mm DT machine guns.

The fact is, the German antitank forces were not prepared to handle the T-34 medium tank. Thus did the Germans evaluate the T-34: "Best and most useful Soviet Russian tank. Fast, mobile, heavily armed and armored. Because of its favorable contours . . . it is hard to attack." From the Soviet point of view, the T-34 had proved itself despite its initial problems; the tank soldiers had high hopes for this type. Its main weakness was poor visibility from inside. It lacked a commander's cupola. A further disadvantage was that only a few T-34s were fitted with a radio set. Command vehicles, in order to direct attacks by their own tanks, had to drive ahead of the front. The Germans soon found that out, concentrated their fire on those tanks and, by shooting them down, made the units leaderless.

In 1941, 3,014 T-34 tanks were delivered to the Red Army, the greater part in the second half of the year. On June 22, 1941, they

Inside the fighting compartment is the 100 mm 1944 model cannon (D-10 S), as well as a Tsch-19 telescope visor.

During the hard fighting in the Stargard-Arnswalde area of Pomerania in mid-February 1945, German troops were able to set this SU-100 medium self-propelled mount afire. Because of the long gun barrel projecting far to the front, the SU-100's freedom of movement in forest or town combat was limited.

Various views of the SU-100 medium self-propelled mount. This vehicle belongs to the collection of the Military History Museum in Dresden.

and many older tanks were in the mechanized corps consisting of two armored divisions and one mechanized infantry division each. Ideally, they were to have over 1,000 tanks. Most of the T-34s were lost during the combat in the border areas. The high losses and lack of replacements forced the disbanding of these corps. The T-34 saw service in much smaller units, independent tank battalions, brigades, and regiments. An independent tank regiement, for example, had three tank companies, one equipped with T-34s. Tank brigades formed in December 1941 had one T-34 company. The heavy tank company used KV tanks, while the light company had the hopelessly obsolete T-26.

The Politburo of the Central Committee of the Communist Party of the Soviet Union had already made two decisions in a special meeting on June 25, 1941:

1. Concerning production of armor steel and the KV tank,
2. Concerning the further production of the KV, T-34 and T-50 tanks, artillery tractors and Diesel engines for tanks in the third and fourth quarters of 1941.

In the course of carrying out these decisions, important personnel and material capacities of the Soviet economy were made available for tank production, and the removal of important tank factories and supplier firms to behind the Urals was prepared. They were to be moved out of German reach. An important role in this was played by the Chief of the People's Commissariat for the Tank Industry, V. Malyshev. Among other things, the "Krasnoye Sormovo" (red Sormovo) factory was included in T-34 production and could deliver its first tanks in October 1941. At almost the same time, the Kharkov Locomotive Factory was relocated in the Urals. Here the factory was merged with the Nishni Tagil auto factory and others to form the Stalin combine. Under winter weather conditions, sometimes outdoors, series production of the T-34 began. On December 25, 1941, the first 25 tanks left the factory. In the period from June 1941 to September 1942, though, the Stalingrad Tractor Factory was the main supplier of T-34 medium tanks. Until combat

The T-44 medium tank, 1944 model. Because it was not possible to carry a 100 mm tank gun in the turret of the T-34/85, this tank appeared at first with the proved 85 mm gun. It was also armed with a coaxial 7.62 mm machine gun in the turret. A second machine gun was installed in the armored hull and was operated by the driver. Thus a fifth crewman was not needed.

To make a modern heavy tank, the Red Army's armored troops and the Russian armament industry at first followed the multiple-turret concept at the end of the thirties. The goal was combining greater firepower with strong armor. The SMK heavy tank of 1939 had a 76.2 mm and a 45 mm tank gun as well as three 7.62 mm machine guns. The crew consisted of six men. The top speed is listed at 35 kph.

activity reached Stalingrad, 3,600 tanks were completed there. During 1942 the Ural Heavy Machinery Company "Ordshonikidse" in Sverdlovsk began to produce tanks. The People's Commissariat for the Tank Industry set up the Ural-Kirov Tank Factory in Chelyabinsk for the same task. It had been formed in the process of moving the Kirov works in Leningrad and the Kharkov Diesel Engine Factory, and merging them with the Chelyabinsk tractor Factory. It went down in history under the name of "Tankograd."

It took much effort to keep increasing production of the T-34, which had meanwhile become the most important Soviet tank. Of the T-34 with the 76.2 mm tank gun (later designated T-34/76) alone, the following numbers were produced until production ended in 1944:

Year	Number	Year	Number
1940	117	1943	15,712
1941	3,014	1944	3,723
1942	12,533	Total	35,099

During the 1939-40 winter war between the Soviet Union and Finland, the 20th Heavy Tank Brigade carried out troop testing of the T-100 (Sotka). This very retouched photo shows one of the test vehicles.

To be able to achieve this vast production, it had been necessary to set up eight large tank factories, six factories to produce tank hulls and turrets, as well as three engine production factories in the eastern Soviet Union, far from the battlefields. Further rates

Very similar tactical and technical figures to those of the SMK were shown by the T-100 (Sotka) heavy tank, likewise built and tested in 1939. Its listed weight varies from 56 to 58 tons.

On the basis of the T-100 heavy tank (Sotka), a heavy self-propelled artillery mount was built in 1939 and designated SU-100 U. The armored vehicle weighed 60 tons, had a six-man crew, and was armed with a 130 mm cannon. Its armor was at most 80 mm thick.

The KV-1 heavy tank, 1940 model, weighed 43.5 tons and was armed with a 76.2 mm 1939 model tank gun (L-11) and three or four DT machine guns. It is easy to tell it from later series. It had a tank gun with a very short barrel, and the cast mount cover was tilted from top to bottom.

Also among the identifying marks of the KV-1 1940 model was the angular turret with rear extension, made of 35 to 90 mm armor plate.

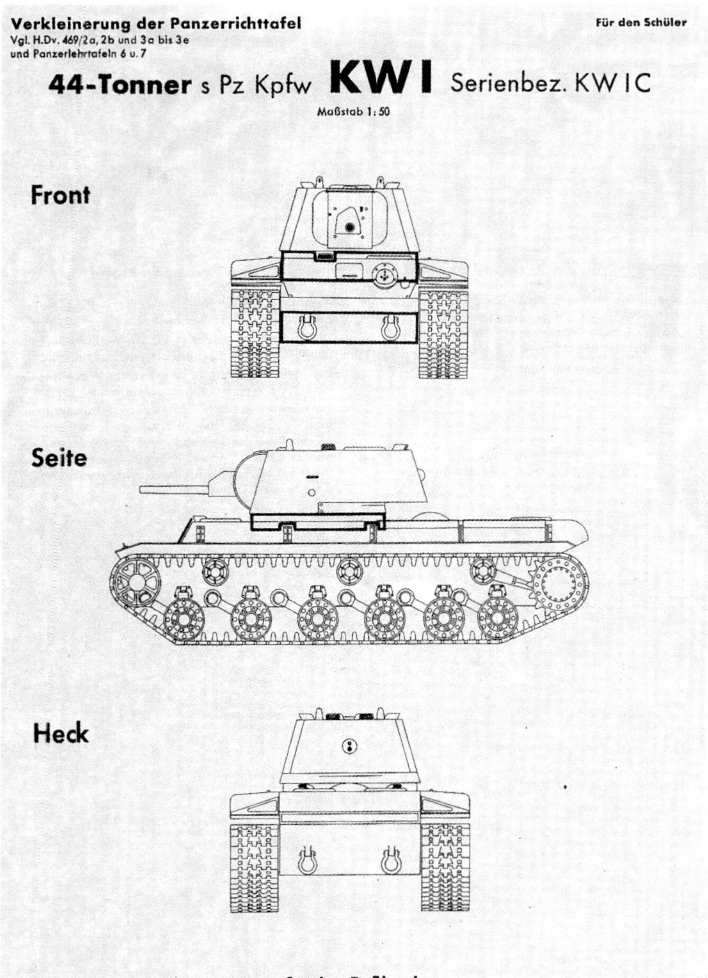

A picture of a 1940 model KV-1 heavy tank on a German tank recognition chart.

of increase were achieved by the introduction of new or improved production technology. These included the fast welding process. In part, turrets or parts were pressed thereby.

Steady improvements to the tank itself took place, resulting from requests from the armored troops at the front; but they were also a result of the antitank defense that grew stronger in 1942-43. The transition from hull to turret showed itself to be a weak spot. In the German tank shot tables (H.Dv.469/3 e), this was particularly noted. The Soviet tankbuilders tried to solve this problem quickly. Steel plates were welded to the hull, and similar reequipping kits were sent to the front. In 1942, completely cast turrets for the T-34 were introduced. This means served particularly to increase the monthly tank production. Production of the old-type turret continued as well. Meanwhile, the big turret hatch had been replaced by two round ones. In the winter of 1942-43, production of a more simplified hexagonal turret was begun. As of the summer of 1943, this model appeared with a cylindrical commander's cupola. The latter was a long-needed improvement, making it easier for the tank commander to observe the battlefield. A disadvantage was that in the war year of 1943 not all T-34s could be equipped with a radio set. T-34 tanks with rubber-saving running gear appeared in 1942. This did not bring any benefits, but it helped ease the rubber shortage. Later, when enough rubber was available, this was given up. Wider running-gear parts were modified during the war. This applied to tracks, which were now made by casting, and chains whose links had more grip. The handling of the T-34 was improved with the introduction of a five-speed gearbox.

In 1943 the model of a new tank, the T-43, appeared. Components such as armament, engine, gearbox, and running gear were like those of the T-34. The torsion-bar suspension was new, replacing the coil springs used until then. The reason for this was that the springs needed more space, impinging on the space in the fighting compartment.

This almost undamaged 1940 model KV-1 heavy tank is examined with great curiosity by German soldiers. The most unbelievable rumors circulated about these Russian giant tanks at first. On the engine cover is an antitank shell for the 76.2 mm tank gun.

During the battles in the western border areas of the Soviet Union in Jule and July 1941, many KV tanks were lost because of minor mechanical problems. These two pictures suggest this by the opened engine-room hatch (above) and the towing cable. Also note the machine-gun mounts in the back of the turret and the pistol loopholes in the turret sides with the covers pushed out (below).

This 1940 model KV-1 heavy tank was badly damaged in a German air raid and had to be abandoned. The pictures were taken in the northern sector of the eastern front in July 1941.

At the driving test center of the Army Weapons Office center in Kummersdorf near Berlin, a special commission of the Army High Command examines tanks captured at the front. Undamaged vehicles were brought back to Germany and examined there, part of the extensive activity caused by the reverses in the German Army's antitank defenses caused by the modern Russian tanks.

The armor was now thicker (bow and sides 75 mm, turret 90 mm). The fighting weight rose to 34 tons, and the speed and off-road capability were slightly under those of the T-34. The development of the T-43 was halted and its introduction to the armored troops was not approved.

The costly combat of 1943 made the Soviet tank soldiers painfully aware of a problem that had meanwhile become very important: the armament of the T-34 was too weak against the new German tanks. It was still armed with the 76.2 mm F-34 tank gun. Its penetrating power against armor plate was no longer sufficient in battle, especially against the Panzer V "Panther" (Sd.Kfz. 171) and Panzer VI (Sd.Kfz. 181). The later Marshal of the Soviet Union, Armored General M. J. Katukov, wrote about the fierce tank battles at the Kursk Bogen early in July 1943 in his book "At the Head of the Advance," published in Moscow in 1974. He had been ordered to lead counterattacks with his tanks, of which he wrote: "What success could be expected from an attack against tank forces that

Later production runs of the 1940 model KV-1 heavy tank had a welded covering for the roller mantlet. The 76.2 mm 1939 model tank gun (L-11) with a 2323.5 mm barrel (L/30/5) was retained.

In this close-up shot, the welded cover of the roller mantlet in the turret can be seen clearly. The impacts of armor-piercing shells look like scars on the turret and hull but did not penetrate the armor.

In the German Army Service Manual 469/3 a "Tank Gun Tables-Tank destroyers" of February 2, 1942, the 3.7 cm tank destroyer gun was given scarcely a chance of success in firing on the front armor of the 1940 model KV-1 heavy tank. An effect could be achieved only by firing at hatches or vision slits. The side and rear armor could only be penetrated at ranges under 100 meters when hard-core ammunition (Antitank Shell 40) was available. The situation was very similar for the somewhat more powerful 5 cm Tank Destroyer Gun 38, which could have an effect within 250 meters with a favorable impact angle. The German antitank defenses were extremely ineffective.

were not only far superior to ours in numbers, but also in armament and equipment? We had to keep this fact in mind. The Tigers with their 88 mm guns could fire on our tanks from a range of almost two kilometers, thus beyond the range of the 76.2 mm guns of our T-34s. Thus the enemy could carry on a successful firefight against us at long range. . . . Under these conditions, was it not practical to wait with the counterattack? . . . The very first reports from the battlefield . . . made it clear that we had made the wrong decision."

According to Russian sources, the Red Army at the Voronesh Front, from July 5 to 13, 1943, reported 1,223 tanks as total losses. The 5th Guard Army, belonging to the strategic reserve of the Red Army High Command, and only entering the battle on July 12, lost 377 tanks and self-propelled guns as total losses on that day. Some armored corps lost up to 60% of their vehicles, mostly T-34 tanks.

The now-insufficient firepower of the T-34 could not be essentially improved by the introduction of undercaliber shells (BR-350 P) for the 76.2 mm F-34 tank gun. They made it possible to penetrate 92 mm of armor at 500 meters, but only 58 mm at 1,000 meters. The slight increase in performance would not be sufficient indefinitely. A new main weapon for the T-34 had to be found. A long-barreled 85 mm tank gun that had been investigated years before in principle for use in tanks was considered. Its development led during 1943 to the T-34/85.

Tactical - Technical Data (T-34, 1940 model)

Crew: 4 men
Weight: 26.3 tons
Armament: 1 76.2 mm caliber L-11 (1939 model) tank gun, with 76 rounds,
2 or 3 7.62 mm caliber DT machine guns, with 2898 to 4725 rounds
Armor plate:
Hull: Front: 45 mm
Sides: 45 mm
Rear: 40 mm
Top: 15-20 mm
Bottom: 15-20 mm
Turret: Front: 45 mm
Sides: 45 mm
Rear: 45 mm
Top: 16 mm
Powerplant: V-12 cylinder 4-stroke W-2/34 Diesel engine
Performance: 500 HP at 1800 rpm
Fuel capacity: 540 liters
Power to weight: 19 HP/ton
Length: 5920 mm
Width: 3000 mm
Height: 2400 mm
Ground clearance: 400 mm
Top speed: 53 kph
Range: 400 km
Climbing degree: 35 degrees
Spanning ability: 2500 mm
Climbing ability: 900 mm
Wading ability: 1220 mm
Specific ground pressure: 0.64 kp/sq. cm.

This July 1941 photo shows a KV-1 heavy tank from a lot built at the beginning of the year. It has become stuck and had to take 38 hits (as far as can be seen) in batttle with German antitank defenses. The two periscopes in the front part of the turret top can be seen.

These two photos show the destructive effect of German aerial bombs on KV-type heavy tanks. Torn-off turrets (above) or fully smashed bodies often resulted from dive-bombing, as here in August 1941.

These two close-up photos again show the effects of shots on the armor of the 1940 model KV-1. The turret sides and rear had 75 mm armor plate.

Tactical - Technical Data (T-34, 1941 model)

Crew:	4 men
Weight:	28.0 tons
Armament:	1 76.2 mm caliber F-34 (1940 model) tank gun, with 76 rounds,
	2 7.62 mm caliber DT machine guns, with 2898 to 4725 rounds
Armor plate:	
Hull: Front:	60 mm
Sides:	40-45 mm
Rear:	45 mm
Top:	15-20 mm
Bottom:	15-20 mm
Turret: Front:	60 mm
Sides:	52 mm
Rear:	52 mm
Top:	16 mm
Powerplant:	V-12 cylinder 4-stroke W-2/34 Diesel engine
Performance:	500 HP at 1800 rpm
Fuel capacity:	540 liters
Power to weight:	17.8 HP/ton
Overall length:	6100 mm
Hull length:	6920 mm
Width:	3000 mm
Height:	2450 mm
Ground clearance:	400 mm
Top speed:	53 kph
Range:	400 km
Climbing degree:	35 degrees
Spanning ability:	2500 mm
Climbing ability:	900 mm
Wading ability:	1120 mm
Specific ground pressure:	0.66 kp/sq. cm.

Officers of the Red Army armored troops complained that the KV-1 heavy tank was considerably heavier than the T-34 medium tank but, with the 76.2 mm tank gun, did not have heavier armament. The tanks often got stuck, destroyed bridges, and often broke down because of their unreliable powerplant. This picture shows a 1940 model KV-1 that got stuck.

Tactical - Technical Data (T-34, 1942 model)

Crew:	4 men
Weight:	28.5 tons
Armament:	1 76.2 mm caliber F-34 (1942 model) tank gun, with 100 rounds,
	2 7.62 mm caliber DT machine guns, with 3150-3600 rounds
Armor plate:	
Hull: Front:	60 mm
Sides:	40-45 mm
Rear:	45 mm
Top:	15-20 mm
Bottom:	15-20 mm
Turret:[11]	
Front:	60 mm
Sides:	52 mm
Rear:	52 mm
Top:	16 mm
Powerplant:	V-12 cylinder 4-stroke W-2/34 Diesel engine
Performance:	500 HP at 1800 rpm
Fuel capacity:	540 liters
Power to weight:	17.5 HP.ton
Length overall:	6100 mm
Hull length:	5920 mm
Width:	3000 mm
Height:	2450 mm
Ground clearance:	400 mm
Top speed:	53 kph
Range:	400 km
Climbing degree:	35 degrees
Spanning ability:	2500 mm
Climbinmg ability:	900 mm
Wading ability:	1120 mm
Specific ground pressure:	0.68 kp/sq. cm.

11. Depending on where they were built, T-34s were delivered in 1942-43 with different turrets. Thus records of armor thickness differ.

Antitank shells of the German 8.8 cm anti-aircraft gun have penetrated the gun-mount armor of a KV-1.

Front view of a 1940 model KV-1 heavy tank. The driver sat in the middle of the vehicle. To the left of the driver's visor is a movable 7.62 mm machine gun in a ball mantlet. Two other machine guns of this type were in the turret, one of them to the right of the 76.2 mm 1939 model tank gun (L-11). The second was in the rear of the turret, also in a ball mantlet.

Tactical - Technical Data (T-34, 1943 model)

Crew:		4 men
Weight:		30-30.9 tons
Armament:		1 76.2 mm caliber F-34 (1942 model) tank gun, with 100 rounds,
	2 7.62 mm	caliber DT machine guns, with 3150 rounds
Armor plate:		
Hull:	Front:	60 mm[12]
	Sides:	40-45 mm
	Rear:	45 mm
	Top:	15-20 mm
	Bottom:	15-20 mm
Turret:	Front:	75 mm
	Sides:	52 mm
	Rear:	52 mm
	Top:	16 mm
Powerplant:		V-12 cylinder 4-stroke W-2/34 Diesel engine
Performance:		500 Hp at 1800 rpm
Fuel capacity:		830-850 liters
Power to weight:		16.7 HP/ton
Length overall:		6070 mm
Hull length:		5920 mm
	Width:	3000 mm
	Height:	2650 mm[13]
Ground clearance:		400 mm
Too speed:		53 kph
Range:		365-465 km
Climbing degree:		35 degrees
Spanning ability:		2500 mm
Climbing ability:		900 mm
Wading ability:		1120 mm
Specific ground pressure:		0.72 kp/sq. cm.

Until the war with Germany began, about 700 heavy tanks of the 1940 and 1941 KV-1 models had been delivered to the tank units of the Red Army. Most of them were lost in battle in the border areas.

12. Some 1943 T-34s were delivered with 110 mm front hull armor. This version was often referred to as T-43, but this was not correct.
13. Data apply to the turret type with commander's cupola, delivered as of summer 1943.

The KV-2 artillery tank was built only in 1941-42 and continued the tradition of support tanks, armed with large-caliber guns, on T-26 and BT chassis. On the chassis of the KV-1 a considerably larger turret was mounted, armed with a 152.4 mm 1938-40 model tank howitzer and two 7.62 mm DT machine guns. Four members of the six-man crew worked in the turret.

This picture gives an idea of the size of the turret. It weight is listed at 12 tons. On uneven ground it was difficult to swing it to the side.

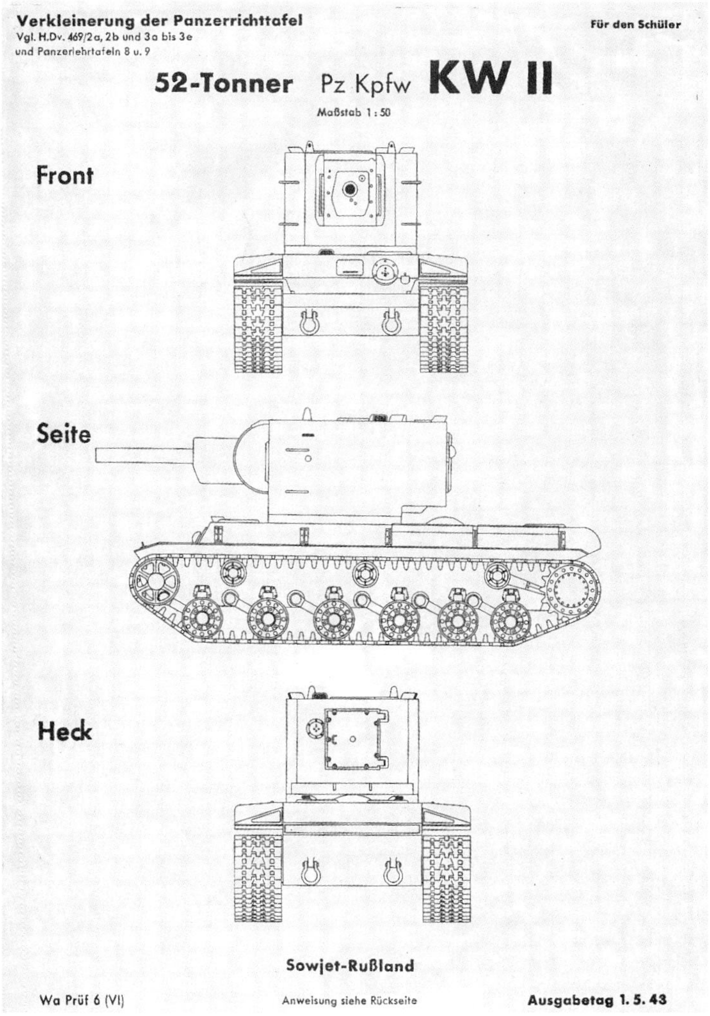

A picture of the KV-2 artillery tank on a German tank recognition chart.

The experience bought with heavy losses during the Kursk Bogen combat was one subject of a meeting of the State Defense Committee on August 25, 1943, in which representatives of the People's Commissariat for the Armor Industry also participated. Here the modernization of the T-34 was decided on. A decision as to what weapon the T-34 should be armed with in the future had already been made in the spring of 1943. The chief designer of Artillery Factory No. 92, V. G. Grabin, had suggested a long-barreled 85 mm tank gun at that time. This suggestion had found favor at a special meeting of the State Defense Committee in April 1943. Contracts for developing such a weapon were given to three development bureaus. The work group of V. G. Grabin turned to a project for an 85 mm gun for the KV-3 heavy tank, already worked out in 1940. To be able to install it in the T-34, it had to be modified. The designation of this weapon was 85 mm Tank Gun ZIS-53.

A different work group, under the direction of General F. F. Petrov, worked during the first half of 1943 on two variations of an 85 mm gun that was later used in the KV-85 and IS-1 heavy tanks and the SU-85 self-propelled mount.

The third variant of the 85 mm tank gun took form in the development bureau of Artillery Factory No. 92 in Gorki. In charge was the young designer A. Savin. By the end of the summer of 1943, the first tests of the prototype of the new tank gun were already being made at a troop training camp near Gorki. For this, the weapons had been mounted in slightly modified T-34 turrets. It became obvious very soon that the turret had to be enlarged, because the cramped space inside the turret would limit the crew's activities. It was also determined that a two-man turret crew was not capable of achieving the technically possible rate of fire. The turret had to be enlarged. The People's Commissariat for the Armor Industry assigned this task to a development bureau in the Krasnoye Sormovo factory. Within a very short time, a three-man turret with strengthened armor, capable of holding an 85 mm tank gun, was created. Among the further improvements were a larger turret turning-circle diameter (1,600 mm), and an improved ventilation and

The 152.4 mm 1938/40 model tank howitzer of the KV-2 artillery tank fired explosive shells weighing 51.07 kilograms. This gun could shoot down or wipe out nests of resistance during tank attacks. As a rule, artillery tanks operated from the second line or fired on their targets from behind cover.

observation system. From the start, a cylindrical observation cupola for the commander was included. The new turret was tested in the autumn and accepted for series production, which took place in the foundry of the "Krasnoye Sormovo" factory. Parallel to this, the old turrets for the 76.2 mm gun continued to be built.

But this did not end the development of a T-34 with a more powerful tank gun. Problems turned up. The 85 mm gun from V. G. Grabin was not yet finished. It turned out that installing the gun in the new three-man turret would cause an unacceptable limitation of its elevation range. The weapon had to be changed again. At the end of 1943, the first two test tanks were fitted with the new guns at the artillery factory. Extensive tests followed. The State Defense Committee approved the official introduction of the T-34/85 into the armored troops of the Red Army on December 15, 1943. Meanwhile, testing of the gun from Grabin's development bureau continued, and faults appeared again. Since no further delays in delivering the improved T-34 to the front were wanted, it was decided to use the 85 mm gun from General Petrov's development bureau. It showed bad ballistic performance and was seen as a transitional solution until the faults of the ZIS-53 could be rectified. In great haste the modification of the gun was tackled. Parallel to that, testing went on in January 1944. From the cooperation of the development bureau of Factory No. 92 (A. Savin) and the Central Design Bureau of the Artillery came the final form of the 85 mm tank gun, approved for introduction at the end of the month and officially

Effective armor protection and high firepower were gained for the KV-2 heavy tank at the cost of mobility (26 kph). The unreliable powerplant was no help either. Thus many KV-2 tanks broke down on the march and were lost.

Front and side views of a KV-2 heavy tank. The armor and armament of these giants made the tanks look unbeatable.

Two KV-2 heavy tanks that were lost during fighting near Dubno in July 1941.

designated 85 mm Tank Gun ZIS S-53 (1944 model). By the end of 1944, 11,778 guns of this type had been built. The gun had a 4,645 mm barrel and fired antitank shells with a muzzle velocity of 792 meters per second, and undercaliber shells at 1200 m/sec. The former could pierce 88 mm of armor plate at 500 meters and 81 mm at 1,000 meters (at a 60-degree angle). For the 4.9-kilogram BR-365 P undercaliber shell, the values were 138 and 100 mm. A Tsch 16 tank aiming scope with a 16-degree field of vision and fourfold magnification was used.

Naturally, the T-34/85, as it was delivered first to several guard armored regiments at the end of March 1944, was a compromise. The larger turret had an unfavorable shape, with the lower part and the transition to the hull proving to be extremely sensitive to shots. But the advantages balanced out these failings. The compromise enabled an increase in performance for the most important Soviet tank without large-scale changes or new designs, and without having to give up any offensive strength. The increased weight was kept within strict limits, so that the tank's mobility was not weakened.

Production of the T-34/85 made quick progress, so that in the course of 1944 the T-34 with the 76.2 mm tank gun could be taken out of production. In all, the following numbers were produced:

Year	Total
1943	100
1944	11,000
1945	18,330
Total	29,430

Captured T-34/85 tanks were quickly and thoroughly evaluated by the Germans. The first printed matter with references to how it could be fought against most successfully was distributed in May 1944 and states: "The gun, larger and with a longer barrel than that of the previous T-34, allows the tank to fire from longer ranges." It was expected that the T-34/85 would be the most often-used tank in the Red Army in the future. The production figures confirm this impression.

Tactical - Technical Data (T-34/85, 1944 model)

Crew:		5 men
Weight:		32.0 tons
Armament:		1 85 mm caliber ZIS-53[14] tank gun (1944 model), with 56-60 rounds,
		2 7.62 mm caliber DT machine guns, with 1890 rounds
Armor plate:		
Hull:	Front:	60 mm
	Sides:	45 mm
	Rear:	45 mm
	Top:	20-23 mm
	Bottom:	22 mm
Turret:	Front:	45-75 mm
	Sides:	75 mm
	Rear:	75 mm
	Top:	20 mm
Powerplant:		V-12 cylinder 4-stroke W-2/34 Diesel engine
Performance:		500 HP at 1800 rpm
Fuel capacity:		840 liters
Power to weight:		15.6 HP/ton
	Length overall:	8150 mm
	Hull length:	6100 mm
	Width:	3000 mm
Height:		2720 mm
Ground clearance:		400 mm
Top speed:		50 kph
Range:		300 km
Climbing degree:		35 degrees
Spanning ability:		2500 mm
Climbing ability:		730 mm
Wading ability:		1300 mm
Specific ground pressure:		0.81-0.85 kp/sq. cm.

Flamethrowing tanks were built on the basis of all T-34 tank types. The OT-34 1943 model had an AT-41 or ATO-42 flamethrower

14. At first a D-5-T 85 mm tank gun was installed.

In this picture, the large rear hatch in the massive turret of the KV-2 heavy tank can be seen. It was opened to load the 36 shells and cartridges for the tank gun.

This KV-2 got stuck and was put out of action by German close-combat antitank fighters, as was the BA-10 1937 model armored scout car, in the battles near Dubno in June 1941.

in place of the bow machine gun, plus a tank with 100 liters of oil. The tank weighed 30.9 tons and corresponded to the tank in terms of its other armaments. The OT-34/85 built in 1944 was very similar. Flames from 60 to 100 meters long were possible with the AT-42.

As of 1942, T-34s with the PT-3 rolling mine removal device were used to clear paths in antitank and antipersonnel minefields. The removal speed is stated as 10 to 18 kph, giving a mine-free path twice 1.2 meters wide. In 1944 the T-34/85 was also fitted with this mine removal device. It was used by armored engineer regiments, which had 22 T-34s and 18 PT-3 mine removal devices.

Other special tanks based on the T-34 were bridgelaying and earth moving tanks. In 1944 the T-34 T medium armored towing tractor reached the troops; it was a turretless old-type T-34 modified for towing. Its numbers were limited. In the Red Army's armored units it was customary to tow disabled armored vehicles with tanks.

Much greater importance was gained by the T-34 as the basic design for numerous self-propelled mounts. Departing from the designs and experimental types of prewar times, based on tanks of various types, a wholly different concept was now followed. The self-propelled mounts on the proved T-34 chassis were conceived as casemate vehicles in the rigid body of which a large-caliber artillery weapon could be mounted as in comparable tanks. The model was the German assault gun.

In the summer of 1942, a team of designers, including S. J. Kotin, worked on the development of a medium self-propelled gun, designated SU-35. A 122 mm howitzer was installed in a casemate body on the T-34 chassis. Testing followed, and in December 1942 it was decided to introduce the vehicle into the Red Army under the designation of SU-122. In that year 25 of them were delivered.

Year	Number
1942	25
1943	630
1944	493
Total	1148

In the spring of 1943 the first self-propelled gun regiments were formed, and equipped with 17 SU-76 and eight SU-122 guns. As of April, such regiments were formed with four or five batteries of five guns each, all of the same type. Their task was supporting the

Numerous hard blows from armor-piercing shells of different calibers show the effectiveness of the armor protection of the heavy Russian tanks.

Two pictures of a KV-2 heavy tank that was put out of action by a bomb that hit the right side of the hull. The barrel of the 152.4 mm 1938/40 model tank howitzer has been shot through just ahead of the mount. An explosive shell is stuck in the mouth of the barrel.

The many souvenir photos of German soldiers taken in 1941 show that the KV-2 heavy tank was a favorite subject for snapshots.

infantry in attacks and defending against enemy tank attacks. The 122 mm 1938 howitzer had a traverse field of 20 degrees and an elevation range from -3 to +25 degrees. It fired explosive and anti-tank shells. Later, hollow-charge shells were also added for anti-tank use. The last SU-122 self-propelled mounts built were recognizable by a changed gun mantlet, which was ball-shaped like that of the SU-85. In 1943 the SU-122 P self-propelled mount was tested. This was an attempt to install a 122 mm 1931/37 corps cannon to create a vehicle to fight against heavy tanks. It did not go beyond this test. A self-propelled mount with this gun was built later, using the IS chassis.

Tactical - Technical Data (SU-122, 1943 model)

Crew:	4-5 men
Weight:	30.9 tons
Armament:	1 122 mm caliber 1938 (M-30 S) howitzer, with 40 shells and cartridges
Armor plate:	
Hull: Front:	45 mm
Sides:	45 mm
Rear:	45 mm
Top:	20 mm
Bottom:	10 mm
Upper body:	
Front:	45 mm
Sides:	45 mm
Rear:	45 mm
Top:	20 mm
Powerplant:	V-12 cylinder 4-stroke W-2/34 Diesel engine
Performance:	500 HP at 1800 rpm
Fuel capacity:	800 liters
Power to weight:	16.2 HP/ton
Length overall:	6950 mm
Hull length:	5930 mm
Width:	3000 mm
Height:	2150 mm
Ground clearance:	400 mm
Top speed:	55 kph
Range:	600 km
Climbing degree:	30-33 degrees
Spanning ability:	2500 mm
Climbing ability:	730 mm
Wading ability:	1300 mm
Specific ground pressure:	0.68 kp/sq. cm.

The use of heavy armored tanks and armed vehicles (such as the Panther and Tiger) by the Germans caused the Soviet armored troops big problems. With the usual armament of the medium and heavy tanks (76.2 mm F-34 tank guns) they were hard to fight against. For that reason, self-propelled mounts with high-performance guns were requested to support the tanks. The attempt to arm the SU-122, already in series production, with a 122 mm corps cannon (SU-122 P) failed. At the Uralmash works in Chelyabinsk the project of a self-propelled mount on T-34 chassis and armed with an 85 mm gun was built; it came from the development bu-

Because of the heavy turret and the two-piece ammunition for the howitzer, the fire of the KV-2 was rather ponderous. The gun was aimed and fired only from a standstill.

Production of the KV-2 heavy tank in the form shown here (1940 model), recognizable by its vertical turret front and rounded roller mantlet, was halted during 1941.

In this picture, the weighty barrel of the 152.4 mm 1938/40 model tank howitzer is easy to see. The barrel was 3697 mm long (L/24) and had a screw breech. For targeting, a T-5-152 1938 model targeting scope (near the gun) and a PT-5 panoramic scope (on the turret top) were available.

reau of General F. F. Petrov. The gun was mounted in a ball mantlet at the front of the upper body. A traverse field of 20 degrees and an elevation range from -5 to +20 was possible. Eight to ten rounds per minute could be fired. The maximum shot range was 13,700 meters; against tanks, ranges up to 1,500 meters were practical. The BR-365 antitank shell was fired with an initial velocity of 792 meters per second, the undercaliber shell at 1,030 m/sec, giving penetration of 102 and 145 mm of armor plate at 500 meters. The SU-85 was used in pure self-propelled gun regiments or in self-propelled gun brigades. These in turn were part of mechanized or armored corps. From German reports of January and February 1944 it can be seen that the SU-85 self-propelled mount turned out to be very vulnerable to shots; it was stated: "A direct hit usually means a total loss."

A few specimens of the KV-2 heavy tank were used by the Germans. Their designation was "Tank KV II-754 (r) -Russian Klim Woroschilow" (the German spelling of "Voroshilov"). This picture was taken in the "Soviet Paradise" display in the Berlin Pleasure Garden on May 9, 1942.

In the Russian literature it is said that only a small number of KV-2 tanks were built. Actually more than 300 tanks of this type were delivered in 1940-41. The great majority were lost to the Germans in the summer of 1941.

There were 750 SU-85 built in 1943 and 1,300 in 1944. Arming the T-34 medium tank with an 85 mm tank gun put the purpose of the SU-85 in question; thus it was replaced by the SU-100 during 1944.

Tactical - Technical Data (SU-85, 1943 model)

Crew:	4 men
Weight:	29.2-29.6 tons
Armament:	1 85 mm caliber D-5 S-85 (later D-5 S-85 A) gun, with 48 rounds
Armor plate:	
Hull: Front:	45 mm
Sides:	45 mm
Rear:	45 mm
Top:	20 mm
Bottom:	20 mm
Upper body:	
Front:	45-75 mm
Sides:	45 mm
Rear:	45 mm
Top:	20 mm
Powerplant:	V-12 cylinder 4-stroke W-2/34 Diesel engine
Performance:	500 HP at 1800 rpm
Fuel capacity:	865 liters
Power to weight:	16.8 HP/ton
Length overall:	8150 mm
Hull length:	5930 mm
Width:	3000 mm
Height:	2400 mm
Ground clearance:	400 mm
Top speed:	47-55 kph
Range:	350 km
Climbing degree:	35 degrees
Spanning ability:	2500 mm
Climbing ability:	730 mm
Wading ability:	1300 mm
Specific ground pressure:	0.81 kp/sq. cm.

The successor to the SU-85, the SU-100 self-propelled mount, appeared in the second half of 1944. In the same basic body, this vehicle carried a 100 mm D-10 S gun from the development bureau of F. F. Petrov. Along with the TSch-19 targeting scope, the gun was mounted in a ball mantlet. The BR-412 antitank shell, weighing 15.6 kg, was fired with a muzzle velocity of 900 m/sec. The best ranges against armored vehicles were those up to 1,200 meters. Armor-piercing ammunition could penetrate 162 mm of armor at 500 meters and 150 mm at 1,000 meters. Like the later versions of the SU-85, the SU-100 had a cylindrical observation cupola for the commander on the right side of the upper body.

In 1944, 500 self-propelled mounts were completed at the Uralmash works in Chelyabinsk. In 1945, 1,175 more were made. As of the end of 1944, they replaced the SU-85 in the equipment of the medium self-propelled gun regiments of the mechanized and armored corps, as well as the self-propelled gun brigades established at the end of 1944.

The KV-2 heavy tank with angled turret armor and angular roller mantlet with ribbed sides was known in the Red Army only as a test version. A number of photographs taken by German soldiers in the summer of 1941 show that there were more than a few examples of it.

In the summer of 1941, heavy tanks from several production runs of the KV-1 type were fitted with added armor, giving a thickness of 110 mm. The weight rose to 47.5 or 48 tons, from which mobility and off-road capability suffered.

A stuck KV-2 of the experimental or final version, photographed in July 1941. Details of the turret structure (angled front, roller mantlet) and the engine-room cover can be seen.

Here is a KV-1 heavy tank, 1940 model, that is still armed with the short 76.2 mm tank gun. The added armor on the bow and ahead of the driver can be seen. The armor plates on the turret were screwed on. Note the cutouts for the vision slit and pistol loophole.

A KV-1 with thicker armor, and with its turret torn off by the air pressure from an exploding aerial bomb. Note the added armor plate!

Tactical - Technical Data (SU-100, 1944 model)

Crew:		4 men
Weight:		31.6 tons
Armament:		1 100 mm caliber D-10 S cannon, with 34 rounds
Armor plate:		
Hull:	Front:	45 mm
	Sides:	45 mm
	Rear:	45 mm
	Top:	20 mm
	Bottom:	20 mm
Upper body:		
	Front:	45-75 mm
	Sides:	45 mm
	Rear:	45 mm
	Top:	20 mm
Powerplant:		V-12-cylinder 4-stroke W-2/34 Diesel engine
Performance:		500 HP at 1800 rpm
Fuel capacity:		865 liters
Power to weight:		16.4 HP/ton
Length overall:		9450 mm
Hull length:		5930 mm
	Width:	3000 mm
	Height:	2240 mm
Ground clearance:		400 mm
Top speed:		50 kph
Range:		310 mm
Climbing degree:		35 degrees
Spanning ability:		2500 mm
Climbing ability:		730 mm
Wading ability:		1300 mm
Specific ground pressure:		0.80 kp/sq. cm.

The medium tank family found its conclusion for the time being in the Soviet Union during World War II with the design of the T-44. The tank appeared in the summer of 1944 at the development bureau of A. A. Morosov, who had performed great service through his collaboration in the creation of the T-34. Prototypes were built and designated T-34/100, but it turned out that the T-34/85 turret was not suitable for mounting the 100 mm D-10 T tank gun. Therefore the T-44, like its predecessor, had to be armed with an 85 mm tank gun. In 1945, 200 tanks were produced. A new feature that pointed the way for postwar tank development in the Soviet Union was the hull design of the T-44. By installing the engine transversely it was possible to shorten the length of the hull, use vertical bulkheads and save weight. The tank appeared very compact and compressed. The armor was also strengthened to 90 mm.

If one wishes to evaluate all the Red Army's medium tanks of World War II together, one cannot but choose the T-34 as the most practical and balanced combination of the three most important qualities of armored combat vehicles: *high mobility, effective armor protection, and the firepower of its weapons*. They determined the value of this tank. In addition, it was ideally suited to large-series production, as shown by the number of more than 64,000 tanks produced.

Two KV-1 heavy tanks with added armor, shot down on a runway outside Leningrad and photographed in July 1941. Some of the Russian tank soldiers fought desperately and were able to slow the advance of Army Group North units.

Tactical - Technical Data (T-44, 1945 model)

Crew:	4 men
Weight:	31.9 tons
Armament:	1 85 mm caliber 1945 (ZIS-S-53) tank gun, with ? rounds,
	2 7.62 mm caliber DT machine guns, with ? rounds
Armor plate:	
Hull: Front:	90 mm
Sides:	75 mm
Rear:	30-90 mm
Top:	15-20 mm
Bottom:	15-20 mm
Turret: Front:	90-120 mm
Sides:	75 mm
Rear:	75 mm
Top:	-
Powerplant:	V-12-cylinder 4-stroke W-44 Diesel engine
Performance:	520 HP at 2000 rpm
Fuel capacity:	642 liters
Power to weight:	16.6 HP/ton
Length overall:	7650 mm
Hull length:	6090 mm
Width:	3150 mm
Height:	2410 mm
Ground clearance:	430 mm
Top speed:	51 kph
Range:	235 km
Climbing degree:	32 degrees
Spanning ability:	2500 mm
Climbing ability:	1000 mm
Wading ability:	1300 mm
Specific ground pressure:	0.84 kp/sq. cm.

3. Heavy Tanks 1939-1945

In August 1938, essential decisions about the armored vehicles of the Red Army were made at a meeting of the State Defense Com-

In a German report on Red Army tanks in the autumn of 1941, based on Russian data and statements from prisoners, one can read of the KV heavy tank: "These KV types have technical and tactical faults. Many operating problems, little mobility and low speed make them unpopular in the Russian Army. Operatively they are of limited or no use, because of difficulties in crossing road bridges and short life spans (100 operating hours normally; lasting 300 operating hours is mentioned with special praise)."

This KW-1 with added armor was shot down by a German 8.8 cm anti-aircraft gun, which was for a long time the only weapon for effective use against the modern Russian tanks. The holes made in the 75 mm rear armor by antitank shells can be seen.

Ahcracteristic features of the KV tanks with added armor were the big screw-heads on the turret and hull sides (upper half). Not all of the tanks had armor added, or it was sometimes limited to the front half.

Another photo of a KV-1 with added armor. The movable machine gun is missing from the left side of the hull. Note the unique cover!

mittee of the Soviet Union. They were to influence development into the mid-forties. A directive issued on this subject called the designers' attention more strongly than before to tanks with more effective armament and heavier armor. Concrete determinations concerned, among others, the development of a heavy penetration tank, among whose primary tasks was the destruction of antitank guns. It was to be used in place of the T-28 and T-35. Designing such a heavy tank began without delay. Mostovenko wrote of it: "In 1938 two heavy tanks were designed, with armor that was to provide protection against shell fire. Three turrets were originally planned, but in the process of the developmental work they were reduced to two. The retention of multiple turrets corresponded to the thinking of the time about the role of heavy tanks. . . . This was justified as long as shell-safe armor was promoted; but if this also had to provide protection against shells, the result had to be a considerable gain in weight."

L. E. Lytshev, who worked as a designer in the Kirov factory in Leningrad in the thirties, also remembered the beginning of a new generation of heavy Soviet tanks: "At that time one held the view that a heavy tank with multiple turrets and guns had especially good combat qualities. But we saw that this resulted in poorer maneuverability and increased vulnerability." In 1938 S. J. Kotin presented three reworked projects at the Kremlin in Moscow, two of them having two turrets and one just one turret. Josef Stalin, as Secretary-General of the Communist Party of the Soviet Union, took a lively interest in these proposals for new heavy tanks. A decision was made to the extent that all three designs were authorized for further development, building and testing of prototypes. From the two twin-turret tank projects came the T-100 "Sotka" and SMK (Sergei Mironovich Kirov, Soviet politician murdered in 1934) tanks. The two looked almost exactly alike, had a main turret raised high in the center with a 76.2 mm gun, and a lower turret farther forward, with a 45 mm gun. The large turret could be turned 360 degrees, the smaller one 180 degrees. For the noticeably long chassis, running gear with eight small, independently sprung road wheels was suggested.[15] The tracks were directed above by four return roll-

15. Torsion bars were used for the suspension.

Because of its high fighting weight and the lack of towing tractors with enough power, heavy tanks of the KV type were seldom reused by the Germans. Their designation was "Tank KW Ia-753 (r) - Russian Klim Woroschilow" for the 1940 model (shown here). KV tanks with added armor were "Tank KW Ib-755 (r) - Russian Klim Woroschilow."

As with the T-34 medium tank, the KV-1 heavy tank was also armed in 1941 with the 76.2 mm 1940 model tank gun (F-34) with 3170 mm barrel (L/41.5). At first the older, angular turret was retained.

This 1941 model KV-1 heavy tank was shot down in the northern sector of the eastern front in the winter of 1941-42. Leningrad, besieged by the Germans, was a center of heavy tank production, thus they were often seen there.

The 1941 model KV-1 heavy tank's still usable older versions were still used in independent tank regiments and brigades in the autumn of 1941. A company was supposed to have five to ten of them.

ers on each side. The T-100 weighed 56 tons, the SMK, though, only 45 tons. The crews consisted of six or seven men. The armor, 60 mm thick, was laid out so that it provived reliable protection from armor-piercing 37 mm shells. Both tanks had 400 HP gasoline engines as powerplants. Tanks of this type saw their only front action in the 1939-40 winter war against the Finns in Karelia, where they had been sent for front testing.

In the winter war against Finland, two KV tanks also saw service, having been sent directly to the front from the factory in Leningrad. The KV tank was the third of the projects proposed in 1938, and differed from the other two test models in having only one turret. Its development had begun in February 1939 at S. J. Kotin's development bureau. N. L. Duchov had been named responsible designer. The first prototypes were already built in September of that year. The omission of more turrets and guns saved weight, which allowed heavier armor. Thus this tank stood out during its testing for its mobility, very high for its weight class. The front testing of two pre-series tanks in Finland was so convincing that on December 19, 1939, its introduction to the armored troops could be authorized. Series production began in the summer of 1940; in that year 141 tanks of the type were completed. Thus the decision was finally made in favor of single-turret heavy tanks. This development caught on outside Russia only in the ensuing years.

The KV tanks built before the beginning of 1941 had armor at most 75 mm thick, which offered reliable protection against fire from antitank guns, even from very close range. The specified ground pressure was stated at 0.75 kp/sq. cm., a very favorable value for a 43.5-ton tank, attained above all through the use of very wide tracks. The Diesel engine produced 600 HP and allowed a top speed of 35 kph. The angular turret held a 76.2 mm L-11 tank gun in a roller mantlet and a coaxial 7.62 mm DT machine gun. Another machine gun of that type was in a ball mantlet at the rear of the turret. The third machine gun, likewise in a ball mantlet, was mounted in the front of the hull. This was the basic arrangement of the weapons. As for the performance of the guns, with the 6.3 kilogram BR-350 antitank shell (muzzle velocity 612 m/sec), 66 mm of armor could be penetrated at a range of 500 meters. Along with the maximum of 114 tank-gun rounds, there were 6.23-kilogram F-34 explosive shells (muzzle velocity 610-635 m/sec).

In connection with the effective armor, which could not be penetrated by either the German 3.7- and 5-cm antitank guns or the 5- and 7.5-cm guns of the Panzer III and IV, the heavy armor of the KV got the reputation of being invulnerable. Its service consisted of supporting medium and light tanks. To be able to do this even

The hull of a KV-1 heavy tank with added armor on the bow and driver's area. The turret has been blown off.

Armor-piercing shells have hit this 1941 model KV-1 several times and put it out of action. The steel road wheels can be seen clearly.

In 1941 the Russian tank industry was able to develop a completely cast turret for the KV-1 heavy tank. Its weight is listed as about seven tons, and the entire tank attained a weight of 48 tons. Externally the tank could be recognized by the rounded turret shape.

more effectively, another type of heavy tank, first called the "KV with the large turret," was created. Later it was designated KV-2 or KV-2 A. With it, the Red Army followed the tradition, already arisen in the thirties, of the artillery tank, that was supposed to use its large-caliber guns to hold down or destroy enemy antitank defenses. This tradition reached its high point in the KV-based artillery tanks. In a turret 1,450 mm high, a 152.4-mm 1938/40 tank howitzer was mounted. The gun barrel was 3,700 mm long (L/24/5) and weighed 1.36 tons in itself. Explosive shells weighing 51.1 kg were fired with an initial velocity of 432 m/sec to distances of 5,000 meters. Armor-piercing ammunition was likewise available; the shell weighed 40 kg (initial velocity 508 m/sec). For aiming, a drum sight with a shortened aiming scope was used. The KV-2 was actually a self-propelled artillery gun with a turning turret. The firing height was stated as 2,500 mm, and the tank's overall height was a striking 3,250 mm. The KV-2 weighed 52 tons, almost ten tons more than the "KV with a small turret" (KW-1, 1940 model), and was resultingly less mobile.

In 1940 and 1941 a total of over 330 KV-2 and KV-2 A tanks were built at the Kirov works in Leningrad. The KV-2 A was an improved version, which could be recognized externally by the modified roller mantlet. During 1941 KV production was halted.

The existence of heavy tanks with shell-safe armor was a surprise for the German Army in the summer of 1941. It is not difficult to choose individual statements from the many combat descriptions of that time to indicate the shock that the first meeting with the Red Army's heavier and heaviest tanks caused the German soldiers. The following excerpt is from the account of a war correspondent about the defensive combat of an infantry division on June 23-24 near Grodno:

"Loud engine noise from all sides—clouds of dust rise up all around us, the steel tank waves roll up from three sides at once. One is short of breath from excitement. . . . The sun is already low on the horizon. . . . New attacks break forth from several directions. Shock wedges that are to push against weak points. And then the gun barrels rise from the horizon, a high turret becomes visible, a gigantic tank body. Tanks! Giant tanks such as we have never seen before! Giants of steel stamp over the slope toward us! Russian 52-ton tanks with a 15-cm gun! Crippling fear falls over us. Then the antitank guns are called in; out of all their barrels our fire roars, but

This 1941 model KV-1 with cast turret was captured almost undamaged by the Germans and photographed in January 1942. On the extra fuel tank in the middle, the usual German designation for tanks of this type ("52 t") is painted.

A shot-down 1941 model KV-1 heavy tank. Note the very wide (650 mm) tracks; despite the high fighting weight, they allowed a comparatively low specific ground pressure (0.80 kp/sq. cm.).

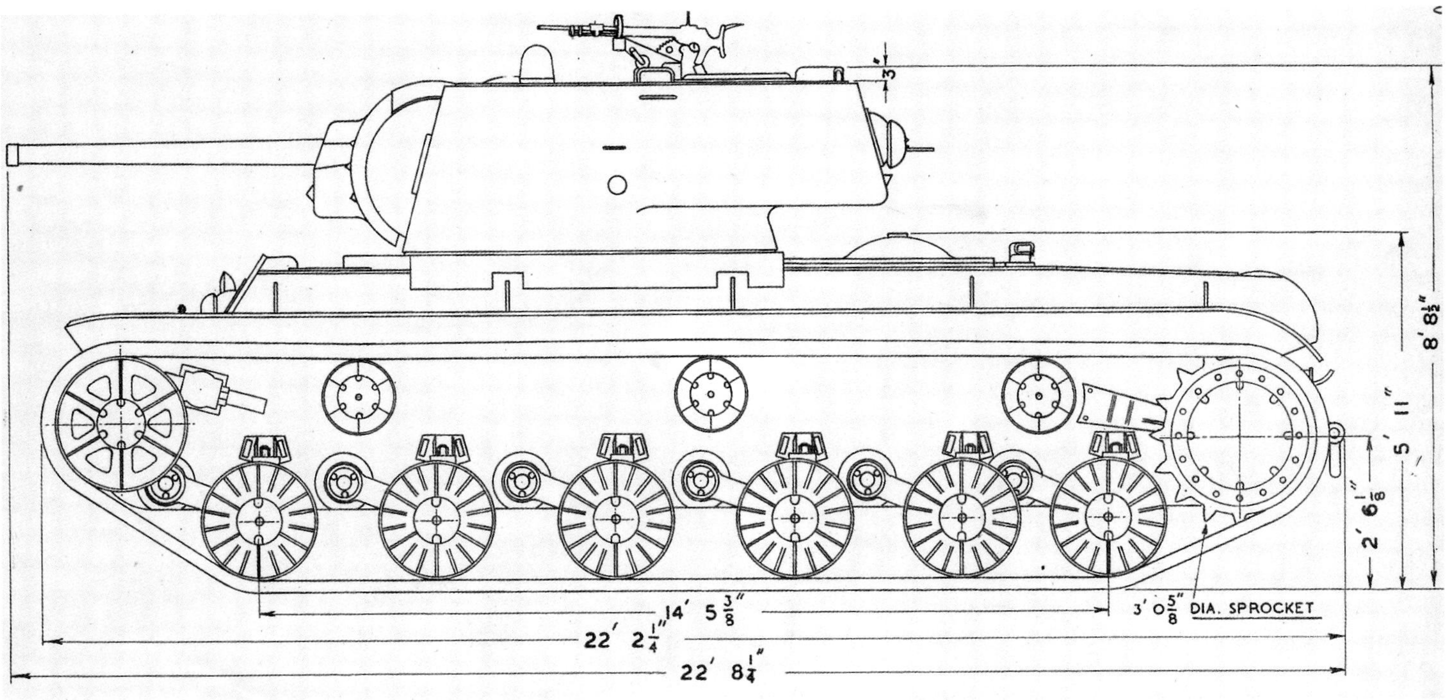

Four-side views of the 1941 model KV-1 heavy tank.

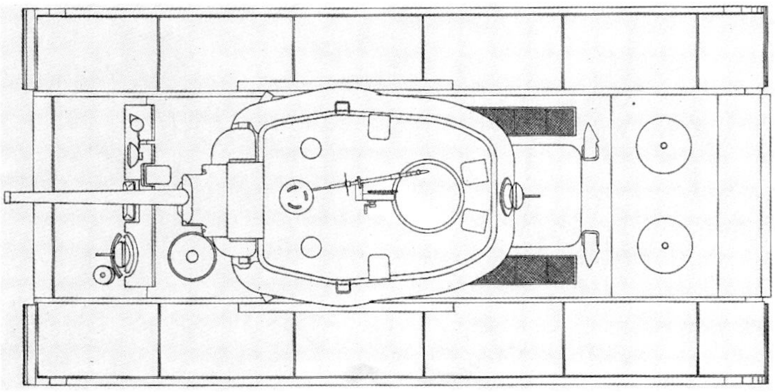

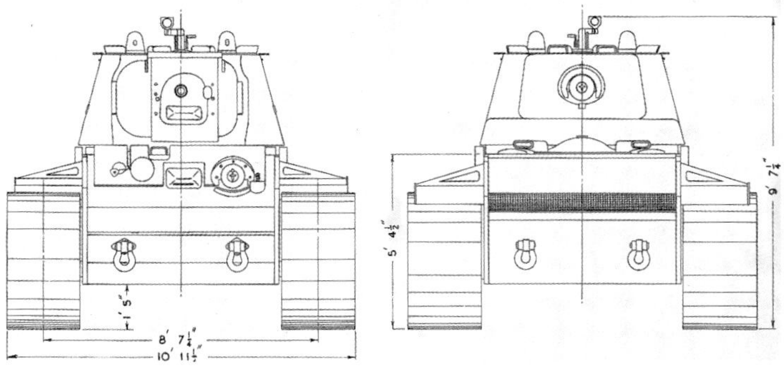

A side view of the 1941 model KV-1 heavy tank.

Two 1941 model KV-1 heavy tanks with cast turrets. The long barrel of the 76.2 mm 1940 model tank gun (F-34). clearly visible here, could achieve good results at 500 meters against armor up to 69 mm thick. This weapon was regarded by the Red Army's armored troops as too weak, but their requests for a heavy tank with greater firepower could not be met until 1943.

The KV-1 S made from the autumn of 1942 on had less thick armor and could be recognized by the rounded [p. 50] cast-steel turret with a small commander's cupola. This type of heavy tank had greater mobility. Its production was halted in the late summer of 1943.

the light armor-piercing weapons can do nothing here. Like rubber balls the shells bounce off the mighty steel walls. . . . The antitank soldiers fight wildly, as if possessed. The tank is their deadly enemy. They let it advance to the closest range, fire cold-bloodedly, as they have learned to do, at its weakest points.

"They fire until the armor plates glow from the heavy impacts and the boring of the antitank shells. . . . Before the last man sinks down over his gun, he fires the last shot."

Much less dramatic and characterized by his usual objectivity are the reports that the Chief of the Army General Staff, Generaloberst Franz Halder, wrote in his war diary:

"June 24, 1941 . . . New heavy tanks! June 25, 1941: . . . Individual reports of newly arrived Russian tanks come in: Weight 52 tons, front armor 37 cm (?), side armor 8 cm, armament 15.2 cm gun and 3 machine guns, crew five men. Speed 30 kilometers per hour, radius of action 100 km. Possible defense: 5 cm antitank gun penetrates under the gun turret, 8.8 cm Flak apparently penetrates on the sides too (still questionable) . . ."

During 1940, the KV-1 began to be equipped with a turret whose armor plates were welded together. The new primary weapon in 1941 was the 76.2 mm F-34 tank gun also used in the T-34, with a longer 3,150 mm (L/41.5) barrel. Another modification was made

This KV-1 S heavy tank was shot down within a German position and provided a welcome addition to its cover. The commander's cupola and the movable 7.62 mm DT machine gun at the rear of the turret can be seen. The KV-1 S was used by independent heavy tank regiments of the Red Army, with 21 tanks apiece, beginning in October 1942.

A close-up shot of a KW-1 S heavy tank's turret, with the stopper of the pistol loophole hanging out and the crude workmanship of the cast steel armr easy to see. Shot damage from previous action was covered by welded-on armor plates.

During the Kursk Bogen fighting in Jul;y 1943, this KW-1 S heavy tank was totally destroyed. The 12-cylinder Diesel engine can be seen right behind the fighting compartment.

A test model of a heavy tank with a 122 mm tank howitzer. This model was tested as a KV-9.

in the summer of that year, when the hull armor was increased from 105 mm to 110 mm by the addition of plates. Armor plates 25 to 35 mm thick were also attached to the sides and rear of the turret. The fighting weight thus increased noticeably, to 47.5 tons. A short time later, production of a completely cast turret for the KV-1 began. Its armor was up to 120 mm thick, raising the weight to 48.0 tons. Of course the tank's speed decreased to 29 kph. General Katukov, during a talk that he had with the Secretary-General of the Communist Party of the Soviet Union and Chairman of the Council of the People's Commissars, Josef Stalin, on September 17, 1942, complained, saying: "The heavy KV and the T-60 and T-70 . . . are not popular among the soldiers. . . . The KV, Comrade Stalin, is heavy, ponderous and thus not maneuverable. It overcomes obstacles only with difficulty, quite the opposite of the thirty-four. In addition, it damages bridges and causes a lot of destruction. It is armed with the same gun as the T-34. So what advantages does the heavy tank offer us in battle? Yes, if it had a bigger gun, then we could get along with its high weight and the other design faults."

When war broke out between Germany and the Soviet Union (the Great Fatherland War), the Kirov works were moved from Leningrad to Chelyabinsk. The factories set up at the new location had taken up tank production again within a few weeks. It was possible to increase production of the KV, so that in the second half of 1941, 933 KV tanks could be delivered to the front.

Experience in battle showed that the mobility of the KV had to be improved again, and that the reliability of several components left something to be desired. These problems had accompanied the KV tank from the beginning and had lost no importance with the later additions to the armor and the resulting increase of weight.

In the second half of 1942 the tank was modernized again. The work was directed by designer N. F. Shashmurin. The thickness of the armor was decreased, which had a good effect on the speed and

The last production run of the KV heavy tank was a small KV-85 series built in the autumn of 1943. The most noteworthy innovation was the use of an 85 mm D-5 T tank gun, housed in a new; likewise cast turret with an observation cupola. The three 7.62 mm DT machine guns used earlier were retained.

Shot-down heavy tanks of the KV-85 type, from the 27th independent Guard Tank Penetration Regiment. This unit was divided into four companies with five tanks each. Another tank was used by the regimental staff. This picture was taken early in December 1943, after the regiment had suffered heavy losses in battle with a German tank-destroyer unit.

On the basis of the KV-1 heavy tank, the KV-8 flamethrowing tank was created in 1942. Its weight is stated as 44 to 46 tons, its armor was 75 to 95 mm thick. The tank, which did not differ from other tanks of the type in terms of mobility (35 kph), had a four-man crew. It was armed with a 45 mm 1938 model tank gun that was falsified to look like a 76.2 mm gun. To the right of the gun was an ATO automatic powder flamethrower, for which 670 liters of oil and 63 [p. 51] fuses were carried. It could fire 52 to 55 bursts of flame. On the left side of the hull was a movable DT machine gun. The tank carried 110 shells and 2772 rounds of machine-gun ammunition.

The SU-152 appeared in 1943 as a heavy self-propelled artillery mount, and was used in the heavy self-propelled gun regiments of the Red Army. These were made up of two units with six SU-152 guns and one T-34 medium tank each. A third tank of the type was used by the regimental staff.

off-road capability; the tank could now reach 42 kph, and the fighting weight was now only 42.5 tons. The trasnsmission and primary armament were simplified and their reliability was increased, while the cooling and lubrication systems were improved. Externally, the tank was recognizable by a small commander's cupola on the turret and the backward-sloping top armor of the hull. The tank was designated KV-1 S and went into series production in the autumn of 1942. An important request of the armored troops, which can also be found in Katukov's criticism of the KV, could not yet be fulfilled in the KV-1 S—that for stronger armament. Heavy tanks were again to be capable of fulfilling their real task, the support of light and medium tanks. The last series-produced version of the KV was the KV-85, which was built in small numbers as of the autumn of 1943. To the modified hull of the KV-1 S was added the cast turret developed for the future IS-1 heavy tank, with the 85 mm D-5 T tank gun. The turret armor was about 100 mm thick, and the weight went back up to 46 tons. Now there was room for only four crewmen in the tank. In addition, the usual previous armament for heavy tanks was changed, namely three machine guns. The KV-85 had two. One of its identifying marks was a large commander's cupola.

The Germans first encountered the KV-85 in the first half of December 1943 in the sector of Army High Command 16 of the Army Group North. The 27th Guard Regiment, which had had twenty heavy tanks of this type in its four combat companies, was hit hard by the German defenses. Examinations of shot-down tanks showed that all tanks were well and thoroughly equipped. Amaze-

The SU-152 heavy self-propelled artillery mount was built on the chassis of the KV-1 S. It fulfilled tasks that the KV-2 heavy tank had been intended for in 1940-41, but had a lighter weight, was lower and more maneuverable, and stood out for its higher firepower.

This SU-152 heavy self-propelled artillery mount was met by the German antitank defenses. As a result of the ammunition having been set afire inside the vehicle, the body, with 50- to 75-mm armor, burst. The German soldier standing at right holds a 40-kilogram antitank shell in his hands.

In the autumn of 1943 a new heavy tank, designated IS-1 or IS-85, was ready for testing. Like the KV-85, it was armed with an 85 mm D-5 T tank gun and three 7.62 mm DT machine guns. Its armor reached a thickness of 90 to 120 mm. The top speed of the 44-ton tank was listed as 37 kph. A tank of this type had a four-man crew.

After the IS-1 heavy tank did not meet the requirements of the Red Army armored troops with either an 85 mm D-5T (IS-85) or a 100 mm tank gun (IS-100), the final version with the 122 mm tank gun appeared at the end of 1943. It was designated IS-2.

ment resulted when it was learned from the German evaluation report of December 11, 1943, that all the tanks that had been seen had gone into battle with a 10-P radio set built in 1943. Until then this obviously had not been taken for granted. The four-man crew was composed of the commander (second lieutenant), driver (technical lieutenant), mechanic (also loader), and gunner (artillery sergeant).

The KV-85 was only a transitional model; after 130 of them were delivered, production was stopped. The IS heavy tank took its place.

The production statistics for tanks of the KV series are as follows:

Year	Number			
	KV-1	KV-2/KV-2 A	KV-1 S	KV-85
1940	141	102	334	
1941	1121	232	1232	
1942	1753	780	130	
1943			452	130
Totals	3015		Grand Total: 4711	

Besides a few test models based on the KV, including the LV-1 S with 122 mm gun and the KV-2 with 85 mm gun, this type of tank achieved great importance as the KV-8 flamethrowing tank. Various series of the heavy tank were used, but usually the KV-1 S. The flamethrower, an automatic ATO-41 powder type, was mounted in the roller mantlet of the turret along with a 45 mm tank gun, which was made to look like the 7.62 mm gun by means of a sheet-metal dummy.

Among the tank's equipment were 670 liters of oil, which gave 52 to 55 bursts of flame, and 63 ignition cartridges for the flamethrower. The range of the flamethrower was 46 meters. For the 45 mm 1938 tank gun, 116 rounds were carried, and for the four 7.62 mm DT machine guns a total of 2,772 rounds. The weight of the KV-8 is stated as 44.0 tons.

The 122 mm 1943 model tank gun (D-25 T) with its roller mantlet. Just the barrel and breech weighed almost two tons. The barrel was 5648.6 mm long (L/46.3), and its antitank shells could penetrate 140 mm of armor plate at a distance of 500 meters.

During the combat in East Prussia in the spring of 1945, this IS-2 heavy tank was shot down. With its 122 mm tank gun the Stalin tank could hold its own in battle, even with the German King Tiger, and had the advantage of being 25 tons lighter. The Russian tank's disadvantage was that its turret crew needed much time to load the two-piece (shell and cartridge) ammunition.

Tactical - Technical Data (KV-1, 1940 model)

Crew:		5 men
Weight:		43.5 tons
Armament:		1 76.2 mm caliber 1939 (L-11) tank gun, with 111-114 rounds,
		3-4 7.62 mm caliber DT machine guns, with 3024 rounds
Armor plate:		
Hull:	Front:	75 mm
	Sides:	75 mm
	Rear:	60-75 mm
	Top:	30-40 mm
	Bottom:	30-40 mm
Turret:	Front:	90 mm
	Sides:	75 mm
	Rear:	75 mm
	Top:	35 mm
Powerplant:		V-12 cylinder 4-stroke W-2-K Diesel engine
Performance:		600 HP at 2000 rpm
Fuel capacity:		600-615 liters
Power to weight:		13.8 mm
	Length:	6750 mm
	Width:	3320 mm
	Height:	2710 mm
Ground clearance:		450 mm
Top speed:		35 kph
Range:		335 km
Climbing degree:		36 degrees
Spanning ability:		2800 mm
Climbing ability:		900-1200 mm
Wading ability:		1450-1600 mm
Specific ground pressure:		0.75 kp/sq. cm.

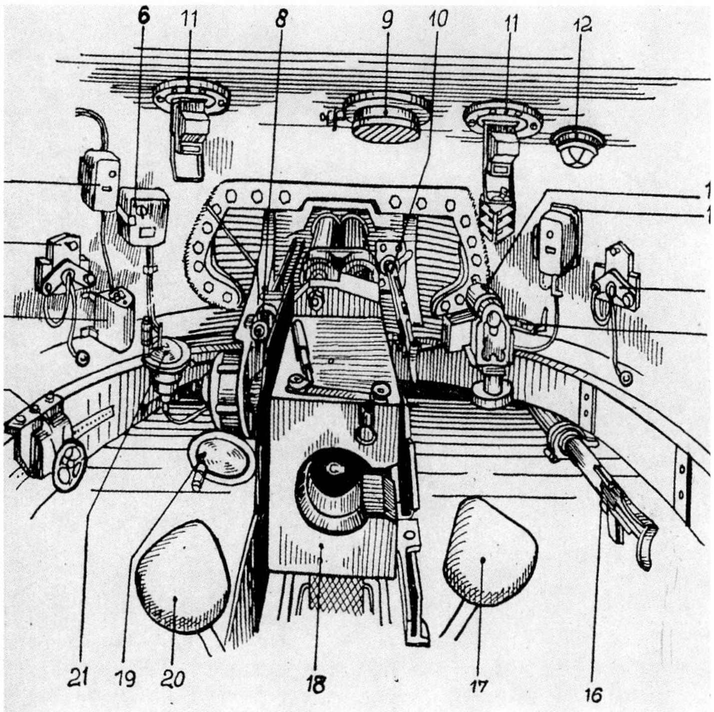

A look into the fighting compartment inside the turret.

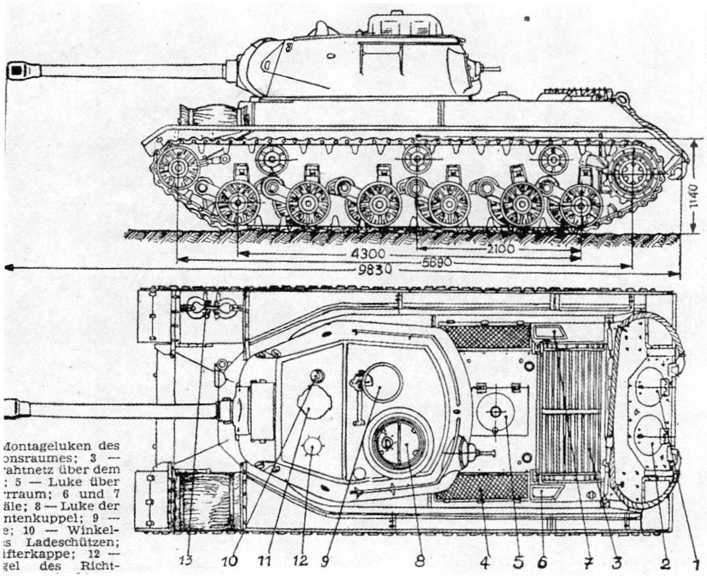

Three-side views of the IS-2 heavy tank, 1943 model.

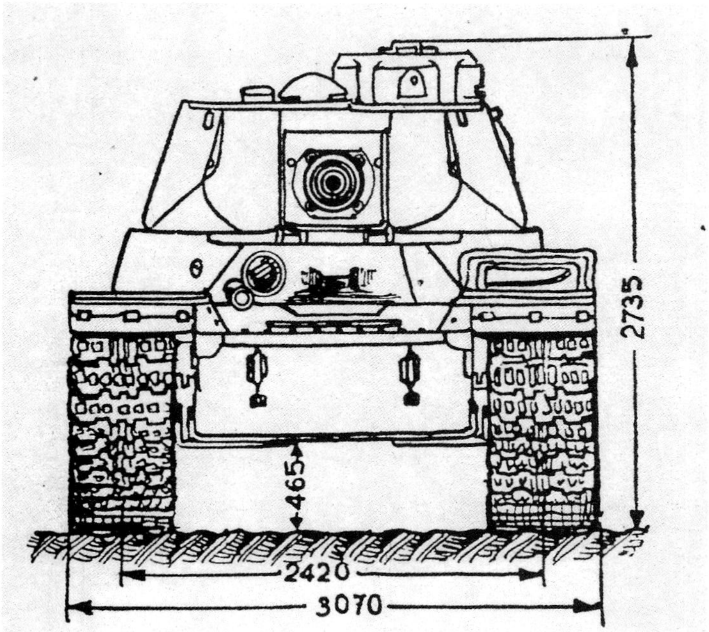

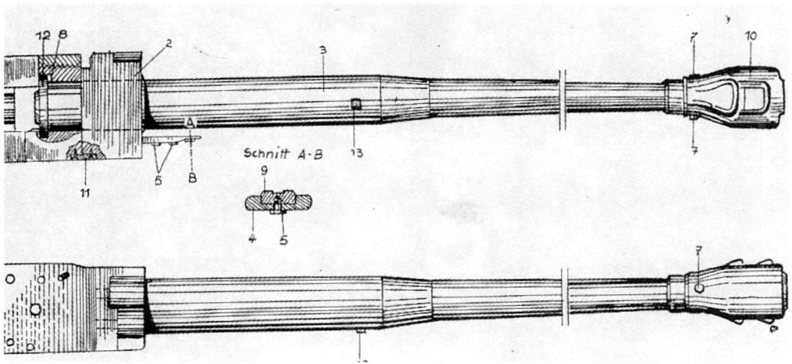

The barrel of the 122 mm 1943 model tank gun (D-25 T): 1. Base, 2. Tension screw, 3. barrel, 4. rails, 5. Holding screw, 6. Wire, 7. Screw, 8. Wedge, 9. Wedge, 10. Muzzle brake, 11. Wedge, 12. Barrel band, 13. Barrel recoil indicator plate.

In marching position, and also when loaded on a train, the barrel of the 122 mm tank gun had to be turned to the back and lashed down.

Tactical - Technical Data (KV-1, 1941 model)

Crew:		5 men
Weight:		47.5 tons
Armament:		1 76.2 mm caliber 1940 (F-34) tank gun, with 111-114 rounds,
		304 7.62 mm caliber DT machine guns, with 3024 rounds
Armor plate:		
Hull:	Front:	110 mm
	Sides:	75-110 mm
	Rear:	75 mm
	Top:	30-40 mm
	Bottom:	30-40 mm
Turret:	Front:	110 mm
	Sides:	110 mm
	Rear:	110 mm
	Top:	35 mm
Powerplant:		V-12 cylinder 4-stroke W-2-K Diesel engine
Performance:		600 HP at 2000 rpm
Fuel capacity:		600-615 liters
Power to weight:		12.6 HP/ton
	Length:	6250 mm
	Width:	3250 mm
	Height:	2750 mm
Ground clearance:		450 mm
Top speed:		29 kph
Range:		250 km
Climbing degree:		36 degrees
Spanning ability:		2800 mm
Climbing ability:		900-1200 mm
Wading ability:		1450-1600 mm
Specific ground pressure:		0.78 kp/sq. cm.

These pictures show a completely destroyed IS-2 heavy tank of the early series (1943 model). The angular front section of the armored hull, with an opening driver's hatch, is typical. The weighty commander's cupola on the turret allowed good all-around vision. To its right is the loader's hatch, in the middle is the ventilator, and just in front of that is the gunner's periscope.

These pictures, taken at an army base in East Germany after the war's end, also show an IS-2 heavy tank, 1943 model. The attachments added to both sides of the forward half of the hull as storage boxes were not originally part of the early-type IS-2.

Rear view of an IS-2 heavy tank, 1943 model. The front part of the armored hull is cast, while the rear part is made of rolled armor plates 90 mm thick. Note the exhaust ports on both sides.

During 1944 the IS-2 heavy tank reached the troops at the front with a better-shaped shot-deflecting front body. The driver's visor was eliminated, replaced by only a vision slit.

Tactical - Technical Data (KV-1, 1942 model)

Crew:		5 men
Weight:		48.0 tons
Armanent:		1 85 mm caliber 1942 (F-34) tank gun, with 111-114 rounds, 3 7.62 mm DT machine guns, with 3024 rounds
Armor Plate:		
Hull:	Front:	100 mm
	Sides:	90-130 mm
	Rear:	75 mm
	Top:	30-40 mm
	Bottom:	15-20 mm
Turret:	Front:	120 mm
	Sides:	120 mm
	Rear:	120 mm
	Top:	40 mm
Powerplant:		V-12 cylinder 4-stroke W-2-K Diesel engine
Performance:		600 HP at 2000 rpm
Fuel capacity:		600-615 liters
Power to weight:		12.5 HP/ton
	Length:	6250 mm
	Width:	3250 mm
	Height:	2750 mm
Ground clearance:		450 mm
Top speed:		29 kph
Range:		250 km
Climbing degree:		36 degrees
Spanning ability:		2800 mm
Climbing ability:		900-1200 mm
Wading ability:		1450-1600 mm
Specific ground pressure:		0.80 kp/sq. cm.

Tactical - Technical Data (KV-2, 1940 model)

Crew:		6 men
Weight:		52.0 tons
Armament:		1 152.4 mm caliber 1938/40 tank howitzer, with 36 rounds, 3 7.62 mm caliber DT machine guns, with 2475-3087 rounds
Armor plate:		
Hull:	Front:	75 mm
	Sides:	75 mm
	Rear:	60-75 mm
	Top:	30-40 mm
	Bottom:	30-40 mm
Turret:	Front:	110 mm
	Sides:	75 mm
	Rear:	75 mm
	Top:	35 mm
Powerplant:		V-12 cylinder 4-stroke W-2-K Diesen engine
Performance:		600 HP at 2000 rpm
Fuel capacity:		610 liters
Power to weight:		11.5 HP/ton
Length overall:		6800 mm
	Hull length:	6670 mm
	Width:	3350 mm
	Height:	3250 mm
Ground clearance:		450 mm
Top speed:		26 kph
Range:		250 km
Climbing degree:		30 degrees
Spanning ability:		2700 mm
Climbing ability:		1200 mm
Wading ability:		1600 mm
Specific ground pressure:		0.90 kp/sq. cm.

Tactical - Technical Data (KV-1 S)

Crew:		5 men
Weight: 42.5 tons		
Armament:		1 76.2 mm caliber 1942 (F-34) tank gun, with 100 rounds,
		3 7.62 mm caliber DT machine guns, with 3024 rounds
Armor plate:		
Hull:	Front:	40-75 mm
	Sides:	60 mm
	Rear:	40-75 mm
	Top:	30-40 mm
	Bottom:	30-40 mm
Turret:	Front:	82 mm
	Sides:	82 mm
	Rear:	82 mm
	Top:	-
Powerplant:		V-12 cylinder 4-stroke W-2-K Diesel engine
Performance:		600 HP at 2000 rpm
Fuel capacity:		615 liters
Power to weight:		14.2 HP/ton
	Length:	6750 mm
	Width:	3250 mm
	Height:	2750 mm
Ground clearance:		450 mm
Top speed:		42-43 kph
Range:		330 km
Climbing degree:		36 degrees
Spanning ability:		2800 mm
Climbing ability:		1200 mm
Wading ability:		1600 mm
Specific ground pressure:		0.74 kp/sq. cm.

During the heavy fighting in the area between Arnswalde and Stargard, Pomerania, in February 1945, the Germans were able to capture these two Stalin tanks almost undamaged. The IS-2 was regarded as particularly hard to fight against. Since November 1944 it was used at the front by the heavy guard tank brigades of three regiments, each with 65 tanks.

This 1944 model IS-2 heavy tank belonged to the 1st Czechoslovakian Tank Brigade at the end of World War II. In addition, this type of tank was used in Polish units that fought alongside the Red Army against the German forces.

Russian guard tank soldiers on their heavy tank, photographed near Altendamm in northeastern Germany early in 1945.

Tactical - Technical Data (KW-85)

Crew:		4 men
Weight:		46.0 tons
Armament:		1 85 mm caliber 1943 (D-5 T) tank gun, with 70 rounds,
		2 7.62 mm caliber DT machine guns, with 3276 mm
Armor plate:		
Hull:	Front:	60-76 mm
	Sides:	60 mm
	Rear:	40-75 mm
	Top:	30-40 mm
	Bottom:	30-40 mm
Turret:	Front:	100-110 mm
	Sides:	100-110 mm
	Rear:	110 mm
	Top:	30 mm
Powerplant:		V-12 cylinder 4-stroke W-2-K Diesel engine
Performance:		600 HP at 2000 rpm
Fuel capacity:		615 liters
Power to weight:		13.1 HP/ton
Length overall:		8600 mm
Hull length:		8600 mm
	Width:	3250 mm
	Height:	2800 mm
Ground clearance:		400 mm
Top speed:		42 kph
Range:		330 km
Climbing degree:		40 degrees
Spanning ability:		2700 mm
Climbing ability:		900-1200 mm
Wading ability:		1200 mm
Specific ground pressure:		0.77 kp/sq. cm.

When the development of heavy self-propelled mounts began in the Soviet Union in the thirties, numerous test vehicles with large-caliber guns on the chassis of the T-35 heavy tank came into being.

The 1945 model of the new IS-3 heavy tank did not arrive in time to take part in combat in World War II. Emphasized in its further development were a lower body and shot-deflecting armor on all sides. Thus arose a tank whose shape soon earned it the nickname of "the armored turtle."

There followed a heavy self-propelled mount with a 130 mm cannon, based on the T-100. Series production never came to pass for either the tank or the self-propelled gun.

In the war the idea of creating heavy self-propelled gun mounts was taken up again. The concept of such a vehicle was influenced by the German assault gun, which carried a 75 mm gun in a casemate upper body. In 1942, under the direction of S. J. Kotin, a vehicle was created on the basis of the KV heavy tank. Prototypes were designated KV-6 and KV-7. The KV-6 self-propelled mount carried a fixed upper body with 76.2 mm gun and two 45 mm guns with a traverse field of 15 degrees; the elevation range ran from -5 to +15 degrees. The KV-7 vehicle looked very similar, but carried two 76.2 mm guns. The armor was 75 mm thick, the weight of the self-propelled mount with its five- or six-man crew was between 44 and 45 tons. Advantageous for such a heavily armed vehicle was its overall height of some 2,400 mm (the KV-1 with its turret was 2,750 mm high!). A disadvantage was the fact that its single shots were no more effective than those of the turret tank. Thus the further developmental work concentrated on installing a gun of

After World War II, IS-2 heavy tanks were sold to several member nations of the Warsaw Pact. This picture shows a 1944 model in use by a heavy tank unit of the National People's Army in East Germany.

Note the rooflike sloping form of the front armor. Along with the 120 mm thickness of the armor in this area, effective protection against heavy armor-piercing shells (APDS) was provided.

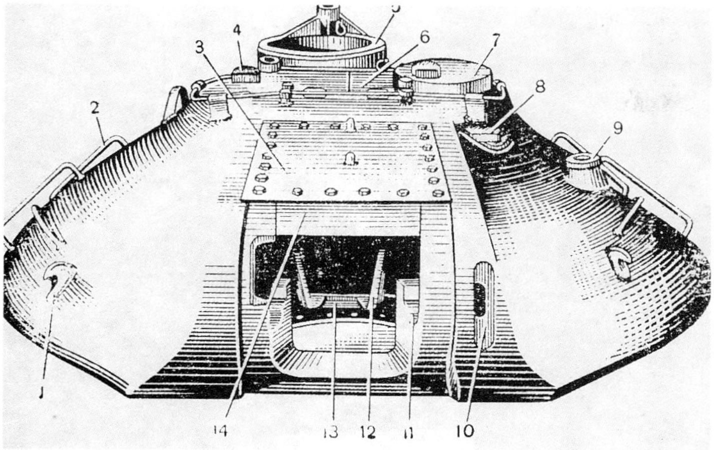

A drawing of the turret area, showing the armor that was 200 to 230 mm thick in front.

larger caliber, which meant that the casemate had to be enlarged as well. The 152.4 mm howitzer-cannon of the corps artillery, intended for direct fire, was chosen. The gun was available under the designation of 1937/43 (ML-20 S). Prototypes were built at the Uralmash factory in Chelyabinsk and designated KV-14. Testing was successful, so that series production could begin in 1943. The final designation was SU-152.

For an armored vehicle weighing 45.5 tons, the SU-152 was remarkably low (2450 mm). The armament was noteworthy: The 152.4 mm howitzer-cannon could fire shells weighing 39.94 to 43.56 kg with an initial velocity between 600 and 900 m/sec. The shot ranges were 700 to 750 meters in direct fire, the maximum range was 12,200 meters. The gun's traverse field was 12 degrees, the elevation range from -5 to +18 degrees. The shell and cartridge case were loaded separately, which kept the rate of fire comparatively low, two to three rounds per minute. For targeting a KT-5 or ST-10 telescopic sight was used. The armor was up to 75 mm thick. Thanks to the powerful W-2-K Diesel engine, a top speed of 43 kph was possible.

The SU-152 self-propelled gun was used by the heavy self-propelled gun regiments of the mechanized and armored corps. The SU-152 had its premiere on the battlefields of the Kursk Bogen in July 1943. In all, 704 vehicles of this type were completed. In 1944 the SU-152 was replaced by the ISU-152, which used the chassis of the "Stalin" tank.

This 1945 model IS-3 heavy tank, photographed in October 1997, now belongs to the collection of the Military Technical Museum of the Historical institute of the Czech Republic in Lesany.

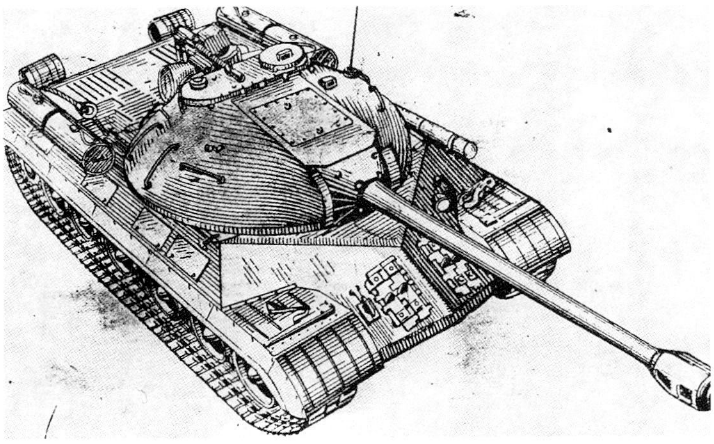

The IS-3 heavy tank seen from above. Note the large tank-gun servicing hatch in the turret.

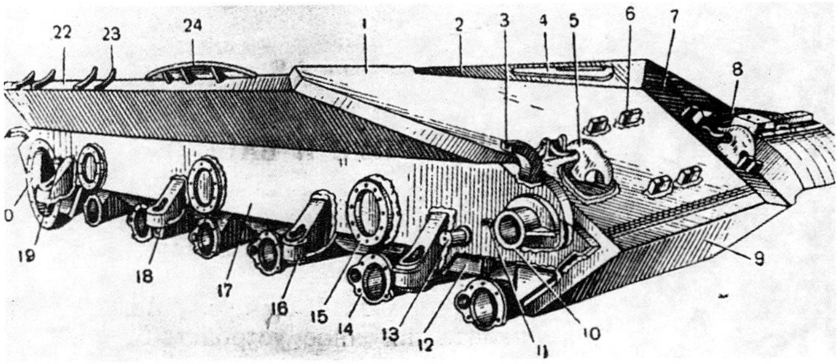

Interesting details of the hull structure of the IS-3 heavy tank are shown in this drawing.

Tactical - Technical Data (SU-152)

Crew:	5 men
Weight:	45.5 tons
Armament:	1 152.4 mm caliber 1937/43 (ML-20 S) howitzer-cannon, with 20 rounds (shells + cartridge cases)
Armor plate:	
Hull: Front:	50-60 mm
Sides:	60 mm
Rear:	60 mm
Top:	30 mm
Bottom:	30 mm
Upper body:	
Front:	60-75 mm
Sides:	50 mm
Rear:	55 mm
Top:	20-30 mm
Powerplant:	V-12 cylinder 4-stroke W-2-K Diesel engine
Performance:	600 HP at 2000 rpm
Fuel capacity:	600-615 liters
Power to weight:	13.2 HP/ton
Length overall:	8950 mm
Hull length:	6750 mm
Width:	3250 mm
Height:	2450 mm
Ground clearance:	440 mm
Top speed:	43 kph
Range:	120-330 km
Climbing degree:	36 degrees
Spanning ability:	2700 mm
Climbing ability:	1200 mm
Wading ability:	1600 mm
Specific ground pressure:	0.85 kp/sq. cm.

Tanks of the KV type proved to be successful designs for a heavy battle tank. By the end of 1942, they remained the most powerful tanks on the battlefield. Among the chief requirements for further development of the KV were increasing firepower and effective armor protection with simultaneous improvement of mobility. This was a hard task to carry out. The KV-85 with its 85 mm D-5 T tank gun could not be a lasting solution to this problem, since the development of the T-34/85 medium tank with the same armament in the autumn of 1943 was almost finished. The effectivity of German antitank guns and tanks had increased in 1943. Now 75 mm guns could penetrate up to 108 mm of armor plate at 500 meters (at a 60-degree angle); for 88 mm guns (8.8 cm antitank cannon 43 L/71) under the same conditions, the values were between 185 and 217 mm. At the same time, increasing numbers of heavily armored tanks appeared in the German armored units. For the Red Army's armored troops, therefore, the development of heavy tanks with better armor protection and higher-performance tank guns had priority. The work had already started in the spring of 1942 in a development bureau under the leadership of N. F. Shashmurin. Various test models were built, including the KV-9 with a 122 mm howitzer, and the KV-13. Shashmurin himself reported after the war: "I too began my activity as a tank designer in the thirties at the Kirov works in Leningrad. In the rough war years I had to move to the well-known Takograd in the Urals. There the IS-2, a heavy tank with stronger armament and better armor protection than the KV ever had, was built, without making the fighting weight higher."

By the end of 1943 the ISU-122 heavy self-propelled artillery mount with the 122 mm 1931/43 cannon (A-19) was delivered to heavy sehlf-propelled gun regiments. It was usede by mechanized and armored corps of the Red Army. Its main task was fighting off heavy armored vehicles.

Except for the gun and its mount, the ISU-122 heavy self-propelled artillery mount, 1944 model (also ISU-122a), was identical to the same vehicle with the 122 mm 1931/43 model cannon (A-19). The new 122 mm 1943 model cannon (D-25-S) was externally recognizable by the muzzle brake.[p. 54] It had an ST-10 panoramic targeting scope and a Tsch-17 telescope for aiming.

Along with the SU-152 heavy self-propelled artillery mount on KV-1 S chassis, such a vehicle was built at the end of 1943 on the basis of the new IS-1 heavy tank. The 152.4 mm 1937/43 model howitzer-cannon (ML-20-S) was recognizable by the long muzzle brake with slits on the sides. It also carried a DSchK 38 (12.7 mm caliber) anti-aircraft machine gun, one or two 7.62 mm machine pistols, and 25 F-1 hand grenades.

The new tank project was called IS (for Josef Vissarionovich Stalin), a name that gave it a particular significance in this patriotic time.

The IS project was finished in the autumn of 1943, and several test models were built. After only a short test, a commission of the State Defense Committee of the Soviet Union approved the introduction of the tank to the armored troops. In December 1943, series production began under the designation of IS-1 or IS-85. It was armed with the 85 mm D-5 T tank gun developed by General F. F. Petrov. Its weight was only slightly more than that of the KV-1 S, and the IS-1 was considerably better armored, as the more strongly differentiated armor was placed more practically on the particularly vulnerable sections of the hull and turret. The turret was cast; the hull consisted of cast and rolled parts welded together.

The designers had improved the gearbox. A two-stage planetary link clutch was installed, which much improved maneuverability over that of the old KV. The IS tank stood out with its high degree of operating safety. When the components were designed, quick changes under field conditions were kept in mind.

The armament with the 85 mm tank gun was not satisfactory; therefore at the end of 1943 a 100 mm gun from V. Grabin's development bureau was installed. By that time 102 Stalin tanks had been delivered. Here the designers still regarded the army's requests for stronger armament in the new heavy tank as not yet fulfilled. At the end of 1943 they began to work on a 122 mm tank gun. It was based on the 122 mm 1931/37 corps cannon, a Red Army corps artillery gun. General A. A. Petrov was again responsible for the project. A slightly shortened barrel of the corps cannon was combined with the upper mount of the 85 mm D-5 T tank gun. By the end of December 1943, the IS with the new gun was being tested. The gun performed well with a simply working muzzle brake, which was replaced later by a double one. Other improvements involved the introduction of a wedge breech, which allowed the rate of fire

The ISU-152used by the heavy self-propelled gun regiments of mechanized and armored corps proved to be especially valuable support vehicles for the battle groups fomposed of riflemen, tanks and self-propelled guns because of the considerable effect of their 43.56 kilogram explosive shells.

Front views of the ISU-152 heavy self-propelled artillery mount. The tank gun with its massive protective armor can be seen on the eight side. Below on the left is the driver's visor, and on both sides of the gun mount are pistol loopholes in the 75 mm front armor.

to be increased. Because the ammunition was loaded in two parts, this was still limited. On December 31, 1943, the 122 mm 1943 tank gun (D-25 T) was confirmed as the primary armament of the IS tank. It could fire 25-kilogram tank shells at an initial velocity of 790 m/sec, and they could penetrate 140 mm of armor at 500 meters.

In January 1944 the first IS with the 122 mm gun were finished at Chelyabinsk. Their official designation was now IS-2. The heavy tanks were used by the heavy guard tank regiments. Only in November 1944 were heavy guard tank brigades formed, with three regiments of 65 IS-2 tanks each.

As for the Germans, who first saw the IS-2 in February 1944 during the heavy combat near Korsun-Chevchenkovski, they officially evaluated the tank as follows: "Newest heavily armored and very heavily armed tank (counterpart of the 'Tiger"); future standard type of heavy tank, hard to fight." The data were taken from Tank Recognition Chart 2, Soviet Russian Tanks, as of July 1, 1944 (addendum to H.Dv. 469/2a). Lieutenant Alfred Regeniter, Kinght's Cross bearer and platoon leader in the 3rd Battery of Assault Gun Brigade 276, reported on his first meeting with the Red Army's new heavy tank: "The battery led an attack in the Steinkrug area of East Prussia on the afternoon of October 21, 1944. But we had hardly left our beginning positions . . . when we sighted a "Josef Stalin" 122 tank at 2000 meters. We fired eight antitank shells, whose tracer lights were wonderful to see. They all bounced off, although the gun is wonderfully accurate." The armor, up to 160 mm on the front of the hull and 100 on the turret, naturally offered reliable protection against shells from the 7.5 cm Assault Gun 40 of Regeniter's assault gun. The Pursuit Tank IV/70 with its 7.5 cm Antitank Gun 42 only achieved sufficient penetrating power against the IS-2 beyond 800 meters. Only the 8.8 cm Tank Gun 43 of the Tiger tank was able to fight the Stalin tank already at a longer range.

Before World War II ended, the IS-2 was modernized. The installation of an improved targeting scope was meant to assure accurate targeting even at long ranges. At the same time, the roller mantlet in the turret was widened. In the second half of 1944 the IS-2 was supplied with a more favorably shaped front armor on the hull. The tank driver was given a sight slit in place of an observation hatch. Only after the war did further modernization result in the driver being given a sufficiently big window. The other three crewmen were in the turret, which held, besides the already described 122 1943 tank gun (D-25 T), a coaxial 7.62 mm DT machine gun in the roller mantlet. Another machine gun of that type was in a ball mantlet in the rear of the turret, and a third machine gun was mounted rigidly in the hull to the driver's right. A new feature of Soviet heavy tanks was the use of a DSchK 38 (12.7 mm caliber) anti-aircraft machine gun on the commander's cupola.

In all, the following numbers of IS tanks were produced:

Year	Number
1943	102
1944	2252
1945	1500
Total	3854

In 1945 some IS-2 heavy tanks were already being rebuilt into IS-2 T heavy armored towing tractors. After World War II, repair companies obtained BTT-1 heavy armored tractors. These were vehicles based on discarded ISU-122 and ISU-152 heavy self-propelled mounts. The guns were removed and a winch and a folding jack were installed or attached. The crew consisted of two men.

Armored and unarmored wheeled and tracked vehicles and armored trains of the Red Army, 1930-1945

Among the notable creations of the armament industry in the Soviet Union, from the beginning of its development, were as many interchangeable components as possible for the various combat and transport vehicles. Armored and unarmored artillery towing tractors used running gear, powerplants and other important parts that came from tank construction. Armored scout cars, armored railcars and armored trains were equipped with weapons and turrets that had been developed for tanks and could now be supplied from current production. The following photos provide some examples:

The "Komitern" (*Above*) heavy artillery tractor was developed at the Kharkov Tractor Works beginning on 1934 and approved for series production in the following year. It was made by using chassis parts of the T-24 medium tank, and was used in heavy artillery regiments for towing the 152.4 mm howitzer-cannon. The engine produced 132 HP, and the maximum speed was 30 kph.

Tactical - Technical Data (IS-1, 1943 model)

Crew:		4 men
Weight:		44.0 tons
Armament:		1 85 mm caliber 1943 (D-5 T) tank gun, with 59 rounds,
		3 7.62 mm caliber DT machine guns, with 2520 rounds
Armor plate:		
Hull:	Front:	120-160 mm
	Sides:	90 mm
	Rear:	60 mm
	Top:	20-30 mm
	Bottom:	20-30 mm
Turret:	Front:	100 mm
	Sides:	90 mm
	Rear:	60-90 mm
	Top:	30 mm
Powerplant:		V-12 cylinder 4-stroke W-2-IS Diesel engine
Performance:		600 HP at 2000 rpm
Fuel capacity:		800 liters
Power to weight:		14.1 HP/ton
Length overall:		8560 mm
	Hull length:	6770 mm
	Width:	3070 mm
	Height:	2730 mm
Ground clearance:		460 mm
Top speed:		37 kph
Range:		150 km
Climbing degree:		30-36 degrees
Spanning ability:		2500 mm
Climbing ability:		1000 mm
Wading ability:		1300 mm
Specific ground pressure:		0.78 kp/sq. cm.

The "Komitern" heavy artillery tractor was fairly seldom seen in the battles against the Germans in the summer of 1941. These two pictures show typical features of the running gear with elements of the T-24 medium tank.

A more powerful version of the "Komitern" tractor was the "Voroshilovetz", likewise used as a heavy artillery tractor in the corps artillery regiments of the Red Army. The powerplant, a W-2 Diesel engine, was also used in the T-34 medium tank and KV heavy tank. The suspension had been improved.

In the German D 50/12 recognition chart for foreign vehicles, the "Voroshilovetz" heavy artillery tractor was listed as "Artillery Tractor Stalin 607 (r)." The vehicle shown here was at the driving test center of the Army Weapons Office in Kummersdorf near Berlin in 1943.

Tactical - Technical Data (IS-2, 1944 model)

Crew:		4 men
Weight:		46.0 tons
Armament:		1 122 mm caliber 1943 (D-25 T) tank gun, with 28 rounds (shells and cartridge cases)
		3 7.62 mm caliber DT machine guns, with 2330 rounds,
		1 12.7 mm caliber DSchK 38 AA machine gun, with 250 rounds
Armor plate:		
Hull:	Front:	120-160 mm
	Sides:	90 mm
	Rear:	60-90 mm
	Top:	20-30 mm
	Bottom:	20-30 mm
Turret:	Front:	100 mm
	Sides:	90 mm
	Rear:	60-90 mm
	Top:	30 mm
Powerplant:		V-12 cylinder 4-stroke W-2-IS Diesel engine
Performance:		600 HP at 2000 rpm
Fuel capacity:		800 liters
Power to weight:		11.3 HP/ton
Length overall:		9830 mm
Hull length:		6770 mm
Width:		3070 mm
Height:		2730 mm
Ground clearance:		460 mm
Top speed:		37 kph
Range:		150 km
Climbing degree:		30-36 degrees
Spanning ability:		2500 mm
Climbing ability:		1000 mm
Wading ability:		1300 mm
Specific ground pressure:		0.80 kp/sq. cm.

The further development of the IS-2 led to various combat vehicles that served experimental purposes. Special emphasis on the shape of the armor of tanks typified the heavy IS-3, which was delivered in small numbers to heavy guard tank regiments as of January 1945. The Germans heard of this new Red Army heavy tank for the first time as early as January 12, 1945. A Red Army major, when questioned, had reported of a tank called "Chtchuka" (...), which had very low and oval shapes and was superior to the Tiger. Actually, the IS-3 never saw action against the German troops. It had its premiere in the victory parade in the ruins of Berlin after the weapons had gone silent in Europe.

In the mechanized artillery regiments of the Red Army's divisional artillery in the late thirties, somewhat lighter ST-3 and STS-5 artillery tractors were often found. The six-ton vehicles reached 25 kph. A curious feature was that the engines were started with gasoline and switched to Diesel fuel while running.

Tactical - Technical Data (IS-3, 1945 model)

Crew:		4 men
Weight:		45.8 tons
Armament:		1 122 mm caliber 1944 (D-25 T) tank gun, with ? rounds,
		1 7.62 mm caliber DT machine gun, with ? rounds,
		1 12.7 mm caliber DSchK 38/43 AA machine gun, with ? rounds
Armor plate:		
Hull:	Front:	90-120 mm
	Sides:	90 mm
	Rear:	no data
	Top:	no data
	Bottom:	no data
Turret:	Front:	200-230 mm
	Sides:	75-115 mm
	Rear:	75-115 mm
	Top:	30 mm
Powerplant:		V-12 cylinder 4-stroke W-2-IS Diesel engine
Performance:		600 HP at 2000 rpm
Fuel capacity:		780 liters
Length overall:		10,000 mm
Hull length:		6670 mm
Width:		3200 mm
Height:		2440 mm
Ground clearance:		430 mm
Top speed:		40 kph
Range:		190 km
Climbing degree:		30-36 degrees
Spanning ability:		2700 meters
Climbing ability:		1000 mm
Wading ability:		1300 mm
Specific ground pressure:		0.79 kp/sq. cm.

The successor model of a heavy self-propelled mount for the SU-152 was a similar vehicle on the chassis of the IS tank, production of which began at the end of 1943. Once again, Kotin's design bureau at the "Uralmash" works in Chelyabinsk was responsible for this development. Since basic design problems had been solved successfully in the SU-152 already, the work went ahead quickly. Within a few weeks prototypes were finished. Along with the already tested 152.44 mm 1937/43 howitzer-cannon (ML-20 S), the installation of a 122 mm 1931/43 corps cannon was planned, in order to have available a pursuit tank to attack strongly armored targets at long ranges. For testing purposes, an even more powerful gun, the 152.4 mm BL-8 cannon, was even installed in 1944. The vehicle was designated SU-152 BM. From German High command reports (Army High Command. Foreign Armies East Department, notice of a lecture on February 4, 1944) it can be seen that even more heavily armed self-propelled mounts were being developed in Soviet design bureaus. An SU-12 with a 203 mm howitzer, with a fighting weight of about 50 tons, is mentioned.

In the summer of 1941, light self-propelled mounts appeared as makeshift means of strengthening antitank defense in the Red Army. The ST-3 and STS-5 artillery tractors were fitted with light armor for this purpose. In the rear body a 45 mm 1937 model antitank gun, identical in performance to the tank gun of the same caliber, was mounted. The Kharkov Tractor Works delivered about 100 of these vehicles.

In 1942 the ST-3 and STS-5 artillery tractors were used as self-propelled mounts for the BM 13 reactive launcher. In place of the loading bed, these vehicles had a folding-up launching rack for sixteen 132 mm rockets, with a range of 8410 mm.

In the latter thirties, light armored artillery tractors for divisional artillery guns were also built on the basis of the 1933 model T-26 light tank. In parades on Red Square in Moscow this tractor was seen towing a 76.2 mm 1936 model divisional cannon.

A very noteworthy vehicle was the "Komsomoletz" (T-20) light armored artillery tractor, which was developed and introduced into the Red Army at the end of the thirties. It was used by the tank-destroyer units of mechanized infantry divisions for towing 1937 and 1942 model 45 mm antitank guns. The road wheels and tracks were those used on the T-38 M-2 amphibious tank.

The "Komsomoletz" had a fighting weight of 3.4 to 4.01 tons, measured 3400 x 1850 x 1580 mm, and was fitted with 6- to 16-mm riveted and screwed armor. On the right side at the front was a ball mantlet holding a 7.62 mm DT machine gun, for which 756 rounds were carried.

Prototypes of the heavy self-propelled mount with the 122 mm gun were presented and designated ISU-249 (Project 249). The first vehicles delivered were armed with a 122 mm 1931/43 cannon (A-19). The final solution was planned to use a 122 mm 1943 cannon (D-25 S), but its development had not yet been finished when series production of this self-propelled mount began. This emphasizes once again the haste with which the Soviets tried to get such vehicles into front action. In 1943 there were 35 ISU-152 or ISU-122 heavy self-propelled mounts delivered. The final designation of Project 249 was decided on as ISU-122. Alternatively armed versions were built in 1944. The ISU-122 BM, which was armed with a 122 mm BL-7 cannon, might be mentioned. The barrel length was 6,220 mm (L/60).

There were also ISU-122 E and ISU-130 test models. The latter was armed with a 130 mm cannon.

While the serial number of the ISU-152 was unchanged when it was built with the 1937/43 howitzer-cannon (ML-20 S), there was a change for the ISU-122 after a small series was built with the 122 mm 1931/43 cannon (A-19). A gun of the same caliber with the 1943 model designation (D-258) was installed, recognizable externally by the double-acting muzzle brake. The barrel length was somewhat shorter (L/43 instead of L/46.3 in the 1931/43 A-19 model). The gun, which was mounted in an external ball-shaped mantlet, weighed 2.365 tons in all. The rate of fire remained low, limited by the ammunition that was loaded in two pieces; two or three shots per minute were possible. The maximum shot range was stated as 8,000 meters, and the most favorable range for direct fire as between 700 and 1,000 meters. The antitank shell weighed 25 kilograms and reached an initial velocity of 781 m/sec (800 m/sec for the 1931/43 A-19 model). At 500 meters, 155 mm of armor plate could be penetrated. At 1,000 meters, this became 145 mm. The 1943 gun model had a wedge breech.

Both self-propelled mounts, the ISU-152 and ISU-122, weighed between 45.5 and 46 tons, were sufficiently armored, and had sufficient mobility for a heavy armored vehicle. They were used in the heavy self-propelled gun regiments of the mechanized and armored corps. In the autumn of 1944, heavy self-propelled gun brigades consisting of three regiments were established. These formations were utilized at focal points of attacks to support infantry and tank units of the Red Army. The following numbers of ISU-152 and ISU/122 were produced:

Year	Number
1943	35
1944	2510
1945	1530
Total	4075

Only after the war were these vehicles rebuilt as towing tractors and recovery tanks.

The powerplant for the "Komsomoletz" (T-20) light armored artillery tractor was a 50-horsepower engine. It allowed a speed of 43 to 47 kph; the range is stated as 150 kilometers. Besides seats for the two crewmen in the armored front body, there were benches for six soldiers of the gun crew in back.

Tactical - Technical Data (ISU-152, 1944 model)

Crew:	5 men
Weight	46.0 tons
Armament:	1 152.4 mm caliber 1937/43 (ML-20 S) howitzer-cannon, with 20 rounds (shells and cartridge cases) 1 12.7 mm caliber DSchK 1938/43 AA machine gun, with 250 rounds
Armor plate:	
Hull: Front:	60-90 mm
Sides:	90 mm
Rear:	60 mm
Top:	20-30 mm
Bottom:	20-30 mm
Upper body:	
Front:	75 mm
Sides:	60 mm
Rear:	60 mm
Top:	22-30 mm
Powerplant:	V-12 cylinder 4-stroke W-2-IS Diesel engine
Performance:	600 HP at 2000 rpm
Fuel capacity:	520-560 liters
Power to weight:	10.9 HP-ton
Length overall:	9050-9180 mm
Hull length:	6770 mm
Width:	3070 mm
Height:	2480 mm
Ground clearance:	460-470 mm
Top speed:	35-37 kph
Range:	220 km
Climbing degree:	36 degrees
Spanning ability:	2500-2700 mm
Climbing ability:	1000-1200 mm
Wading ability:	1300-1500 mm
Specific ground pressure:	0.81-0.82 kp/sq. cm.

There were different layouts of the armored body of the "Komsomoletz". The vehicle shown here has a screwed-on front section to hold the 7.62 mm DT machine gun in a ball mantlet and a separate vision opening. Behind the front body is the rear section with a shield to protect the gun crew.

Towing tractors of the "Komsomoletz" type captured by the Germans were designated "Armored Artillery Tractor 630 (r)" and used mainly in tank-destroyer units. Behind the tractor are a single-axle limber and a likewise captured 45 mm 184/1 (r) Russian 37 antitank gun.

Another light armored self-propelled mount for antitank guns was built in the autumn of 1941 at Factory No. 92 in Gorki. It was designated ZIS-30. On the "Komsomoletz" light artillery tractor, a 57 mm antitank gun, 1941 model (ZIS-29), was mounted with a gun shield. The tractor also carried a 7.62 mm DT machine gun in the armored body.

Between 1927 and 1931, about 100 BA-27 armored scout cars were built. They were armed with a 37 mm tank gun and a 7.62 mm machine gun, and their turrets were those of the MS-1 light tank.

The BA-10 armored scout car, built since 1937, was fitted with the turret of the T-26 1937 model light tank minus its extensive rear extension.

Small numbers of BA-27 M armored scout cars (a modernized version from the thirties) were still seen during the battles with the Germans in the summer of 1941.

This picture of a BA-10 armored scout car, 1935 model, was taken during the Spanish Civil War. The three-axle reconnaissance vehicle, weighing over five tons and only lightly armored, had the turret of the 1933 model T-26 light tank and carried 49 shells for its 45 mm tank gun and 2000 rounds for the two 7.62 mm DT machine guns.

Numerous 1937 model BA-10 armored scout cars were lost by the Red Army during the defensive fighting in the summer of 1941. Their comparatively heavy armament could not make up for their light armor (6 to 15 mm), insufficient off-road capability and mobility (the 4-cylinder 4-stroke GAZ-M-1 gasoline engine produced 50 horsepower). These pictures were taken in July 1941.

Tactical - Technical Data (ISU-122, 1944 model)

Crew:	5 men
Weight:	45.5-46.0 tons
Armament:	1 1943 (D-25 S) cannon, with 20-30 shells and cartridge cases

1 12.7 mm caliber DSchK 38/43 AA machine gun, with 250 rounds

Armor plate:		
Hull:	Front:	60-90 mm
	Sides:	90 mm
	Rear:	60 mm
	Top:	20-30 mm
	Bottom:	20-30 mm
Upper body:		
	Front:	75-90 mm
	Sides:	60 mm
	Rear:	60 mm
	Top:	22-30 mm
Powerplant:		V-12 cylinder 4-stroke W-2-IS Diesel engine
Performance:		600 HP at 2000 rpm
Fuel capacity:		520-560 liters
Power to weight:		10.9 HP/ton
Length overall:		9059-9180 mm
Hull length:		6770 mm
	Width:	3070 mm
	Height:	2480 mm
Ground clearance:		400-470 mm
Top speed:		37 kph
Range:		220 km
Climbing degree:		36 degrees
Spanning ability:		2500-2700 mm
Climbing ability:		1000-1200 mm
Wading ability:		1300-1500 mm

Specific ground pressure: 0.81 kp/sq. cm.

In the four years in which the Soviet Union was in a state of war with Germany, the country's armament industry delivered 96,099 tanks and self-propelled gun mounts to the Red Army. Their high level of quality, along with quantities that Germany could not match, was one of the most important prerequisites for their victory over the German armed forces.

152 mm Tank Howitzer 1938/40

Caliber:	152.4 mm
Barrel length:	3697 mm = L/24
Rifling length:	3117 mm
Number of riflings:	48
Weight overall:	-
Barrel with breech:	1398 kg
Type of breech:	Screw
Elevation range:	-5 to +12 degrees
Traverse range:	360 degrees
Ammunition:	Separate, with cartridge case
Weight of antitank shell:	40 kg
Weight of explosive shell:	51.07 kg
Performance data:	
Initial velocity:	508 m/sec (antitank shell)
Initial velocity:	432 mm (explosive shell)
Shot range:	5000 meters (antitank shell, +8 degree elevation)
Shot range:	5000 meters (explosive shell, +10 degree elevation)
Rate of fire:	2 rounds per minute
Firing:	Mechanical
Targeting:	Tank turret targeting scope T-5 152 mm M.38, Panoramic scope PT-5
Armor-piercing:	No data

The BA-64 light armored scout car was supplied to the mechanized and armored units of the Red Asrmy from 1943 on for use as a reconnaissance and communication vehicle. It was based on an off-road-capable passenger car. With 6- to 10-mm armor, it weighed 2.36 tons and was armed with the 7.62 mm DT machine gun used in almost all tanks.

The turrets of various production runs of T-34 medium tanks were used in 1944-45 for the Project 1124 armored cutter. The two 76.2 mm 1940 or 1942 model tank guns (F-34) gave these armored boats, used on inland waters, a respectable firepower. They also carried two 12.7 mm and four 7.62 mm machine guns. The crew numbered seventeen men.

76 mm 1940 and 1942 Tank Gun (F-34)

Caliber:	76.2 mm
Barrel length:	3170 mm (L/41.5)
Rifling length:	2564 mm
Number of riflings:	32
Weight overall:	-
Barrel with breech:	470 kg, 1942 model = 455 kg
Breech type:	Semi-automatic vertical wedge
Elevation range:	-4.5 to + 29 degrees
Traverse range:	360 degrees
Ammunition:	Cartridges
Weight, antitank shell:	6.3 kg (BR-350 A)
Weight, explosive shell:	6.2 kg (CF-350)
Weight, undercaliber:	3.04 kg (BR-350 P)
Weight, hollow-charge:	3.94 kg (BR-354 A)
Performance data:	
Initial velocity:	662 m/sec (antitank shell)
Initial velocity:	680 mm (explosive shell)
Initial velocity:	965 mm (undercaliber shell)
Shot range:	6000 meters (antitank shell at +8 degrees)
Shot range:	12,000 meters (explosive shell at +12 degrees)
Rate of fire:	5 rounds per minute
Firing:	Mechanical
Targeting:	Tank targeting scope TOD-7, Panoramic targeting scope PT-7
Armor-piercing: (antitank shell)	69 mm at 500 meters, 61 mm at 1000 meters
Armor-piercing: (undercaliber shell)	92 mm at 500 meters, 58 mm at 1000 meters

76 mm 1939 Tank Gun (L-11)

Caliber:	76.2 mm
Barrel length:	2323.5 mm (L/30.5)
Rifling length:	1790 mm
Number of riflings:	32
Weight overall:	-
Barrel with breech:	328 kg
Breech type:	Semi-automatic vertical wedge
Elevation range:	-5 to +24 degrees
Traverse range:	360 degrees
Ammunition:	Cartridges
Weight, antitank shell:	6.3 kg (BR-350)
Weight, explosive shell:	6.21 kg (CF-450)
Performance data:	
Initial velocity:	612 m/sec (antitank shell)
Initial velocity:	610-635 m/sec (explosive shell)
Initial velocity:	no data (undercaliber shell)
Shot range:	- (antitank shell)
Shot range:	7300 meters (explosive shell at +12 degrees)
Rate of fire:	no data
Firing:	no data
Targeting:	Targeting scope I O II-6, Panoramoc scope F.-6
Armor-piercing:	66 mm at 500 meters (armor steel)

76 mm 1938/39 Tank Gun (L-10)

Caliber:	76.2 mm
Barrel length:	2325 mm (L/30/5)
Rifling length:	1790 mm
Number of riflings:	32
Weight overall:	-
Barrel with breech:	433 kg
Breech type:	semi-automatic vertical wedge
Elevation range:	-3 to +25 degrees
Traverse range:	360 degrees
Ammunition:	cartridges
Weight, antitank shell:	6.3 kg
Weight, explosive shell:	6.2 kg
Performance data:	
Initial velocity:	612 m/sec (antitank shell)
Initial velocity:	555-635 m/sec (explosive shell)
Shot range:	-
Shot range:	7300 meters (explosive shell at +12 degrees)
Rate of fire:	4-5 rounds per second
Firing:	no data
Targeting:	no data
Armor-piercing:	no data

Comparison of armor-piercing ammunition used by Russian tank guns in the 1930-1945 period (left to right):
a. 12.7 mm bullet (12.7 mm DSchK 38 machine gun) b. 14.5 mm bullet (only used for the 14.5 mm 1941 model PTRD and PTRS antitank gun) c. 20 mm shell (20 mm 1941 model SchWak tank gun) d. 45 mm undercaliber shell (45 mm 1932, 1934 and 1938 model antitank gun) e. 76.2 mm antitank shell (76.2 mm 1940 and 1942 model tank gun) f. 85 mm antitank shell (85 mm 1943 model D-5 T tank gun) g. 122 mm antitank shell and cartridge (122 mm 1943 model D-25 T tank gun)

Armored railway trains lost none of their importance in the Red Army's operations during World War II. They were used in goodly numbers in defensive and, later, also in offensive action. Older armored trains were often modernized, frequently being fitted with the turrets of light, medium or heavy tanks (including the KV-2). The armored train "Alexander Nevski" (named for a Russian historical hero and commander) was destroyed by the Germans in 1942. Note the crude workmanship of the armor plates.

76 mm 1927/32 Tank Gun (KT-28)

Caliber:	76.2 mm
Barrel length:	1254 mm (L/16.5)
Rifling length:	779 mm
Number of riflings:	24
Weight overall:	540 kg
Barrel with breech:	229 kg
Breech type:	Screw breech with tension trigger and cartridge sealing
Elevation range:	-5 to +25 degrees
Traverse range:	360 degrees
Ammunition:	Cartridges
Weight, antitank shell:	6.5 kg
Weight, explosive shell:	6.2 kg
Performance data:	
Initial velocity:	370 m/sec (antitank shell)
Initial velocity:	381-387 m/sec (explosive shell)
Shot range:	6763 meters (antitank shell, at +15 degrees)
Shot range:	- (explosive shell)
Rate of fire:	2 rounds per minute
Firing:	Mechanical
Targeting:	Tank targeting scope 1930, Panoramic targeting scope 1932
Armor-piercing:	no data (antitank shell)

45 mm 1938 Tank Gun

Caliber:	45 mm
Barrel length:	2072 mm (L/46)
Rifling length:	1650 mm
Number of riflings:	16
Weight overall:	-
Barrel with breech:	113 kg
Breech type:	Semi-automatic vertical wedge
Elevation range:	-6 to +25 degrees
Traverse range:	360 degrees
Ammunition:	Cartridges
Weight, antitank shell:	1.43 kg
Weight, explosive shell:	2.15 kg
Performance data:	
Initial velocity:	760 m/sec (antitank shell)
Initial velocity:	335 m/sec (explosive shell)
Shot range:	3600 meters (antitank shell, at +4 degrees)
Shot range:	2600 meters (explosive shell, at +9 degrees)
Rate of fire:	12 rounds per minute
Firing:	Electric or mechanical
Targeting:	TOD 1932 or TOL tank aiming scope with stabilizer, PT-1 panoramic targeting acope
Armor-piercing:	35 mm at 500 meters (antitank shell)

During World War II the Soviet Union's forces received 7056 tanks from the USA through the lend-lease program. Several thousand tanks also came from Britain and Canada. They were used by the Red Army's armored troops in place of tanks produced in the Soviet Union. The "Matilda" (*Above*) II infantry tank was first used by the Red Army in the fighting against the Germans before Moscow in the winter of 1941-42. With their slow speed, weak armor and other faults, these tanks were not very popular among the Russian soldiers. The two shot-down "Matildas" shown here were photographed during the fighting around Kharkov in the spring of 1942.

45 mm 1934 Tank Gun - electric firing

Caliber:	45 mm
Barrel length:	2072 mm (L/46)
Rifling length:	1650 mm
Number of riflings:	16
Weight overall:	-
Barrel with breech:	113 kg
Breech type:	Semi-automatic vertical wedge
Elevation range:	-6 to +25 degrees
Traverse range:	360 degrees
Ammunition:	Cartridges
Weight, antitank shell:	1.43 kg
Weight, explosive shell:	2.15 kg
Performance data:	
Initial velocity:	760 m/sec (antitank shell)
Initial velocity:	335 m/sec (explosive shell)
Shot range:	3600 meters (antitank shell, at +4 degrees)
Shot range:	2600 meters (explosive shell, at +9 degrees)
Rate of fire:	12 rounds per minute
Firing:	Electric and mechanical
Targeting:	TO-D 1932 tank targeting scope or TOP with stabilizer, PT-1 panoramic targeting scope
Armor-piercing:	35 mm at 500 meters (antitank shell)

Note: Electric firing was added later.

45 mm Tank Gun 1932

Caliber:	45 mm
Barrel length:	2072.5 mm (L/46)
Rifling length:	1650 mm
Number of riflings:	16
Weight overall:	-
Barrel with breech:	123 kg
Breech type:	Semi-automatic vertical wedge
Elevation range:	-6 to +25 degrees
Traverse range:	360 degrees
Ammunition:	Cartridges
Weight, antitank shell:	1.43 kg
Weight, explosive shell:	2.15 kg
Performance data:	
Initial velocity:	760 m/sec (antitank shell)
Initial velocity:	335 m/sec (explosive shell)
Shot range:	3600 meters (antitank shell, at +4 degrees)
Shot range:	2600 meters (explosive shell, at +9 degrees)
Rate of fire:	12 rounds per minute
Firing:	Mechanical
Targeting:	TOD 1932 tank targeting scope, PT-1 panoramic targeting scope
Armor-piercing:	35 mm at 500 meters (antitank shell)

The Kharkov battlefield in the spring of 1942. Most of the Mark III "Valentine" infantry tanks used by the Red Army came from Canada. Their combat value was below that of Russian tanks.

122 mm 1943 Tank Gun (D-25 T)

Caliber:	122 mm
Barrel length:	5648.6 mm (L/43)
Rifling length:	no data
Number of riflings:	44
Weight overall:	1930 kg
Barrel with breech:	-
Breech type:	Semi-automatic vertical wedge
Elevation range:	-3 to +20 degrees
Traverse range:	360 degrees
Ammunition:	Separate, with cartridge case
Weight, antitank shell:	24.9 kg (BR-471 B)
Weight, explosive shell:	24.9 kg (OF-471)
Weight, hollow-charge:	13.2 kg (BP-460 A)
Performance data:	
Initial velocity:	781 m/sec (antitank shell)
Initial velocity:	800 m/sec (explosive shell)
Initial velocity:	550 m/sec (undercaliber shell)
Shot range:	1100 meters (antitank shell, in direct fire)
Shot range:	5000 meters (explosive shell; 15,000 with elevation)
Rate of fire:	2-3 rounds per minute
Firing:	-
Targeting:	Tsch-17 tank telescopic hinged targeting scope
Armor-piercing:	140 mm at 500 meters (antitank shell)

85 mm 1944 Tank Gun (ZIS-S-53)

Caliber:	85 mm
Barrel length:	4641 mm (L/54.6)
Rifling length:	-
Number of riflings:	-
Weight overall:	-
Barrel with breech:	-
Breech type:	Semi-automatic vertical wedge
Elevation range:	-5 to +22 degrees
Traverse range:	360 degrees
Ammunition:	Cartridges
Weight, antitank shell:	9.02 kg (BR-365)
Weight, explosive shell:	9.2 kg (O-365)
Weight, undercaliber:	4.9 kg (BR-365 P)
Performance data:	
Initial velocity:	792 m/sec (antitank shell)
Initial velocity:	792 m/sec (explosive shell)
Initial velocity:	1200 m/sec (undercaliber shell)
Shot range:	- (antitank shell)
Shot range:	- (explosive shell)
Rate of fire:	4-7 rounds per minute
Firing:	-
Targeting:	Tsch-16 tank targeting scope (16-degree firled of vision, fourfold magnification)
Armor-piercing:	81 mm at 1000 meters (at 60 degrees)

20-.. 1941 Tank Gun (SchWak)

Caliber:	20 mm
Barrel length:	1245 mm (L/62.2)
Rifling length:	-
Number of riflings:	-
Weight overall:	40-45 kg
Barrel with breech:	-
Breech type:	Fully automatic
Elevation range:	-
Traverse range:	360 degrees
Ammunition:	Cartridges, 60-shot belt feed
Weight, tank shell:	0.096 kg
Weight, explosive shell:	0.095 kg
Performance data:	
Initial velocity:	750 m/sec (antitank shell)
Initial velocity:	750 m/sec (explosive shell)
Initial velocity:	- (undercaliber shell)
Shot range:	- (antitank shell)
Shot range:	- (explosive shell)
Rate of fire:	800 rounds per minute (theoretical)
Firing:	-
Targeting:	-
Armor-piercing:	24 mm at 100 meters

37 mm 1931 Tank Gun (B-3 (5K))

Caliber:	37 mm
Barrel length:	1665 mm (L/45)
Rifling length:	-
Number of riflings:	-
Weight overall:	-
Barrel with breech:	-
Breech type:	Semi-automatic vertical wedge
Elevation range:	-8 to +25 degrees
Traverse range:	360 degrees
Ammunition:	Cartridges
Weight, antitank shell:	0.665 kg
Weight, explosive shell:	-
Performance data:	
Initial velocity:	800 m/sec (antitank shell)
Initial velocity:	762 m/sec (explosive shell)
Initial velocity:	- (undercaliber shell)
Shot range:	900 meters in direct fire (antitank shell)
Shot range:	7000 meters (explosive shell)
Rate of fire:	12 rounds per minute
Firing:	Mechanical
Targeting:	-
Armor-piercing:	27 mm at 500 meters (antitank shell)

The Mark IV "Churchill" infantry tank saw action in Russia mainly in 1943. It is said that the 5th Guard Armored Army lost 12 Churchill tanks to German antitank fire on the battlefields in the southern Kursk Bogen on July 12, 1943.

Another view of the Kharkov battlefield in the spring of 1942.

These M 3 A 1 light tanks sent from the USA came to grief in a landing maneuver of the Russian Black Sea Fleet at Novorossisk early in February 1943.

85 mm 1943 Tank Gun (D-5 T)

Caliber:	85 mm
Barrel length:	4386 mm (L/51.6)
Rifling length:	-
Number of riflings:	-
Weight overall:	1530 kg
Barrel with breech:	-
Breech type:	Semi-automatic vertical wedge
Elevation range:	-5 to +22 degrees
Traverse range:	360 degrees
Ammunition:	Cartridges
Weight, antitank shell:	9.2 kg
Weight, explosive shell:	9.6 kg
Weight, undercaliber:	4.99 kg
Performance data:	
Initial velocity:	785 m/sec (antitank shell)
Initial velocity:	785 m/sec (explosive shell)
Initial velocity:	1030 m/sec (undercaliber shell)
Shot range:	1100 meters in direct firing (antitank shell)
Shot range:	- (explosive shell)
Rate of fire:	4-7 rounds per minute
Firing: -	
Targeting:	-
Armor-piercing:	110 mm at 500 meters, 100 mm at 1000 meters (antitank shell) 145 mm at 500 meters (undercaliber shell, at 90 degrees)

In 1942-43 the Red Army received a large number of M 3 medium tanks of various series from the USA. This picture shows two M 3 tanks shot down on the battlefield near Kursk early in July 1943.

The greatest numbers of the tanks delivered to the Soviet Union from the USA were by far the most effective type of tank, the M 4 medium tank. It also came from various production runs and was utilized until the war ended. This M 4 A 4 (75 mm) was shot down by the German antitank forces in the summer of 1944.

Appendix I: Production of Armored Vehicles in the Soviet Union 1940-1945

Type	1940	1941	1942	1943	1944	1945	Total
T-26 light tank and variants	1549						1549
BT-7 M fast wheel/track tank	706						706
T-28 medium tank	12						12
Other types:	125						125
T-40 amphibian tank		41	181				225
T-50 light tank		48	15				63
T-60 light tank		1818	4474				6292
T-70 light tank			4883	3343			8226
T-80 light tank				120			120
T-34 medium tank	117	3014	12,533	15,712	3723		35,099
T-34/85 medium tank				100	11,000	18,330	29,430
T-44 medium tank						200	200
KV-1 heavy tank	141	1121	1753				3015
KV-2 & KV-2 A heavy tank	102	232					334
KV-1 S heavy tank			780	452			1231
KV-85 heavy tank				130			130
IS-1, IS-2 & IS-3 heavy tank				102	2252	1500	3584
SU-76, ZSU-37 light self-prop. mount			26	1928	7155	3552	12,661
SU-122 medium self-prop. mount			630	493			1148
SU-85 medium self-prop. mount				750	1300		2050
SU-100 medium self-prop. mount					500	1175	1675
SU-152 heavy self-prop. mount				704			704
ISU-122, ISU-152 heavy self-prop. mount				35	2510	1530	4075
Totals	2752	6274	24,670	24,006	28,933	26,287	112,922

Note: Because of faulty sources, numbers differ.

Appendix II: Data on Production and Losses

Data on production and loss of tanks and self-propelled mounts in the Soviet Union from a report of the General Staff of the German Army (Army High Command, Foreign Armies East Department (IId), of October 10, 1944

Tank and Assault Gun Production[16]

Year	Tanks	Assault Guns	Imports[17]	Total
1941	—	—	7400	7400
1942	14,500	50	4500	19,050
1943	20,350	2500	3650	26,500
Total	42,250	2550	8150	52,950

16. Figures are based on troop reports and factory numbers of shot-down Soviet tanks.
17. Impoted in lend-lease agreement with USA, Canada and Britain.

Red Army tank and assault-gun losses (as of October 8, 1944)

Year	Month	Losses
1941		22,000
1942		16,200
1943		18,850
	June	53 [?]
	July	4150
	August	4050
	September	2160
	October	1530
	November	2070
	December	1460
1944	January	3240
	February	1520
	March	1560
	April	1990
	May	370
	June	610
	July	2140
	August	2310

Appendix III:
Tank and Self-propelled Mount Production in the Soviet Union 1930-1945

Year	Tanks	Self-prop. Mounts
1930	170	
1931	740	
1932	3038	
1933	——	
1934	3565	
1935	3055	
1936	4803	
1937	1559	
1938	2271	
1939	2982	
1940	2794	
1941	6590	
1942	24,660	59
1943	19,994	4194
1944	16,923	12,016
1945	8730	6689
Total	105,383	23,003

Appendix IV: Production Comparison of Important Tank Types in the Soviet Union and Germany

1941-1945

Tank type	Year	Soviet Union	Germany
Light tanks	1941	1907	931
	1942	9553	501
	1943	3463	164
	1944	—	131
	1945	—	—
	Total	14,923	1727
Medium tanks	1941	3014	2325
	1942	12,553	3519
	1943	15,812	5272
	1944	14,723	7730
	1945	18,530	823[1]
	Total	64,612	19,669
Heavy tanks	1941	1353	—
	1942	2533	78
	1943	684	647
	1944	2252	1002
	1945	1500	112[2]
	Total	8322	1114

1. Only to March 1945.
2. Same as above.

Bibliography

H.Dv. 469/3a-e, Antitank Weapons, 3a-3, Tank Shot Tables, Berlin 1942.

Addendum to H.Dv. 469/2a, Tank Recognition Chart 1, Most Important Soviet Russian Tanks, as of January 27, 1942, Berlin 1942.

Addendum to H.Dv. 460/2a, Tank Recognition Chart 1, Most Important Soviet Russian Tanks, as of July 1, 1944, Berlin 1944.

Addendum to H.Dv. 469/2a, Tank Recognition Chart 2, The Soviet Russian Tanks, July 1, 1944, Berlin 1944.

DV-43/12 T-34/85 Tank Handbook, East Berlin, no date.

DV-43/13 SFL SU-100 Handbook (manuscript), East Berlin, no date.

D 41/2 Manual for Russian Equipment, Part 2, Guns, Launchers and their Ammunition from 11/1/1941, Berlin 1941.

D 50/4 Recognition Chart, Foreign Equipment, Vol. 4, Light Guns of 3/20/1941, Berlin 1942.

D 50/12 Recognition Chart, Foreign Equipment, Vol. 12, Motor Vehicles of 3/20/1941, Berlin 1942.

D 612/3 Heigl's Pocket Book of Tanks, Munich-Berlin 1938.

Illustrated Volume 146 a, Enemy Tanks, Part I: T-34 of 5/20/1944, Berlin 1944.

Appendix to Russian Army Pocket Guide of May 15, 1942, Berlin 1942.

Lecture Notice on Type Designations for Russian Assault Guns of 2/4/1944, Foreign Armies East Dept. (II d).

The Most Important Tanks in the Union of Soviet Socialist Republics (USSR) as of 6/1/1941, Berlin 1941.

Coverage of the Russian Assault Guns and KV 85 (Staff officer for antitank fighting Adjutant 4, Addendum ro H.Gru.Kdo. Nord I a 103334/43.

Adameit, Th., Sowjetarmee und Weltrevolution, Berlin-Leipzig 1942.

Antonov, A. S. & Artamanov, B. A., Der Panzer, East Berlin 1959.

Babadshanian, A. Ch., Hauptstosskraft, Berlin 1981.

Barmitzke & Rakula, Bericht über die Finnlandreise von Mitarbeitern der Gustloff-Werke, Suhl und von Rheinmetall Borsig, Berlin, mit Angaben über dort vorgefundene russische Waffen und Fahrzeuge (4/25-5/13/1941).

Cecil, M. K., Kubinka—The Russian Museum of Armoured Vehicles, Victoria, no date.

Ermolina, O. & Bruisov, V., Bronetankovaya Technika, Moscow 1994.

Frieser, K. H., Schlagen aus der Nachand. Die Schlachten von Charkow und Kursk 1943, in: Vorträge zur Militärgeschichte, Vol. 15, Gezeitenwechsel im Zweiten Weltkrieg, Berlin 1996, pp. 101- 135.

Goluschko, I. M., Panzer Erwachen wieder, East Berlin 1981.

Guderian, H., Achtung Panzer! Stuttgart, no date.

Guderian, H., Erinnerungen eines Soldaten, Stuttgart 1986.

Halder, F., Kriegstagebuch, Vol. 3, Stuttgart 1964.

Heigl, F., Taschenbuch der Tanks. Wesen, Erkennung, Bekämpfung, Munich 1926.

Heigl, F., Taschenbuch der Tanks. Addenda, Munich 1927.

Heigl, F., Taschenbuch der Tanks, 1930 edition, Munich 1930.

Katukow, M. J., An der Spitze des Hauptstosses, East Berlin 1979.
Magnuski, J., Ciezkie Dziato Somobienzne ISU, Warsaw 1980.
Magnuski, J., Czotg Ciezki IS, Warsaw 1974.
Magnuski, J., Czotg Sredni T-34, Warsaw 1970.
Magnuski, J., Dziatko Pancerne SU-85, Warsaw 1971.
Magnuski, J., Lekkie Dziato Samobiezne SU-76, Warsaw 1976.
Magnuski, J., Postrach Zachodu "Stalin", Warsaw 1995.
Magnuski, J., Worzy Bejowe 1914-1964, Warsaw 1964,
Magnuski, J., Wozy Bojowe LWP 1943-1983, Warsaw 1985.
Markin, I. I., Die Kursker Schlacht, East Berlin 1960.
Milsom, J., Die russischen Panzer Die Geschichte der sowjetischen Panzerwaffe 1900 bis heute, Stuttgart 1974.
Mironow, W. B., Die stählerne Garde, East Berlin 1986.
Mostowenko, W. D., Panzer gestern und heute, East Berlin 1961.
Muikku, E. & Kuusela, K., Puolustusvoimien Pansarikalusto 1918-1989, Helsinki 1990.
Nehring, Die Geschichte der deutschen Panzerwaffe 1916 bis 1945, Augsburg 1995.
Panow, V. P. & Solarz, J., Czotgi Sowieckie 1939-1945, Warsaw 1996.
Die Panzerkampfwagen der Sowjetunion, in Die Panzertruppe, Vol. 6, 1938, Berlin 1938.
Pataj, S., Artyleria Ladowa, Warsaw 1975.
Pejcoch, I., T-28, in Historie a plastikove modelarstvi, in Vol. 6, 1996, Pargue 1996.
Poor, I., Harckocsik es pancelozott jarmu"vek tipuskönyve, Budapest 1980.
Popjel, N. K., In schwerer Zeit, East Berlin 1981.
Popjel, N. K., Panzer greifen an, East Berlin 1981.
Rein, R. H., Die Entwicklung der sowjetischen Standardpanzer, Parts I-III, in Militärtechnik, Vol. 1-3, 1967, East Berlin 1967.
Senger & Etter, in Dr.F.v. Taschenbuch der Panzer 1943-1954, Munich 1954.
Sergeeba, L. B. et al., Bronetankovaya Technika Sovietskai Armii-Album, Moscow 1966.
Shmelev, I. P., Tanki BT, Moscow 1993.
Slesina, H., Soldaten gegen Tod und Teufel. Under Kampf in der Sowjetunion eine soldatische Deutung, Düsseldorf 1942.
Velek, M. I. & Ovcacik, M., T-34 Tank Fenom'en in Atom, in Vol. 5, 11987, Prague 1987.
Volckheim, H., Der Kampfwagen in der heutigen Kriegsführung, Berlin 1924.
Waffen der Roten Armee (Heeresgruppe Mitte Ic/A.O./Auswertung), Posen 1944.
Warjatinckii, M. & Kolomiez, M., Lechhie Tanki BT-2 I BT-5, Moscow 1995.
Wo kommen die vielen Sowjetpanzer her? in Neue Leipziger Tageszeitung Nr. 41, 2/10/1943, Leipzig 1943.